GUN LAWS BY STATE

RECIPROCITY AND GUN LAWS QUICK REFERENCE GUIDE

2018 Edition

By Bryan L. Ciyou, Esq.

I have Read, Understand, and Agree to the Terms of Access and Use for the GLBS Guide and its Companion Website.

TERMS OF ACCESS AND USE

By opening the *GLBS Reciprocity and Gun Laws Quick Reference Guide, 2018 Ed.*, I/We acknowledge we have read, understand, and agree to the following Terms of Access and Use:

The GLBS Guide was considered, created, researched, and written to provide its readers (herein "You(r)" or "Reader(s)" or "User(s)") with an accurate and authoritative general educational resource tool to explore reciprocal carry of a concealed (or unconcealed, as allowed by law) handgun in a different state by use of Your resident or non-resident license reciprocal legal authority granted by the reciprocal state.

However, the GLBS Guide was not researched and/or written by attorneys admitted in any particular jurisdiction as a specific legal guide to rely upon. In addition, all laws (cases, statutes, rules and regulations, ordinances) are always subject to reasonable, but different, legal interpretation as to meaning and application in a given case under certain facts in a particular moment in time.

As such, the GLBS Guide is not intended to supplant, nor limit, Your need for independent verification of any and all material contained herein and consultation with competent counsel of choice regarding any specific issues. It is only through legal counsel admitted in any given jurisdiction that the facts can be developed, and then considered, under the controlling laws, rules and regulations to answer specific queries.

This type of specific legal analysis is necessarily beyond the general educational objective of the GLBS Guide and for which a bar-admitted attorney in the particular state(s) is needed. Bryan L. Ciyou, Esq., Ciyou & Dixon, P.C. is/are not engaged in rendering legal services hereby, nor is the firm soliciting any client.

Professional contact only may be made through the following contact methods for Bryan L. Ciyou:

Bryan L. Ciyou
CIYOU & DIXON, P.C.
50 E 91st St.
Suite 200
Indianapolis, Indiana 46240
Telephone: (317) 972-8000
Facsimile: (317) 955-7100
E-Mail: bciyou@ciyoudixonlaw.com

Specific and/or general questions are not answered by use of this contact information. All queries should be directed to competent legal counsel in Your jurisdiction.

HOT TRENDS AND NEW FOR 2018

2018 begins with a number of interesting trends facing (lawful) gun owners.

For many Readers, the question this Book helps them wrestle with is self-defense and violent crime.

From the most recent FBI data, violent crime increased for the second consecutive year, while property crime decreased for the 14th straight year (2016). The most recent report shows there were an estimated 1.2 million violent crimes in the U.S. in 2016. By region, violent crime was up in the West and Midwest and down in the South and Northeast (2012).

Against this statistical backdrop, the FBI reported the highest Black Friday background checks level in history in 2014, at more than 175,000 and corresponding with potential gun purchases. And speaking of statistics, women continue to be the fastest growing segment of first-time gun purchasers. The number of background checks conducted by the FBI has more than tripled in the last decade, from 8,952,941 in 2005 to over 27.5 million in 2016.

The market for firearms and ammunition remains somewhat volatile and some consumers are concerned about possible effects on gun laws as a result of the 2016 presidential election. There is often a sharp jump in demand (and by extension prices) in the aftermath of mass shootings or presidential elections, as many people fear that new restrictions on firearm ownership may be passed as a result and start "panic buying" guns and ammo while they are still able to.

Within mainstream media, some stories of lawful self-defense of individual's life by a firearm or third parties are making national news. However, there are many more stories questioning the right to keep and bear arms, from individuals brandishing "toy" guns that are shot and killed by a person believing the firearm is real to injuries by pellet and BB guns.

Under this backdrop and to new laws, Congress has been unable to get any consensus to pass new gun legislation. There does not appear to be any gun cases posed in the United States Supreme Court; however, the President will have four potential appointments and this may dramatically impact the types of gun cases decided by SCOTUS.

However, there are significant "administrative" actions being taken that have a direct impact on the right to keep and bear arms. Under ATF regulations and state actions, individuals who are disqualified for mental illness is being expanded to vast swaths of society, including some Veterans returning from active duty. A new ATF ruling eliminated the requirement that NFA applicants get approval from their Chief Law Enforcement Officer, but added the requirement that NFA trusts obtain fingerprints and photos from all trustees for every NFA purchase.

The other trend—all dangers to the individual right to possess firearms—emerging stems from the United States signing the United Nations Small Arms Treaty. However, it still has to be ratified by the Senate and, thus, is not law yet. Finally, the Attorney General and ATF continue to take a more restrictive approach to the right to private sales to build and liquidate a personal collection. Anyone operating under this exception should take great care to follow the specific language of the U.S. Code and case law applying it, which is increasingly being watered down by cases and jury instructions.

These are all significant Federal trends that those who count private ownership of firearms as a constitutional right should follow. All of these trends are aimed at more restrictions on private gun ownership. Where applicable to this Book, this material is covered in the many legal changes in the laws in the last year.

Within the States, a new "Wild West" is emerging—those states that have a strong preference for private gun ownership and those who do not. To understand this, more densely populated states or cities tend to fall within the "anti-gun" position and lightly populated states with the "pro-gun" stance.

In a few states with a strong gun culture, there have been laws passed that refuse to recognize more restrictive federal gun laws and regulations. In states or cities, with a position against private gun ownership, handguns in particular, a host of laws have been passed to address firearms access.

These changes are noted in the context of this Book. However, understanding the ever-changing nature of law and how it is applied is something that should be researched to Your individual satisfaction before any carry or transportation of firearms.

TABLE OF CONTENTS

NATURAL AND CONSTITUTIONAL RIGHT TO BEAR ARMS

I. United States Constitution

The Second Amendment provides: "A well regulated Militia, being necessary to the security of a free State, the right of the people to keep and bear Arms, shall not be infringed."

II. Natural Law Right to Self-Preservation

There is a natural (or divine) law of the right of resistance and self-preservation. As such, an individual may use firearms for this purpose when the intervention of society may be too late. As such, the Second Amendment to the United States Constitution does not grant this ancient right, but exists to prevent its infringement. *United States v. Cruikshank*, 92 U.S. 542 (1876).

III. Individual Right to Bear Arms

The Second Amendment to the United States Constitution protects the individual right to keep and bear arms; it is not a collective right for the state national guard or federal military. As such, the government cannot ban the entire class of firearms, handguns, overwhelmingly preferred by citizens for self-defense. *District of Columbia v. Heller*, 554 U.S. 570 (2008).

IV. Second Amendment Applies to States by Due Process Clause

The Second Amendment is incorporated and applicable to the states and individuals in the states by the Fourteenth Amendment. *McDonald v. City of Chicago*, 561 U.S. 3025 (2010).

BRIEF HISTORY OF FIREARMS' REGULATION

The constitutional right to keep and bear arms inherently directs a historical component to law itself. In fact, firearms law has a rich history preserved in legislative records (codes) and judicial records (cases).

A somewhat arbitrary point of time to begin exploring this history of firearms regulation is with colonial life, the root of the society in which we now live. Within the colonies, most families (the men) had firearms. And there were a number of laws relating to firearms, particularly focused on discharge and fire hunting.

On the frontier, outside of any notion of an organized society, firearms were an indispensable part of everyday life. It was mainly by a hunter's skill that the frontier family was fed and protected.

In fact, a gun was *the* line of defense against the dangers of the wilderness, lawless bandits, and hostile encounters with Native Americans. Thus, even the most ill-prepared pioneers counted a rifle, or sometimes a pistol, among their minimal possessions. Also, whether by choice or necessity, frontier women were skilled gun-handlers.

As the states settled, most adopted constitutions with the right to keep and bear arms. Open carry of firearms was lawful and normal. Regulation of firearms, as in the colonies (states) to the east, soon followed. Some early statutes prohibited everyone, except travelers, from wearing or carrying concealed weapons.

Practically, this was focused on handguns for the most part because the Kentucky Rifle was over four feet long and not readily capable of being concealed. State-based regulation continued hand-in-hand as the states evolved and life became more industrialized.

Jumping ahead to the 20th Century, the state legislatures ultimately adopted certain provisions of the Uniform Firearms Act.

Among those, the legislatures codified the requirement for a license to carry a handgun, and courts upheld challenges unique to handgun regulation as constitutional, all given the ease of concealability.

V.   Felons May Transfer their Firearms to Third Parties

People convicted of felonies are prohibited from owning firearms, and may be required to surrender any firearms they possess to the government. Felons who have surrendered their firearms to the government may petition a court to transfer those firearms to a third party, such as a friend, as long as the court is satisfied that the recipient of those firearms will not allow the felon to use or have control over them. *Henderson v. U.S.,* 135 S.Ct. 1780 (2015).

PART I: GETTING STARTED

In Part I, the GLBS Guide takes on the daunting task of pulling together 200-plus years of U.S. History and legal developments to get to the current state of affairs governing a person holding a valid license to carry, who is carrying in another state by a reciprocity agreement. Through Part I, the GLBS Guide specifically addresses the scope of reciprocity agreements and the state and federal criminal statutory law most likely to cause a licensee risk. However, states that do not have state-based preemption, whereby the state legislative body makes the majority of gun laws, are legally risky states into which to carry firearms under a reciprocity agreement, if it exists.

While beyond the scope of the GLBS Guide, a number of research tools and suggestions are contained in Part I to aid Readers if this is the case, which also may aid with long-gun questions that Readers may have. These broad research tools applicable to all firearms are found throughout the GLBS Guide. Part I is purely a foundational section to set forth the scope of considerations necessary for lawful reciprocal carry.

The Chapters that accomplish this are the following:

- **Chapter 1: The GLBS Guide and Its Use!**
- **Chapter 2: What is Reciprocity?**
- **Chapter 3: Where is the Law Located?**
- **Chapter 4: Determining Lawful Reciprocal Carry and Law**
- **Chapter 5: Key Definitions**
- **Chapter 6: Common Acronyms**
- **Chapter 7: Myth-Busters**
- **Chapter 8: Recent Decisions & Upcoming Issues**

Chapter One
The GLBS Guide and Its Use

I.   Introduction

With the Internet, there are numerous official state sources, chat rooms, blogs, and materials available on any given state's gun laws and reciprocal carry. These sources are useful depending on the level of question that may arise. However, they are not integrated, and many are based on "updates" that are made from "paper" laws that take days, weeks or months to become available in that format.

In addition, the available resources do not cross the rather bright lines between interstate transportation of a firearm, such as by checking-in baggage on a commercial flight (a federal right), to retrieval of the firearm at the airport and lawful carrying in another state (determined by state law). This is a complex scheme, whether You prefer a single-shot shotgun or bolt-action rifle.

At the next level, carrying a handgun in reciprocal carry (as opposed to lawful transport) brings on an entirely new set of legal complexity because handguns are more highly regulated. And with reciprocal carry, it is occurring in a state in which the non-resident is likely to be unfamiliar or less familiar with its primary criminal law (mostly statutes) that may have a simple provision different from the state that issued the license. If this criminal provision is not followed, it may well result in criminal arrest.

EX **Disclose First Police Contact.** For instance, in Alaska, a person lawfully carrying a concealed handgun under their state's reciprocity agreement with Alaska, would commit a crime if, at the time he or she comes upon a police officer, the person fails to immediately inform the police officer that he or she is carrying a concealed handgun. This is not the law in many other jurisdictions.

2

Thus, determining reciprocity and criminal laws is the central focus of the GLBS Guide.

II.   Connecting the Dots

This GLBS Guide is the first of its kind that ties together and boldly crosses into the invisible lines between transportation versus carry and interaction between state and federal law. Some of these are issues and concerns that law enforcement officers face when they carry off-duty in other states or do so after they retire under H.R. 218 (a federal law). And there is a proliferation of licenses and gun law-making, in some cases complicating the analysis.

To date, such a book has been unable to be written because it faced structural problems that were impossible to overcome. With tens of thousands of gun laws, the book would be too complex a resource to write and print or too simplistic to even be useful. Today however, with handheld, mobile devices being commonplace, this is possible.

Precisely now, this is accomplished by compiling the legal information that most people likely require to stay lawful in most reciprocal situations, be they a civilian carrying under a reciprocity agreement, or an off-duty law enforcement officer. Hyperlinks to official and other sources sweep in the rest of issues that may arise so that You can access, in real time, second or third checks of complex queries or account for unexpected deviations in travel plans.

The GLBS Guide is that tool. The GLBS Guide is apolitical, merely connecting law, although not a tool designed to challenge it directly. That is a different need, and it is well-served by powerful lobbies, such as the NRA [http://gunla.ws/nra] and GOA [http://gunla.ws/goa].

III.   Reciprocity and Criminal Law Focus

As noted, the focus of the GLBS Guide is with the federal and state criminal laws and determining reciprocity agreements themselves. Running afoul of criminal laws with reciprocal carry is the greatest risk, save for an unjustified use of deadly force, as it may mean arrest, conviction and imprisonment. However, it is critical to stay mindful that this *is not* all-controlling law.

Many, if not most, jurisdictions have a vast array of other laws that might impact lawful carry, from cases decided under licensing and penal statutes, for which FindLaw.com [http://gunla.ws/findlaw] provides a powerful resource database to search. Local ordinances are difficult to locate. However, a few powerful online resources [http://gunla.ws/am] along with ATFE [http://gunla.ws/atfe] provide good sources. These are identified for Your future research in various places in the book. However, they are not analyzed herein.

Where useful, hyperlinks are provided to aid with the various other such queries You may face or need to consider in any given state and situation, such as the noted local ordinances and hunting laws. In addition, with reciprocity and criminal law, checking and cross-checking and verifying Your conclusions through multiple sources is always prudent.

IV.   Other Authoritative Resources

To this end, there is no substitute for a knowledgeable person in the proposed state for reciprocal carry, such as the official author of a book on that state's gun laws and/or advice of counsel in that state.

A good staple in Your research is to access (and support) The National Rifle Association's materials, which are comprehensive and available online. Again, the hallmark of good legal research is cross-checking what You discover with multiple sources to ensure

4

its accuracy and timeliness.

V.   Worksheets

In the beginning, determining reciprocity and controlling state and federal law is confounding for most Readers. However, to help You navigate the process, and as a supplement to the GLBS Guide, there are worksheets to aid in Your research for proposed reciprocal carry. This also helps You organize and internalize the material. These are provided at the end of the GLBS Guide.

VI.   Icons

To act as an instructional aide, several icons are utilized throughout the GLBS Guide to make key points, set out examples, or identify problematic areas. They are indented and identified as follows:

AN **Author's Note**. This icon provides commentary on areas of common concern or confusion among Readers. Moreover, this flag is used, at appropriate junctures, to qualify the text. In a few places, this symbol sets forth subjective points or positions held by the Author. Nevertheless, this should not be confused with the law-and-order focus of the GLBS Guide: It is not written to *test* the law.

CA **Caution**. The caution icon highlights the number of factual and legal circumstances where unintended violation of penal law might occur. Many criminal defendants who run afoul of firearms law were otherwise law-abiding citizens who did not properly understand the penal law. In other words, many cases and arrests for firearms violations are not the product of hardened criminals.

CL **Case Law**. The case law icon sets out actual cases on point, typically those decided at the federal level. These are used to illustrate points in the text or how certain cases have changed or developed the law. Again, even with the statutory penal focus of the GLBS Guide, there are significant state and federal cases applying and/or interpreting state or federal statutes.

EX **Example**. The example icon highlights a relevant incident or specific instance of the law and/or its application to illustrate a point in the GLBS Guide to aid the reader's understanding.

HY **Hypothetical**. The hypotheticals flagged by this icon in the GLBS Guide are a common learning tool employed in law school education to illustrate a legal point, ambiguity in the law, or possible application of the law to a specific set of facts.

LC **Legal Concept**. The legal concepts are critical bits of the material that the Reader must understand to make prudent decisions in analyzing firearms matters. Specifically, this icon presents information to help differentiate similar legal issues or matters that might be equated as one and the same, and thereby, obscure the material of the text and analysis to be made therefrom. Grasping and applying these concepts often demarcates the line between lawful and unlawful behavior, criminal, civil and/or regulatory.

NL **New Law**. This icon is employed to highlight changes, refinements, interpretations or important or unique applications of a given firearms law. These not only allow a Reader to more fully understand and follow a particular law, but also provide insight into the complex lawmaking process.

6

VII. Hyperlinks

What makes the GLBS Guide unique is its shortened hyperlinks. These allow easy access to the best state and federal primary law and other quality reference materials. These allow You to delve into technical material, if necessary, to answer specific and/or unique questions.

VIII. Conclusion

We hope the GLBS Guide aids You in determining and exercising concealed, reciprocal carry. This is a learning curve for everyone, and we at Peritus Holdings, Inc., the publisher, welcome Your insights on how to make the GLBS Guide a more accurate, authoritative, timely and complete resource tool. It is only with finding the law and then following the law that gun owners understand what they want to seek to change and, by doing so, keep free of criminal and/or civil issues.

This is what makes America and its legal system the envy of the world; and it ensures a free society.

Chapter Two
What is Reciprocity?

I. Introduction

Congress has made a specific policy statement in the United States Code, Chapter 44 covering firearms, that it is *not* preempting the field in firearms, which it could do (at least arguably) under the authority of the Commerce Clause. Further, under the status of federal firearms law at present, there is no federal license to carry a handgun [http://gunla.ws/title18].

This is where, why and how that reciprocity and reciprocal carry comes into play. The point of departure with the GLBS Guide is with delineating exactly what is meant by the various terms this legal concept embodies and has associated with it, collectively referred to by many Readers by some or all of the following terms:

- Reciprocity
- Reciprocal carry
- Non-resident license
- CCP, CCW, permit, license
- Carrying in another state

II. The Legal Concept and Authority

What these terms refer to, collectively, is a legal scheme whereby certain states that issue licenses to carry a concealed handgun have made agreements with other states so as to recognize *some* or *all* other state licenses to carry a handgun as valid for reciprocal carry in their state. In today's mobile society, precisely understanding the implications of carrying in more than one state is an important starting point to carrying at all. Accordingly, the GLBS Guide dissects the various components of reciprocity.

III. Varying Scope of Reciprocity Agreements

Different states have different scopes to reciprocity, if they have reciprocity at all. The fact that Your state is reciprocal with all states does not mean You can carry in all the states that Your state allows.

LC **Recognizing All States.** Indiana's reciprocity agreement reflects the broadest recognition of other states' licenses: "Licenses to carry handguns, issued by other states or foreign countries, will be recognized according to the terms thereof but only while the holders are not residents of Indiana."

With most states, the legislative body authorizing reciprocity agreements requires the attorney general, state police or a similar agency to verify, at a minimum, that the other state recognizes their licenses for their residents. Hoosiers face a situation in which there are states that do not recognize their license, while Indiana recognizes licenses from all other states.

In the balance of states, the statutory authority requires a written agreement between the states and/or verification that their licensing requirements, particularly in terms of training and qualification with firearms, is as strict as theirs so that the state's residents are ensured the same measure of safe gun-handling by non-residents.

IV. Reciprocity Agreements Change

Finally, reciprocity agreements, once reached between states, might terminate at some point in time, as was recently the case between Florida and Utah; both of these states also have prolific non-resident licensing programs. A number of states signed new reciprocity agreements in 2016, and also revoked a number of agreements.

V.   Conclusion

Do You now understand the legal concept of reciprocity? It is state-based and not a federal right, similar to certain professional licenses, where one state recognizes another's subject to some minor paperwork. There may be no reciprocity between certain states and, therefore, preclude Your carry in that state. It is an imperfect solution, but that is the alternative unless and until Congress passes a federal provision that is signed into law by the President.

Chapter Three
Where is the Law?

I.   Introduction

The law is dynamic and varies from place to place and over the course of time; yet it is created and developed, within the relatively uniform, highly stable, and structured State and Federal legal systems.

How law is made (and who may make it), and particularly the enforcement and prosecution of criminal matters, must be understood by the Reader in order to reach the requisite level of competence as to lawful reciprocal carry. The GLBS Guide provides a depth of coverage on reciprocal carry and on potential criminal implications associated with ignorance on the topic.

In addition, as Your base knowledge increases, You will likely want to delve into firearms' civil and regulatory and ordinance matters. The GLBS Guide, consistent with connecting the proverbial legal dots, provides some material in this chapter for Your future use as You advance Your study.

II.   The Components of (Recipe for) Law-Making

Laws (including firearms laws) are made to meet, actual or perceived, public needs. Assuming a law is passed (by the legislative branch) and signed into law (by the executive branch), it only has to pass Constitutional muster (as decided by judicial branch) to stay on the books, unless it sunsets like the 1994 to 2004 Assault Weapons Ban. These are the three (3) branches of government accounting for all laws.

Because public policy and constitutionality factor into gun laws, they are analyzed:

A.   Public Policy

At the fundamental level, social, political and/or economic policy matters drive lawmaking.

Thus, determining the policy the law attempts to effectuate may drive the analysis of any given legal question, from changing the law to its application.

HY **Mandatory Seat Belt Laws.** A classic example of public policy resulting in laws is demonstrated by the policy underpinning mandatory seat belt laws - the need to preserve life. Simply put, seat belts work in keeping occupants restrained in a motor vehicle in a crash, thereby reducing injury and preserving life. There is little debate about the myriad of benefits from wearing a seat belt or that seat belt laws have saved lives. A permutation of this hypothetical aptly demonstrates the difficulty that any proposal to repeal mandatory seat belt laws would face, hence highlighting how policy drives law (or does not do so). Given the statistics on lives saved by seat belts, it would likely have little legislative momentum; the social, political and economic benefits are too great. Who would support it with a countervailing policy, and what would that policy be?

However, the more that reasonable men and women differ on the merits of a policy, and firearms certainly fits the bill as it has several policy "camps," the more complex the legal analysis becomes: some policy groups firmly believe that guns cause crime; and that if firearms, particularly handguns, were more regulated or prohibited, crime would decrease.

On the other hand, other policy camps strongly embrace the reasoning that a firearm is but a tool to effectively commit crimes, and that in the absence of easily obtained firearms, some other deadly weapon would replace the role that firearms play.

12

This camp believes the actual issue is societal acceptance of violent crime as a fixed and unchanging component of American life, which is masked by focusing on firearms regulation. Inasmuch, this camp believes that law-abiding citizens should be able to possess firearms to protect themselves.

The reason for the complexity in analysis should now be apparent: there are many laws and exceptions to the laws. Why? With hotly contested and competing policies, different policy groups fund public awareness programs and, by lobbying politicians, they push for lawmaking consistent with their views. However, after this lawmaking occurs (if it does), a different policy group may be successful in obtaining an exception to the law through passage of another law that cuts away at the authority of the prior law.

In other words, under sway of policy and/or advocacy groups, the legislatures and/or Congress adopt statutes, which, when signed into law, are then applied, enforced, and developed by State or Federal courts by case law. Ultimately, these evolve with society, for better or worse. This creates layer upon layer of legal complexity that must be peeled back like the proverbial onion to decide what the law is in a particular place.

This is an inefficient legal model. However, this is the model our society envisioned and contracted for by the Founding Fathers vis-à-vis the United States (and States') Constitution. The legal system flowing therefrom ensures the fundamental legal concepts such as Due Process. Above all, freedom.

That said, despite its glaring shortfalls at times, it is, arguably, the best, most advanced system any organized, post-industrial society has implemented to date. Without the rule of law, our society would not exist in its present form. Without our current system, the freedom we experience would be diminished.

B.   Constitutional Limits

Despite the great power of the people to advance and/or change policy, effectuated by the legislative branch, as checked and balanced by the executive branch (veto power) and judiciary (trial courts generally), there are outer limits on the policy-to-statute legislative process and, ultimately, the legal system's enforcement and refinement of these laws.

Statutory law and case decisions — all law for that fact — are constrained by, and must operate within, constitutional parameters. These boundaries are set forth in the United States Constitution and the states' constitutions. These are supreme sources of law from which all laws emanate, meaning they must not be abridged.

As a general rule, constitutional boundaries and thresholds are not reached in lawmaking of the Legislature or Congress, or routine enforcement by the Judiciary, even in firearms cases. However, on occasion, even routine legal matters exceed constitutional limits. This is exactly the case with the *Heller* [http://gunla.ws/heller] and the *McDonald* [http://gunla.ws/mcdonald] cases.

III.   Civil and/or Criminal Violations of the Law

When laws are adopted, they are either civil or criminal. Broadly, civil violations are remedied with monetary award. Criminal violations may also result in a monetary fine, but its significance is in the potential loss of freedom by incarceration and/or removal of certain constitutional rights, such as the right to vote (or right to bear arms as with a felony conviction).

The ultimate arbitrator of a violation of state and/or federal civil and/or penal law is a judge or jury. For purposes of the GLBS Guide, state coverage is limited in scope generally to crimes that could occur because of variances in carry laws between reciprocal states under local, state and federal law.

IV.   Sources of the Law

With the policy identified, if necessary and presupposing the constitutionality of the lawmaking thereupon, civil and, to some extent, criminal law is generated and developed through a number of other sources.

Primary law, namely the state and federal criminal statutes, being the most severe risk in reciprocal carry, is the focus of the GLBS Guide. This is a concern of the majority of Readers with reciprocal carry. And again, however, there are other laws from local ordinances to hunting laws that might dictate something penal or civil by act or omission in carrying under reciprocity.

In executing and enforcing civil, and to some extent, criminal statutes, or the broad policies they seek to foster, the law requires regulation in specific contexts. This is accomplished through precise rule-making by administrative arms of government. The Legislature and/or Congress, as legislative bodies, are too small to accomplish this task. Among other things, these legislative bodies lack the time and technical expertise to do so. For this reason, both create administrative bodies to consider, draft, and adopt rules and regulations, by statutory delegation of authority. Such administrative agencies may even have some responsibilities for defining the elements of a criminal offense.

For this reason, vast quantities of law are found in administrative codes. Administrative bodies of law must, thus, be considered to ensure a complete legal analysis of any given issue. The ATFE's regulations are a good example, as well as the administrative codes of each state.

In addition, within this complicated mix, under state law, some local units of government are empowered to adopt ordinances that are also laws to consider and comply with. Inasmuch, firearms laws may be embodied within any or all of the following sources of law:

A. Federal

- United States Constitution and Amendments
- SCOTUS Decisions (U.S. Supreme Court)
- United States Circuit Courts' Decisions
- Congress Criminal or Civil Statutes Codified in the U.S. Code
- Regulatory Bodies' Regulations Published in the Code of Federal Regulations (CFR)

B. State

- Constitution and Amendments
- Appellate Court Decisions
- Legislative Criminal or Civil Statutes Codified
- Regulatory Bodies' Regulations Published in the state administrative codes
- Local Ordinances

In states without state-based preemption or limited preemption, Readers must comply with local ordinances, which may vary widely and are difficult to locate. Nevertheless, by following this hyperlink [http://gunla.ws/atf] You can access the ATFE publication of all local ordinances published in the Federal Register. You can also look to some of the recognized databases that compile and house local ordinances [http://gunla.ws/am].

CA **Consider All Sources of Law that May Apply in Reciprocal Carry.** Make no mistake about the focus of the GLBS Guide. While it addresses determining reciprocity and state and federal penal law that might be commonly triggered in doing so, all of these (other) sources of law may apply to Your reciprocal carry, particularly private property, hunting, and local ordinances. It is for this reason hyperlinks are provided for Your educational use in assessing this and what additional information You may need.

V. Private Regulations

In addition to the foregoing sources' restrictions, there are private restrictions placed on firearms under property and contract law (these rights are constitutional in nature). For instance, a landowner may lease his/her property with contractual exceptions, stated in the lease, prohibiting firearms. Failure to follow this lease term by the tenant (lessee) might result in the landlord (lessor) bringing a civil action for breach of contract under property and contract law.

In some states, a violation of private rules may not result in a penal violation, but it nonetheless exposes civil liability. On the other hand, in other states, a failure to comply with posted private restrictions is a criminal act and there may be a duty to tell any private party with a possessory interest in the property that You are carrying a handgun. Failure to do so may result in ejection from the property and/or arrest.

VI. The Legal System

The means through which all these statutes, cases, rules, regulations, and agreements are enforced is by state and federal criminal and civil courts. In addition, there are administrative proceedings associated with administrative laws of the states and Code of Federal Regulation ("CFR").

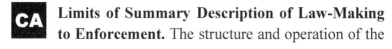 **Limits of Summary Description of Law-Making to Enforcement.** The structure and operation of the

state or federal legal system (each comprised of executive, legislative and judicial branches) could be the topic of an entire manual (and is). The GLBS Guide is not intended to address the minutia of this process and, thus, this Chapter is drastically simplified. Nonetheless, an understanding of the lawmaking process, and the legal system in which it operates through enforcement, globally aids the understanding of firearms law and compliance therewith for all Readers with reciprocal carry or otherwise.

A.   State Law

1.   Criminal Law

Under state criminal codes, criminal acts, including firearms matters related to reciprocal carry, are investigated by state and/or local law enforcement officers ("LEOs"). County prosecutors, district attorneys, or their equals determine whether to charge and commence action by filing a document (an information) or by seeking a grand-jury indictment. This is done in the county where the alleged crime occurred.

In such situations, the state is the victim and it brings the case against the defendant for violation of the relevant penal statute(s). The defendant may be represented by private counsel or by a public defender.

There is a constitutional right to legal representation in criminal cases, or certain quasi-criminal cases, despite lack of financial means. Criminal cases are typically decided by (or anticipated to be decided by) a jury.

2.   Civil

As a general rule, civil litigation is brought by the "plaintiff(s)" against the "defendant(s)" (other terms are "petitioner" and "respondent"). However, the government, such as by the Attorney General, may also bring a case as a plaintiff and the state or local government may sue as a plaintiff and be sued as a defendant.

The county court system in which the case is filed is decided by a more technical issue of preferred venue, and generally is proper where a majority of defendants live, where the property in question is located, or where the act or omission occurred.

The theory of a civil case may be in law or in equity (or both), invoking statutory law, case law and/or common law. Typically, private lawyers handle these cases. Unlike in a criminal case, in civil cases there is no general right to counsel.

Depending upon the type of matter, there may be a right to a jury trial. If not, a judge hears the case in what is referred to as "a bench trial." A bench trial may result in a judgment rendered for the plaintiff in a monetary award or, alternatively, a defense verdict in which the defendant is deemed not guilty and no monies are awarded. There are a number of variations on this trial procedure.

EX **Reciprocal Carry.** A question as to the validity of a Readers' license, or revocation proceedings, and/or return of a handgun confiscated under reciprocal carry would likely be deemed civil in nature and handled in this way or by administrative hearing.

B.   Federal: Criminal and Civil

The federal legal system largely follows the same path. The legal parlance varies, however. With regard to firearms, the matters are usually investigated by the ATF or FBI. An AUSA, who works for the Department of Justice, headed by the U.S. Attorney General, and who is the prosecutor, then decides whether to charge the matter or seek an indictment.

EX **Mistaken Carry in Federal Park Visitor's Center.** A mistake a Reader could make that would land them in federal criminal court would be to inadvertently carry into a visitor's center of a National Park. While state law may allow carry in other parts of the National Park with a license, a visitor's center is a federal facility, and it is a criminal act to carry within the confines of these places.

A trial, if it occurs, is in the United States District Court. As with state court, there is a right to legal counsel. Appeals are taken to the United States Court of Appeals for the Circuit, as a matter of right, and then, if discretionary certiorari is granted, to the Supreme Court of the United States.

As it relates to civil matters, violations of federal civil statutes (such as civil rights) may be brought in federal court; and certain state-based legal matters (federal question or diversity of citizenship, respectively) may be filed in federal court if the parties live in different states and certain threshold damages ($75,000.00) are alleged. Civil appeals track essentially the same process as that for criminal cases.

VII. Federal and State Age Requirements Regarding Firearms

There are several laws regarding how old You must be in order to purchase or carry firearms, and these laws are often confusing. There are certain things You may do at 18 and other that require You to be 21, and these can vary from state to state. Federal law requires that You be at least 18 to buy long guns or ammunition for long guns from an FFL, and 21 to buy handguns or handgun ammunition from an FFL, or to purchase NFA items. Federal law generally prohibits people under the age of 18 from owning or possessing handguns, except under adult supervision. States enact their own laws governing how old You must be to obtain a CCP or buy guns in private transfers, and these laws differ from state to state. A private transfer is a sale between two residents of the same state such as friends, when neither of the parties holds an FFL. In many states, You only have to be 18 to purchase handguns and handgun ammunition from private parties.

In addition, several states such as Indiana allow You to obtain a CCP as soon as You turn 18. Note that most states require You to be 21 to carry a handgun, and include this as a requirement for reciprocity. For example, if state A issues CCPs at age 18 and state B only issues them at age 21, a 20-year-old with a valid CCP from state A could not carry in state B even if the two states have a reciprocity agreement. Likewise, many states allow You to open carry handguns at age 18, even if they don't allow concealed carry until You turn 21.

Some states have stricter rules, for example in New York You must be 21 to even possess a handgun, while Illinois and Washington D.C. generally require You to be 21 in order to obtain a permit to purchase or possess any firearm, even long guns. States with assault weapon bans often require You to be 21 to possess an "assault weapon", even if You only have to be 18 to obtain or possess other long guns.

VIII. Recent Trends in Gun Laws

Firearm laws are changing almost constantly, but most gun laws can be categorized into several distinct patterns, and understanding these trends makes it much easier to make sense of the changing legal landscape. As a rule of thumb, every type of new gun law falls into one of two overarching categories: laws that expand gun rights, and laws that restrict them. There are several distinct trends within both categories. By and large, there is a trend in conservative states such as Texas to expand gun rights (such as by broadening the scope of who can carry guns, where they can be carried, and when force can be used in self-defense), and another trend in liberal states such as New York to pass restrictions on gun ownership (such as assault weapon bans, universal background checks, and restrictions on magazine capacity). In the political debate, these two positions (and the states that adopt them) are generally referred to as being "pro-gun" or "anti-gun" (though many proponents of laws restricting firearms prefer the terms "pro-gun safety" or "pro-gun control" to "anti-gun"). Both sides of the political spectrum have been pushing their states to one extreme or the other with very little common ground. There are a few exceptions to these broad trends, generally when restrictive laws in liberal states get struck down in court. For example, the ability to carry firearms has expanded even in liberal states such as Illinois, and absolute bans on handguns have been repeatedly nullified by courts since the 2008 *Heller* decision.

Pro-gun laws generally fall into one of three categories (each of which may be comprised of several related trends): Laws that expand who can carry guns, laws that expand where guns can be carried, and laws that expand when lethal force may be used in self-defense. A prime example of the first trend is the steady expansion of several types of laws allowing people to carry guns on their person. As of 2013, every state now issues a CCP, and while some states make these permits hard to get, the general trend has been towards making it easier to get a permit by adopting "shall issue" laws which mandate that a CCP must be issued to any applicant who is not legally prohibited from owning guns. In an expansion of who can carry guns a rapidly growing number of states now allow "open carry", i.e., carrying a firearm openly in plain view like police officers do. Currently 45 states allow open carry in some form, and 30 states do not require a permit or license in order to open carry.

Another recent trend is the growth of "constitutional carry" laws, which refers to the legal carrying of a concealed handgun without a license or permit. Many states already allow open carry without a permit; constitutional carry refers specifically to laws allowing permitless concealed carry. In constitutional carry states, a firearm owner may legally carry a concealed handgun without needing a permit. Many states only require a permit to carry a handgun concealed, but not openly. Constitutional carry states do not require a permit for either. The exact nature of these laws can vary between states, so You should always read up on the specific laws of a state before carrying there without a permit. Constitutional carry began in Vermont and is now legal in 13 states. The list of constitutional carry states currently encompasses: Alaska, Arizona, Arkansas (disputed), Idaho (residents only), Kansas, Maine, Mississippi, Missouri, New Hampshire, North Dakota (residents only), Vermont, West Virginia, and Wyoming (residents only). Three states have a limited form of permitless concealed carry: Montana (outside city limits), New Mexico (can carry unloaded gun and loaded magazine, plus concealed carry in vehicle), and Oklahoma (permitless carry for residents of constitutional carry states). Several other states are scheduled to debate reform including Colorado, Indiana, Kentucky, Minnesota, New Hampshire, North Dakota, South Dakota and Texas. Not all of these states are expected to pass reform over the next year, but considering the current trend, the number of states with constitutional carry is likely to grow.

The next big trend is the expansion of places where You can legally carry firearms, such as at work or on college campuses. A growing number of states have laws that protect Your right to carry firearms at work, mainly the right to keep a gun in Your car while parked on Your employer's property. A common example of this is the law recently passed in Tennessee that makes it illegal for employers to punish, fire, or reprimand employees for having firearms legally stored in their private vehicle. Utah and Texas have also recently adopted laws allowing people with a CCP to carry on the campus of any public university. These types of laws generally work by prohibiting employers or schools from adopting or enforcing strict no-gun policies: while carrying a gun at Your work or college may not be illegal in many states, You could be fired or expelled for having a gun, while laws like the one in Texas protect You from being punished for having a gun in a legal manner.

Another example of laws expanding where You can legally carry firearms is the possibility for a National Reciprocity Act, which has been proposed several times before, but now stands a decent chance of passing into law. Critics of the current state-based reciprocity system fear that gun owners crossing state lines with legally registered firearms can land in prison due to the current patchwork of laws. Recently, lawmakers have sought to standardize reciprocity with the National Reciprocity Act of 2017. In its current form, the Act would amend the federal criminal code to permit individuals who are allowed to carry guns in their home states to exercise the rights in any other state that allows concealed carry. Despite its uniform application, the Act does not restrict state and local governments' ability to decide where citizens may or may not carry firearms. It essentially extends the same rights to a non-resident who lawfully carries in their home state the same rights afforded to lawfully carrying state residents. Similarly, the Law Enforcement Officers Safety Act of 2004 resembles both national reciprocity and constitutional carry. It allows police officers (and retired police officers, provided they served for at least 10 years and were discharged in good standing) to carry a concealed weapon in any state or jurisdiction in the U.S. without a permit, regardless of local laws. National Reciprocity would have a similar effect; by allowing people with a valid carry permit issued in one state to carry a concealed weapon in all other states, even states with stricter gun laws.

The National Reciprocity Act is aimed at providing legal gun owners the ability to travel freely between states without having to worry about conflicting state codes or onerous civil suits. Additionally, the Act specifies that a qualified individual who lawfully carries a concealed firearm in another state is not subject to the federal prohibition on possessing a firearm in a school zone. Along with provisions to open up more federal land for hunting, the Act reinforces the existing reciprocity that exists for National Parks and National Wildlife Refuges, but would also lift the ban on firearms on federal lands managed by the Army Corps of Engineers.

Another pro-gun trend is the expansion of self-defense laws. More states have been adopting "castle doctrine" or "stand Your ground" laws, which expand when and where people can use deadly force in self-defense. These types of laws have been in the political spotlight recently due to several high-profile cases (most notably the shooting of Trayvon Martin in Florida). "Castle doctrine" and "stand Your ground" laws explicitly state that people do not have a duty to retreat from an attacker, and may use deadly force if they reasonably believe it necessary to prevent death or serious injury. "Castle Doctrine" laws have been around for over a century, so the recent trend has been towards "stand Your ground" laws. These types of laws are very similar; the difference is that Castle Doctrine only applies to Your home or property (some states extend it to Your place of business or car), whereas "stand Your ground" laws expand upon that and say You have no duty to retreat from an attack that occurs in public. Think of "stand Your ground" laws as a broader version of the castle doctrine that expands Your right of self-defense beyond Your property.

Conversely, there has been a growing movement among more liberal states to restrict gun ownership, especially after the Sandy Hook shooting in 2012. Common trends are expansion of assault weapons bans, limits on "high-capacity" magazines (these are often part of a larger assault weapons ban), and universal background checks. Assault weapon bans (AWB) have been around since the '90s, and many states model theirs after the federal assault weapons ban that was in place from 1994 to 2004. AWBs typically try to restrict or ban semi-automatic rifles such as the AR15. California recently tightened their AWB by expanding the definition of what constitutes a prohibited "assault weapon" and requiring that assault weapons be registered within a certain timeframe or risk being confiscated. The most common anti-gun trend is the expansion of laws that restrict magazine capacity and ban "high-capacity" magazines (usually means magazines capable of holding more than 10 rounds, although the specifics vary from as low as 7 in New York to 15 in Colorado and New Jersey). The final trend is the adoption of universal background check policies. These laws are aimed at closing the so called "gun show loophole" by requiring that all gun sales go through a licensed dealer, who conducts a background check on the buyer for a nominal fee. In states with universal background checks all sales between private parties (such as between friends or between people who meet and arrange the sale online) must go through a licensed dealer and conduct a background check before the buyer may take possession of the firearm. Note that transfers/gifts between family members are often exempt from these requirements, but the details of who counts as family (i.e., immediate relatives only, or a broader definition including aunts/cousins etc.) vary from state to state.

In this same vein is the recent possibility for a Federal law banning "bump stocks." On October 1, 2017, a gunman fired from the 32nd floor of the Mandalay Bay Resort & Casino at a crowd attending a music festival, killing 58 people and wounding 515 others. Of the nearly two-dozen guns authorities discovered in the shooter's hotel room, half were modified with a device known as a "bump stock" or "bump fire stock." A bump stock is an attachment that enables a semi-automatic rifle to fire at a rate similar to a fully automatic rifle by freeing the weapon to slide back and forth rapidly while the trigger finger is held in place. This causes the trigger to be pushed against the trigger finger in rapid succession, allowing one to pull the trigger rapidly enough to create a rate of fire similar to that of machine guns.

Bump stocks are not banned under federal law. However, in the aftermath of the Las Vegas mass shooting, a public debate has begun as to whether bump stocks should be regulated more tightly, or banned altogether. Days after the shooting, the NRA announced that it would support tighter restrictions on such devices. Furthermore, several Republicans in Congress along with President Trump have expressed willingness to consider an outright ban. The mass shooting in Las Vegas is likely to influence potential legislation regarding bump stocks, as well as other gun law legislation that was already in the works.

Another pro-gun trend involves the removal of restrictions placed on suppressors by the NFA. At the federal level, lawmakers have proposed the Hearing Protection Act, which removes suppressors from the regulatory scheme of the NFA, which requires a $200 tax stamp and an exhaustive background check that can take 6-10 months. Under the Hearing Protection Act, suppressors would be regulated like ordinary firearms, meaning they would have to be purchased from an FFL and would require passing an ordinary background check. If successful, suppressors would essentially be regulated as a firearm.

The reduction of restrictions on suppressors has garnered much support from gun owners and hunters who appreciate suppressors' ability to mute the sound of gunfire to a point where hearing damage is limited, as well as reducing noise pollution from shooting ranges, which can be a concern especially if the shooting range is located in or near a city. While the proposed legislation addresses a safety hazard long cited by gun owners and hunters as an unnecessary danger, opponents argue that increasing accessibility to suppressors is a threat to public safety. Congress is expected to vote on this sometime in the winter of 2017 or early 2018, although an exact date has not yet been set.

One final related trend, at least in the state of New York, has been increased regulation of toy guns. In recent years, New York has passed laws requiring that all toy guns (generally meaning props, imitations, and look-a-likes, not airsoft, pellet, or BB guns) must be painted in bright color or made of transparent plastic, so they can be easily identified as toys, and not confused with real firearms. This is intended to reduce accidental shootings where police or bystanders mistake a toy gun for a real gun and shoot the person wielding it, such as the shooting of Tamir Rice. Many states have some laws like this on the books, such as requiring toy guns to have a bright orange barrel tip, and some have more detailed laws governing the appearance of toy guns to make them appear visually distinct from real guns.

IX. Conclusion

With reciprocal carry, the biggest risk is unknowingly violating a federal criminal law, such as school zones, applied differently by overlapping state coverage, violating a federal property restriction, or by differences between state penal laws. The more You understand about who makes law, where laws are reduced to written form, and how laws are enforced, the more You will see commonalities. Thus, the better You will be at strict compliance, which is what is sometimes expected by law enforcement. Ultimately, every choice in life is a risk, and so too is the decision to engage in reciprocal carry. The GLBS Guide hopefully helps reduce this risk of the diversity in laws among the 50 states.

Chapter Four
Determining Lawful Reciprocal Carry & Law

I.   Introduction

The foregoing chapter frames the American legal system: from policy to lawmaking, through civil and criminal enforcement. That said, with the complexity, ambiguity and evolving nature of primary law (cases and statutes), rules and regulations, it is only possible to perhaps provide "the" answer to a precise legal issue at one specific moment in time. Inasmuch, the law cannot just be looked up in a book, including the GLBS Guide, as You will see the more You study it.

II.   How to Make a Decision

For this reason, the prudent Reader who is involved with firearms in any personal or professional capacity should not seek "the" answer in exploring reciprocal carry, generally. Instead, he or she should determine and consider a range of courses of action to address the legal need, thought best as existing on a continuum: the black (not lawful), white (lawful), or gray (maybe lawful/unlawful).

Many, if not most, courses of action, including reciprocal carry, involve the gray areas on a continuum. These gray areas allow our society to work and be flexible enough to meet the needs of the day. However, the gray areas also involve civil and/or criminal and/or administrative risk. In fact, most everyone violates some law, rule or ordinance each day.

III.   Risk Tolerance and Status

A Reader's risk tolerance is thus a valid variable to consider, although it may be more or less unique to a profession. Most LEOs, operating under color of law, have immunity, and if he/she has reasonable suspicion to stop an individual and probable cause for arrest for a firearms violation, it is a matter of professional judgment.

The obvious proof of an improper analysis by a LEO, and such arrest, is dismissal of a case. For the civilian, the risk (and tolerance thereof) may be quite different, as violation may result in arrest and prosecution.

This is the workplace of lawyers, and it consumes a great deal of time for other professionals. Depending upon the Reader's perspective, and risk tolerance, there are a number of ways to reach a decision about a proposed act or omission within this gray area of the continuum, presupposing understanding of the controlling law. Remembering, however, everyone is accountable for his/her personal and/or professional acts.

IV.   Weighing the Risks

After the legal analysis is completed, such as researching the issues under the topical coverage of the GLBS Guide, and a course of action is cross-checked through multiple sources, the course of action, if any, might be selected based on answers to these three (3) threshold questions:

- Is the proposed reciprocal carry within the black areas and clearly impermissible? If so, this is generally the end of the analysis. The proposed course of action may not be engaged in.
- Is the proposed reciprocal within the white areas and clearly permissible? If so, this is generally the end of the analysis. The proposed course of action may be engaged

in.

- Is the proposed reciprocal carry within the gray zone? This creates the need for a second level of analysis.

Thus, if the answer or proposed course of reciprocal carry is "gray" and undetermined, the answers to a number of questions may direct the course to be taken, if any, as follows:

- Is the proposed reciprocal carry worth the loss of freedom if it is criminal?
- Is the proposed reciprocal carry worth the payment of money or administrative action if civil action results?
- What is the objective of the proposed reciprocal carry? Is the objective important, relevant to the risk? If this is self-defense, does the analysis change if You are visiting a crime-laden place versus an area with a very low violent crime rate? Only You can decide.
- What is the political climate at the particular moment in time?
- Are there professional ramifications for the decision?
- How much will it cost for a criminal and/or civil defense, even if the act or omission in connection with the reciprocal carry is ultimately deemed not criminal, under the "beyond a reasonable doubt" standard, or deemed not rising to the level of civil liability, generally under the standard of a preponderance of the evidence?
- Is there ambiguity as to the controlling law and/or its application?

If these questions do not direct a clear determination of a course of action, the Reader is well-advised to seek the opinion of counsel and/or continue the legal inquiry.

V.   Conclusion

Ultimately, Readers are assessing the matter much like an insurance company would do. There may well be states where the political climate and penalty is too great to accept. Insurers do not insure in those states, and You may choose to not carry even with reciprocity. In the balance of the case, the risk will be evaluated and a reasoned decision made, not based on urban legend or a guess, but on real information and data.

Chapter Five
Key Definitions

I. Introduction

Nearly all trades and professions utilize jargon that have a unique meaning known to those only who have some familiarity of the industry. However, with reciprocal carry, this may not be sufficient to prevent a criminal charge. To the extent possible, You should know how the state uses a given term and the differences, if any, between state and federal law.

The term "a gun" may not be sufficient enough to determine lawful from unlawful status (is the "firearm" itself legal) and carry from state to state. A "gun" might be a handgun or a long gun. A handgun, which is generally what reciprocal licenses allow for carry, however, may be a short-barreled rifle or a machine gun depending on how it is equipped.

EX **Glock 18**. Here is what could be an example of where shared common knowledge definitions and terms are insufficient to avoid criminal act:

Mr. Smith intends to travel from his state of residence, State X, to State Y, where there is a reciprocity agreement between. Mr. Smith lawfully travels to State Y and is arrested and informed his carrying and discharge of his handgun is going to subject him to a lengthy stay in State Y's prison and the confiscation and destruction of his weapon. "Why," he asks? Well, as it turns out, the handgun is a lawfully possessed and registered Glock 18 (or a clone), which is capable of fully automatic fire. This makes it a machine gun. Mr. Smith completed ATFE Form 5320.20 for Interstate Transportation of NFA Firearm. However, State Y makes it a crime to possess and discharge a machine gun, and there is no statutory exception for NFA weapons.

In the loose sense, this is a handgun, as about anyone with knowledge of firearms would agree, but in the strict technical sense, it is a machine gun, since a Glock 18 (based on the Glock 17 platform and in 9MM) has a selector switch that allows for more than one shot to be fired for each press of the trigger.

Therefore, both in traveling into another state, and in carrying in that reciprocal state, it is important if not critical to understand federal and state definitions, and the laws of both. To aid with a benchmark, the GLBS Guide sets forth some common terms and specific definitions in this chapter as found in federal law or other useful definitions.

Such definitions inform what a "handgun" is (and what is not), assuming reciprocity in any given state does not cover "long guns" and other necessary terms.

Federal law applies in some places in each state. Some states track federal definitions closely, some do not. With each state, hyperlinks are provided to allow access to state-specific resources, many of which have state-specific definitions of firearms, as well as other helpful material to stay lawful.

II.   Federal Definitions

Antique Firearm: "The term 'antique firearm' means – (A) any firearm (including any firearm with a matchlock, flintlock, percussion cap, or similar type of ignition system) manufactured before 1898; or (B) any replica of any firearm described in subparagraph (A) if such replica – (i) is not designed or redesigned for using rimfire or conventional centerfire fixed ammunition, or (ii) uses rimfire or conventional centerfire fixed ammunition which is

34

no longer manufactured in the United States and which is not readily available in the ordinary channels of commercial trade; or (C) any muzzle loading rifle, muzzle loading shotgun, or muzzle loading pistol, which is designed to use black powder, or a black powder substitute, and which cannot use fixed ammunition. For purposes of this paragraph, the term 'antique firearm' shall not include any weapon which incorporates a firearm frame or receiver, any firearm which is converted into a muzzle loading weapon, or any muzzle loading weapon which can be readily converted to fire fixed ammunition by replacing the barrel, bolt, breechblock, or any combination thereof."

Curio & Relic: Is a type of firearm that You can have mailed straight to Your door, if You possess a Curio & Relic license. For a firearm to be recognized as a Curio & Relic, it must fall into one of the three following categories:

1. *Firearms which were manufactured at least 50 years prior to the current date, but not including replicas of such firearms;*
2. *Firearms which are certified by the curator of a municipal, State, or Federal museum which exhibits firearms to be curios or relics of museum interest; and*
3. *Any other firearms which derive a substantial part of their monetary value from the fact that they are novel, rare, bizarre, or because of their association with some historical figure, period, or event.*

Firearm: "The term 'firearm' means – (A) any weapon (including starter gun) which will or is designed to or may readily be converted to expel a projectile by the action of an explosive; (B) the frame or receiver of any such weapon; (C) any firearm muffler or firearm silencer; or (D) any destructive device. Such term does not include an antique firearm."

Handgun: "The term 'handgun' means – (A) a firearm which has a short stock and is designed to be held and fired by the use of a single hand; and (B) any combination of parts from which a firearm described in subparagraph (A) can be assembled."

Machinegun: "The term 'machinegun' means any weapon which shoots, is designed to shoot, or can be readily restored to shoot, automatically more than one shot, without manual reloading, by a single function of the trigger. The term shall also include the frame or receiver of any such weapon, any part designed and intended solely and exclusively, or combination of parts designed and intended, for use in converting a weapon into a machinegun, and any combination of parts from which a machinegun can be assembled if such parts are in the possession or under the control of a person."

Rifle: "The term 'rifle' means a weapon designed or redesigned, made or remade, and intended to be fired from the shoulder and designed or redesigned and made or remade to use the energy of an explosive to fire only a single projectile through a rifled bore for each single pull of the trigger."

Semiautomatic Rifle: "The term 'semiautomatic rifle' means any repeating rifle which utilizes a portion of the energy of a firing cartridge to extract the fired cartridge case and chamber the next round, and which requires a separate pull of the trigger to fire each cartridge."

Short-Barreled Rifle: "The term 'short-barreled rifle' means a rifle having one or more barrels less than sixteen inches in length and any weapon made from a rifle (whether by alternation, modification, or otherwise) if such weapon, as modified, has an overall length of less than twenty-six inches."

Short-Barreled Shotgun: "The term 'short-barreled shotgun' means a shotgun having one or more barrels less than eighteen inches in length and any weapon made from a shotgun (whether by alternation, modification or otherwise) if such a weapon as modified has an overall length of twenty-six inches."

Shotgun: "The term 'shotgun' means a weapon designed or redesigned, made or remade, or intended to be fired from the shoulder and designed or redesigned and made or remade to use the energy of an explosive to fire through a smooth bore either a number of ball shot or a single projectile for each single pull of the trigger."

III.   Other Common Definitions

Constitutional Carry: Refers to the policy in states such as Vermont that allow anyone who is legally able to possess a firearm to carry it concealed without a permit. These states do not require that You have a valid CCP in order to carry a concealed weapon.

Castle Doctrine: Refers to a type of law governing the use of deadly force in self-defense inside Your home or property. These laws generally state that You have no duty to retreat if attacked in Your home and may use force (including deadly force) if reasonably necessary to protect yourself or others from death or serious bodily injury. Many states have some form of Castle Doctrine law, but the exact details can vary from state to state, so it is important to verify what the law is in Your state.

Duty to Retreat: Refers to a policy in states that do not have castle doctrine or stand Your ground laws. This states that deadly force may only be used as a last resort, and if attacked You are required to flee the threat if it is feasible and safe to do so, and generally may only use deadly force if You are unable to escape. Some states may also require You to surrender Your valuables to a robber if that would safely end the attack. The specifics of what You must try to do before You can legally resort to deadly force vary from state to state, so be sure to learn what the rules are in Your state.

May Issue: Refers to a policy in some states that gives the government and police discretion in deciding whether or not to issue carry permits to applicants. This decision is often left up to the local sheriff, who may have a bias towards or against issuing permits, or may require applicants to have a good reason for wanting a carry permit. Some states with this policy (such as California and New

York) tend to be very stingy with who they issue permits to, often making it almost impossible for an average citizen to obtain a carry permit.

Open Carry: Refers to laws that allow people to carry guns openly, such as in a holster on Your hip. Most states allow You to open carry without a permit, and only require permits for carrying concealed firearms. Open carry laws often apply to transporting firearms in vehicles. Generally, for a gun to be "openly" carried in a vehicle it must be readily visible from outside the vehicle, such as by being placed on the dashboard or passenger's seat.

Preemption: Refers to a state policy that prevents local governments, such as cities and municipalities, from adopting rules or regulations on firearms that are inconsistent with or stricter than the state law. This ensures that laws are uniform throughout the state, rather than being a patchwork of varying laws. States with preemption usually allow local governments to adopt some regulations governing the unsafe discharge of firearms. In states without preemption, gun laws can vary considerably throughout the state, and big cities often adopt stricter gun laws. New York City for example has very strict laws, and has its own permitting system.

Private Transfer: Refers to a sale of firearms between two private citizens who are residents of the same state, as opposed to a sale from a gun store. Private transfers are governed by state law instead of federal law, and these laws vary from state to state. Private transfers may only be conducted if both parties are residents of the same state, as the interstate sale of firearms is subject to federal law. Most states do not require background checks for private sales, and in many states You only need to be 18 purchase handguns in private sales, while You need to be 21 to purchase handguns from a licensed dealer.

Reciprocity: Refers to the policy of states to honor the CCP issued by another state. As an example, if State A has reciprocity with State B that means people with a CCP issued by State B can legally carry firearms in State A. Part IX of this book contains tables showing which states have reciprocity with others. Be mindful that reciprocity can and does change frequently as states either start honoring permits from a new state, or stop honoring permits from a state they used to have reciprocity with. For this reason, it is important to double check what the current reciprocity law is in states You plan to carry in.

Shall Issue: Refers to a policy in most states that anyone who applies for a permit to carry must be granted one as long as they are not legally disqualified from obtaining one (like convicted felons). Under this system, anyone who applies for a permit will automatically be granted one, and local law enforcement do not have discretion to deny applicants (unless they are prohibited from owning guns).

Stand Your Ground: This is a broader version of the Castle Doctrine, and allows the use of deadly force in self-defense when You are outside of Your home or in public areas. These laws generally state that You have no duty to retreat if You are attacked in any place that You have a legal right to be in (not just Your home), and may use force (including deadly force) if You reasonably believe it is necessary to protect yourself or others from imminent death, serious bodily injury, or the commission of a forcible felony. As a rule of thumb, You are generally allowed to use deadly force to protect a third party from harm if that person would have been justified in using deadly force to defend themselves. Many states have some form of Stand Your Ground law, but the exact details can vary considerably from state to state, so it is important to verify what the law is in Your state.

IV.   Conclusion

Careful compliance with the wrong understanding of the term, particularly as to the firearm itself, is unlikely a criminal defense. It is for this reason that the GLBS Guide breaks these down in chapters that address legal issues related to reciprocal carry on a step-by-step basis. Ask yourself, is Your state's definition of the dispositive legal term the same as in a reciprocal state? Would You bet Your freedom on it?

Chapter Six
Common Acronyms

I.   Introduction

There are a number of acronyms that will be used commonly in the GLBS Guide. To make the most of Your research with reciprocal carry and to ensure You have the correct meaning, it is important to understand the acronyms. Some carry two or more meanings, for example, LEO may be "Law Enforcement Officer" or "Law Enforcement Only," the latter associated with magazine and weapons markings during the 1994 to 2004 period encompassing the assault weapons ban. In addition, the terms "CCP, CCW, and CHL" all refer to the same thing and are often used interchangeably.

II.   The Acronyms

AG:	Attorney General
ALJ:	Administrative Law Judge
AMS:	Alternative Misdemeanor Sentencing
AOW:	Any Other Weapon
ATF(E):	Bureau of Alcohol, Tobacco, Firearms and Explosives
AUSA:	Assistant United States Attorney
AWB:	Assault Weapons Ban
CBP:	Customs and Border Protection
CCP:	Concealed Carry Permit
CCW:	Concealed Carry Weapon
CHL:	Concealed Handgun License
CFR:	Code of Federal Regulations
CHINS:	Child in Need of Services
DD:	Destructive Device
DHS:	Department of Homeland Security

DOJ:	United States Department of Justice
EAP.	Emergency Action Plan
FBI:	Federal Bureau of Investigation
FFL:	Federal Firearms License
FOPA:	Firearms Owners Protection Act of 1986
FPC:	Federal Penal Code
GCA:	Gun Control Act of 1968
LEO:	Law Enforcement Officer *or* Law Enforcement Only
MG:	Machine Gun
NCIC:	National Crime Information Center
NCO:	No Contact Order
NFA:	National Firearms Act of 1934
NICS:	National Instant Criminal Background Check System
NRC:	Nuclear Regulatory Commission
PO:	Protective Order *or* Probation Officer
SBI:	Serious Bodily Injury
SBR:	Short-Barreled Rifle
SBS:	Short-Barreled Shotgun
SCOTUS:	Supreme Court of the United States
SOP:	Standard Operating Procedure
SYG:	Stand Your Ground
SVF:	Serious Violent Felon
TSA:	Transportation Security Administration
USA:	United States Attorney *or* United States of America
USC:	United States Code
WMD:	Weapon of Mass Destruction

III.   Conclusion

Even the lowly acronym may have a different meaning associated with it in the firearms community. Try not to assume, but understand the precise meaning attributed to the acronym. This is again, a prudent part of being a gun owner and a necessity to lawful reciprocal carry.

Chapter Seven
Myth-Busters

I.   Introduction

In the reciprocity discussion, there are a number of pervasive myths. Some of this urban legend does not equate to the potential for unlawful acts or omission in carrying a handgun in a reciprocal state. However, to properly comply with the law, it is important to increase Your base knowledge and stay abreast of changes in law over time. Dismissing myths, not inadvertently perpetuating them, is one step in this process. The myths:

II.   "In a Reciprocal State, Follow Law of State Issuing License"

A pervasive and fundamentally unsound view held by many licensees is that in carrying a handgun in a reciprocal state, he or she has to follow the law of the state that issued the license. That is MYTH. *The licensee must follow the laws of any state in which he or she carries a concealed handgun*.

EX **Driver's License Companion.** A driver's license may help You understand the legal distinction if You once held this belief. When You are driving in a state that has a slower speed limit, say 55 MPH, but Your state of residence has a 65 MPH speed limit, You can only go 55 MPH in the state in which You are in. That other state's law applies. Your driver's license is recognized only to allow You to drive there in accordance with the laws of that state.

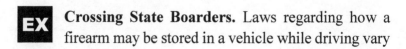 **Crossing State Boarders.** Laws regarding how a firearm may be stored in a vehicle while driving vary

from state-to-state. For instance, an Indiana resident with a CCP is allowed to have a loaded firearm in their vehicle when they travel in Indiana. However, if the licensee drives into the District of Columbia, they must abide by D.C.'s firearm-transfer law and unload the ammunition from their firearm and store it where it is not readily accessible.

III.   "A Federal License Exists"

There is no federal license available to civilians to authorize reciprocity in each and every other state. These bills are routinely floated in Congress, but have yet to become law. If they should ever pass, it is likely there will still be a great number of exceptions in deference to states and state sovereignty. This is a MYTH.

Some of this confusion likely stems from the passage of H.R. 218, titled the "Law Enforcement Officers' Safety Act of 2004." This federal law allows qualified off-duty and certain retired police officers to carry a concealed handgun in any other state, subject to following some state restrictions, such as on government property. This only applies to this narrow set of people.

IV.   "A CCP Cannot be Revoked"

As an example, any time a licensee is convicted of a felony, he or she is disqualified from possessing a firearm. The license is *de facto* revoked at that time. Several states have provisions that require a court to notify the licensing agency (often an arm of law enforcement) to suspend the license and begin the revocation process.

In other states, there is an affirmative duty on the licensee to self-disclose certain life developments that may call into question their status as a licensee, such as a conviction for domestic violence. A license to carry can be revoked, and statements to the contrary are MYTH.

V.   "A License Allows Carry in All Places in State"

A number of licensees believe their license to carry in their state of issuance or in reciprocal states allows carry in all places in that state. However, this is a MYTH. In even the most liberal states vis-à-vis gun rights, there are a number of places a person cannot carry a handgun with a license.

VI.   "The Second Amendment Allows Carry in All Places"

Many believe that the Second Amendment allows carrying of a handgun or other firearm or its possession in all places, at all times. This view is a MYTH and is not supported by even the U.S. Supreme Court's most favorable Second Amendment analysis.

The *Heller* decision set out that the right to have firearms, including a handgun, is an individual right, not a collective right of the states' National Guards, police, and U.S. Government. The *City of Chicago* case applied the constitutional right to bear arms applied to the states through the Due Process Clause of the Fourteenth Amendment. Neither case indicated handguns could not be regulated.

VII.   "Federal Law Only Applies to Federal Property"

Under the Supremacy Clause of the U.S. Constitution, federal law is supreme to state law and Congress has adopted firearms regulation, including handguns, at airports and schools that regulates or prohibits firearms, even with a license. The violation of these provisions may subject the person to arrest, prosecution, and imprisonment in the federal system. This view of federal law too is MYTH.

VIII. "The Safe Passage Provision Covers Extended Stays"

FOPA's Safe Passage Provision (SPP) protects those who are transporting firearms for lawful purposes from local restrictions that would otherwise prohibit passage. So long as the driver complies with state and local laws governing transportation of firearms, the driver may make briefs stops and be protected under the SPP. The view that the SPP protects gun owners during *extended* stops is a MYTH.

EX **Extended Stops**. An Indiana gun owner properly stores and transports his assault rifle while traveling through Chicago and stops overnight there. Despite the fact that his assault rifle was legal in Indiana and properly stored in his vehicle, the gun owner would be in violation of Chicago's municipal code banning possession of assault rifles. The gun owner is protected under the SPP only if his stops in Chicago are brief. Here, the overnight stay would not be protected under the SPP.

IX. "You Don't Need a Background Check to Buy a Gun at a Gun Show"

Known as the "Gun Show Loophole," this is a common misconception. Anytime anyone buys a firearm from an FFL, they must undergo a background check, even at a gun show. Confusion arises over the fact that in many states, private transactions between two residents of that state do not require a background check. If You meet up with someone to buy or sell a gun, no background check is required, in many states. Gun shows are popular locations for private parties to meet to perform gun sales; some people go to gun shows for the purpose of buying or selling guns to other patrons. As long as neither party holds an FFL, these transactions generally do not require a background check. The vast majority of vendors at gun shows are FFL holders, however, and You must undergo a background check when buying a firearm from them.

X.   Conclusion

To advance reciprocity, it is important to have meaningful discussions on the topic with accurate information. Hopefully, You do not (or no longer) subscribe to any of these myths. Some of them could literally land You in federal prison.

Chapter Eight
Recent Decisions & Upcoming Issues

I. 'Shall Issue' Law Suits

Two landmark cases involving the Second Amendment recently reached SCOTUS: District of *Columbia v. Heller* (2008), declaring an individual has a right to own a firearm, and *McDonald v. City of Chicago* (2010), affirming the Second Amendment applies to the States. *Peruta v. California* was set to be the third major case to be heard by the Supreme Court in a decade. However, in June 2017, the Supreme Court declined to hear *Peruta*, letting stand a 9th Circuit Court of Appeals determination that there is no Constitutional right to carry concealed weapons in public.

Essentially, the problem in *Peruta* came down to "shall issue" vs. "may issue." California law allows county/municipal officials to require applicants to demonstrate "good moral character" and "good cause" before they "may" issue a concealed carry permit. The 9th Circuit upheld the Constitutionality of California's law. In his dissent to the Supreme Court's decision to not hear *Peruta*, Justice Thomas wrote: "Even if other Members of the Court do not agree that the Second Amendment likely protects a right to public carry, the time has come for the Court to answer this important question definitively."

More recently, however, the U.S. Court of Appeals for the District of Columbia Circuit ruled in a line of "may issue" challenges that the District government must grant handgun carry licenses to D.C. residents on the same basis that carry permits are issued in most states. In particular, D.C. may not limit carry permits only to persons who prove a "special need for self-protection distinguishable from the general community as supported by evidence of specific threats or previous attacks that demonstrate a special danger to the applicant's life." Instead, D.C. must follow the standard American system: issuing permits to adults who pass a fingerprint-based background check and a safety training class.

Though this ruling only affects Washington, D.C., it might have national consequences. The outcome in Washington, D.C., or any one of several other similar cases currently being challenged, could end up before the U.S. Supreme Court and determine, once-and-for-all, if the "may issue" qualifier is a prior restraint on citizen's ability to exercise a Constitutional right. [http://gunla.ws/mus5], [http://gunla.ws/cslb] & [http://gunla.ws/wm07]

II.   Assault Weapons Bans & The Second Amendment

Are assault weapons and large-capacity magazines (LCMs) protected under the Second Amendment? A recent decision from the 4th Circuit Court of Appeals has created uncertainty regarding how much protection the Second Amendment provides to weapons that are suited more for military use rather than civilian use. In 2008, the U.S. Supreme Court ruled in *Heller* that, although the Second Amendment is not absolute, a complete ban on a class of weapons (handguns), even for a lawful purpose, violates the Constitution. In the wake of the 2012 Sandy Hook shootings, three states – Connecticut, New York, and Maryland – passed laws banning "assault weapons."

Keeping in line, the 4th Circuit Court of Appeals recently ruled in *Kolbe v. Hogan Jr.* that Maryland's ban on assault-style weapons and LCMs is constitutional. The *Heller* decision stated that the Second Amendment does not extend protection to weapons that are "dangerous and unusual." Attempting to stay in line with the *Heller* holding, the 4th Circuit found that the weapons and LCMs banned by Maryland's law are dangerous and unusual because they are "exceptionally lethal weapons of war." Departing from the "common-use" test as proscribed in *Heller*, the 4th Circuit created what seems to be a "most useful in military service" test.

Assuming the plaintiffs will not give up after this defeat, the next step will be the Supreme Court of the United States. There is no guarantee the Supreme Court would agree to here this case, but the 4th Circuit's circumvention from *Heller* may weigh heavily in its decision. [http://gunla.ws/heller] & [http://gunla.ws/wkko]

III.   Domestic Violence & Gun-Owners' Rights

In June of 2016, the U.S. Supreme Court ruled that those convicted of domestic abuse can be barred from buying or owning a gun for life – even if the violence was "reckless" instead of "intentional." The 6-2 ruling in *Voisine v. United States* analyzed the Constitutionality of the 1996 Lautenberg Amendment to the GCA, which regards those convicted of domestic violence misdemeanors the same as felons in prohibiting gun ownership.

The plaintiffs argued that prior convictions should not count for federal purposes because a "reckless" assault is not the "use of physical force" required by federal law. The Supreme Court disagreed and retained the broad definition of domestic violence. By retaining a broad definition, the Court dismissed the argument that gun laws do not cover domestic violence crimes in which the abuser's intent is not clearly violent. This could give states greater discretion in restricting and confiscating firearms owned by those convicted of "reckless" domestic abuse.

Or, as evidenced by a May 2016 New Jersey appellate court ruling, it could justify "presumptive confiscation" of firearms from anyone even accused of domestic violence. The New Jersey appellate court upheld a lower court's ruling that law enforcement officers had Constitutional authority to confiscate a man's guns following a domestic violence arrest.

In June 2013, Arthur Vinogradsky's wife obtained a restraining order against her husband. As police were removing firearms from the home, they arrested the husband for possessing high-capacity magazines and hollow-point bullets. The wife later dismissed her complaint and Vinogradsky completed a pretrial intervention program, which spared him a criminal conviction on the weapons charges. The judge, however, stripped him of gun ownership rights, finding that he assaulted his wife and committed a crime. [http://gunla.ws/09jd]

IV.   Machine Gun Bans & The Second Amendment

In June 2016, the Fifth Circuit Court of Appeals ruled in *Hollis v. Lynch* that the NFA/FOPA's machine gun ban does not violate the Second Amendment. The story began when, complying with the registration requirements for automatic firearms and paying the $200 tax, Aubrey Hollis, on behalf of his revocable trust, filed a Form 1 with the ATF(E) to manufacture an M16 machine gun. His Form 1 was approved, but then revoked by the ATF(E) two days later. Their basis for the revocation was that a trust was not listed as a "person" under a provision of the GCA, and therefore, it reverted back to Hollis the individual. The ATF(E) stated that since the ATF(E) is prohibited from approving any private person's application to manufacture and register a machine gun, the original approval was issued by mistake.

Hollis filed his complaint against the AG and the ATF(E) seeking to overturn both the NFA and the ban on private ownership of machine guns manufactured after May 19, 1986. Hollis argued that the M16 is suitable for military use, and is thus protected under *Miller* and *Heller*. The Court disagreed, claiming that the individual right protected by the Second Amendment only applies to weapons "that are possessed at home and are in common use at the time for lawful purposes like self-defense." Further, they found that "the Second Amendment does not create a right to possess a weapon solely because the weapon may be used in or is useful for militia or military service. The Court concluded that machine guns are "dangerous" and "unusual" within the meaning of *Heller* and therefore not in common use, and thus, not protected under the Second Amendment.

The Court also disagreed with Hollis' interpretation of the meaning of a "trust" and found that, though not explicitly included in the GCA's definition of a "person," Hollis himself would in fact possess the machine gun and therefore is subject to the ban. A similar case from the 3rd Circuit Court, *U.S. v. Watson*, was ruled the same on nearly identical grounds. Going forward, this case means that the 1986 ban on machine guns remains valid and is unlikely to be overturned in court.
[http://gunla.ws/jzdn] & [http://gunla.ws/61hh]

V.   Medical Marijuana & Gun Rights

Recreational marijuana use is legal in eight states and the District of Columbia. In these areas individuals may buy and use marijuana without noting it on a background check to purchase firearms. However, if You live in any of the twenty-nine states where medicinal marijuana is available and you have a prescription, the federal government can prohibit You from legally purchasing a firearm.

In August 2016, the 9th Circuit Court voted unanimously to reject *Wilson v. Lynch*, a suit filed by a Nevada woman who tried to buy a firearm after obtaining a medical marijuana card. The gun store refused to sell her a firearm, citing a federal rule banning firearm sales to illegal drug users. Despite the fact that many states have legalized marijuana for medicinal or recreational use, the federal government still classifies marijuana as an illegal Schedule I drug. The ATF(E) requires gun sellers to assume a person with a medical marijuana card uses the drug, and recently updated the language on the form 4473 so it explicitly says that use of marijuana, even if legal under state law, is illegal under federal law and makes one a prohibited person. The Cole memo, which directs the DOJ from enforcing federal law in states where recreational or medical marijuana is legal, does not apply to gun ownership.
[http://gunla.ws/3n6m]

VI. Mental Health Lifetime Gun Ban

In September 2016, the 6th Circuit ruled the GCA, which bans anyone "who has been adjudicated as a mental defective or who has been committed to a mental institution" from owning a firearm, could violate the Second Amendment.

The ruling revives a lawsuit – *Tyler v. Hillsdale County Sheriff's Dept.* – filed by a Michigan man who was involuntarily committed thirty years ago following an emotional divorce. He had not had any mental-health issues since then, but was prohibited from purchasing a firearm due to the federal law banning gun possession by anyone who has been committed to a mental institution.

Although the Director of the ATF(E) is empowered to restore the rights of those who can demonstrate they are not a danger to public safety, Congress defunded the review program in the 1990's and has not appointed a director since 2006. For this reason, Tyler maintains the GCA creates a permanent ban on his Second Amendment rights. The Court reiterated that there are compelling reasons for prohibiting people currently or recently suffering from mental illness from possessing a gun. However, they found that none of the government's evidence squarely answered the key question at the heart of the case: "Is it reasonably necessary to forever bar all previously institutionalized persons from owning a firearm?" [http://gunla.ws/jl9a]

VII.   Virtual Plans & Real Firearms

The First Amendment protects most speech from prior restraint or censorship by the government. However, technology has begun to test the boundaries of traditional First and Second Amendment doctrine. In December 2016, a Texas-based 3D-printer filed a motion asking the 5th Circuit Court for a rehearing of an earlier ruling that essentially made it illegal for anyone to share gun-design files online. In *Defense Distributed v. United States Department of State*, the 5th Circuit refused to suspend a regulation restricting publication of computer-aided design (CAD) files that enable the public to print guns or gun parts using a 3D printer.

If sharing CAD code is considered speech, it would be protected by the First Amendment, which would hamper the government's ability to regulate the physical objects that are printed. This question is especially important when the object at issue is an untraceable weapon.

Defense Distributed describes itself as a nonprofit organization committed to promoting Second Amendment rights by "facilitating global access to information related to the 3D printing of arms" and publishing this information online for free. In 2013, Defense Distributed published a file for the world's first entirely 3D-printable handgun.

Defense Distributed argues that in reaching its ruling, the 5th Circuit disregarded precedents set by the Circuit Court, as well as the U.S. Supreme Court. This case is expected to be litigated for years and could ultimately engender precedent-setting First and Second Amendment rulings.
[http://gunla.ws/l5qs]

PART II: INTERSTATE TRANSPORTATION

Even though there is no federal license or permit to carry between states or statutes making licenses reciprocal, the way firearms are transported to reciprocal states comes from federal law. Specifically, federal law requires states to allow a person to transport any lawfully possessed firearm from any lawful place to any other lawful place.

Of course, there are a number of restrictions, including that the firearm be unloaded and not accessible during travel. Without this, state-based reciprocity would be severely limited: unless two (2) reciprocal states were contiguous, it would be difficult or impossible for the civilian to lawfully transport the firearm (which would be a handgun with reciprocal carry) to the reciprocal state. The conditions on how interstate transportation is lawfully executed depend on the mode of travel.

The most common are addressed in the following chapters, noting again this *is not reciprocal carry*:

- **Chapter 9: Right to Interstate Transportation**
- **Chapter 10: Flying by Commercial Airline Scheduled Flight**
- **Chapter 11: Amtrak**
- **Chapter 12: Bus Lines**
- **Chapter 13: Driving by Private Transportation**

Chapter Nine
Right to Interstate Transportation

I.   Introduction

In most circumstances (unless You could travel by, and in, personal transportation through reciprocal states only), the state-to-state right of reciprocity would not be able to be exercised without engaging federal rights to move firearms among the states.

This is a key federal statute and critical legal concept to gather and understand, along with the fact this right exists as to handguns and long guns, but the GLBS Guide only addresses carrying a handgun in a reciprocal state.

However, as noted in the preface to Part II, the means by which the person is traveling, private versus public, dramatically changes how the firearm (i.e., handgun) must be packaged. In addition, this federal right is fundamentally different from the right to reciprocal carry (a right by state law) and You will not be able to exercise control over the firearm until You arrive in the reciprocal state — at least to stay in compliance with the law.

II.   Commerce Clause

Congress did not preempt the firearms' field in adopting extensive regulation of NFA weapons (machine guns, short-barreled rifles, short-barreled shotguns, and suppressors), GCA, nor as a part of its significant regulation of FFLs, or penal restrictions on firearms at airports, and school zones.

However, Congress did recognize the potential for problems to emerge when a lawful firearms' possessor moves a firearm between one lawful place in one state to one lawful place in another state, if the firearm was prohibited or restricted somewhere in between.

Under its authority through the Commerce Clause to address matters that affect interstate commerce (i.e., travel across state lines), Congress adopted a statute, Chapter 44 of the U.S. Code [http://gunla.ws/title18] covering "Firearms." Statutes therein make unenforceable any state law to the contrary. In other words, Chapter 44 expressly affords You the right to interstate transportation of firearms from one lawful place to another lawful place.

III.   Federal Code Provision

Because of its power and importance, it is set forth in pertinent part, as follows:

> "Notwithstanding any other provisions of any law or any rule or regulation of a State or any political subdivision thereof, any person who is not otherwise prohibited by this chapter from transporting, shipping, or receiving a firearm shall be entitled to transport a firearm for any lawful purpose from any place where he may lawfully possess and carry to any other place where he may lawfully possess and carry such firearm . . . ."

IV.   DOJ Directive

Nevertheless, some states and/or their LEOs ignored this provision or misunderstood its application. This included local police officers working at J.F.K. International Airport who threatened through-passing passengers with arrest because of checked firearms moving between two (2) lawful places by commercial passenger flight, with at least one (1) firearm being confiscated.

At the behest of Representative Don Young, by letter of June 18, 2003, who was outraged at this situation, the DOJ investigated and agreed the local police were in violation of the Gun Control Act.

The local police were advised of the laws they were violating.

This is the provision that ultimately allows interstate transportation of Your handgun for reciprocal carry in a reciprocal state under a reciprocity agreement and Your resident or non-resident license to carry. The provision it requires depends on the means of transportation and is addressed next.

V.   Conclusion

The federal right to interstate transportation fosters any given state law affording reciprocal carry. However, they are not one and the same right. The right to interstate transportation requires certain packaging and disclosures that the firearms are being transported, always being unloaded and not readily accessible to You. Reciprocity addresses only carrying a handgun in a loaded condition.

Chapter Ten
Flying by Commercial Airline Scheduled Flight

I. Introduction

Before September 11, 2001, the process of placing a firearm in checked luggage and flying with it to another U.S. location was largely left to the airlines and its passengers. In fact, many Readers in the 30+ age range probably remember flying on about anyone's ticket and just walking to the gate without any screening.

In the top-down look at aviation security, the Transportation Security Administration ("TSA") came into existence. Ultimately, the TSA promulgated specific rules for flying with firearms in checked luggage, removing some of the ambiguity or inconsistent enforcement of airline rules for flying with firearms. Airlines can still have their own rules and do, but largely track TSA's requirements.

Links to the pages of major carriers that address their rules:

- American: [http://gunla.ws/aa]
- Southwest: [http://gunla.ws/sw]
- United: [http://gunla.ws/united]
- Delta: [http://gunla.ws/delta]

Any person who desires to fly with firearms in checked baggage should carefully study the TSA [http://gunla.ws/tsa] and airline's most current rules, regulations and policies just prior to departure. Each and every rule and regulation must be followed. There are several general, universal requirements a passenger must follow in every check-in associated with passenger flight and a checked firearm (i.e., a handgun for purposes of reciprocity).

II. TSA Requirements

A. Unload the Firearm

Although it should not have to be said, the first requirement is that the firearm must be unloaded. Point the gun in a safe direction and check to see that it is unloaded. Re-check manually (finger in the chamber/cylinder) and visually inspect it.

Remember, and apply, the universal gun safety rules:

Rule I: (Treat) All Guns As Always Loaded.

Rule II: Never Let the Muzzle (the end of the barrel where the bullet comes out) Cover Anything You Are Not Willing To Destroy.

Rule III: Keep Your Finger Off the Trigger Until Your Sights are on the Target.

Rule IV: Be Sure of Your Target.

Generally speaking, it is a bad idea to be manipulating and unloading a firearm that will be checked into luggage in the confined space of a car after arriving at the airport. This is a recipe for an accidental discharge. Also remember, many times where an "unloaded" firearm has discharged and killed an unintended victim, it was with the last round in the chamber. For instance, dropping the magazine in an auto-pistol does not extract the chambered round.

B. Declare the Firearm

At the first point to do so, the firearm must be declared to the airline check-in. In the hustle of modern-day airports, this is easy to forget. In addition, it is shockingly easy to neglect to account for the carry gun that a person may lawfully wear as a part of police officer

60

or civilian apparel. Every major airport has had a seasoned civilian CCP or police officer enter security still wearing his or her carry gun.

One effective way to prevent the latter is by patting down the areas of Your own body where You routinely carry a firearm. Think from head to toe to ensure no firearm or ammunition remains on Your person, which may be a carry gun and not the one being checked.

A related consideration goes for carry-on luggage, which, for avid shooters, may have an errant bullet, knife or otherwise prohibited item contained within it. A preferred practice is maintaining separate "shooting" clothing and baggage in a separate home closet and never intermixing them.

C.   Transport in Hard-Sided Case

TSA requires a hard-sided case for checked firearms. If the destination You are flying to is where reciprocal carry will occur, this would be a defensive handgun. The case must be able to be locked and the key maintained by the flyer. There are limits, however, including amount of ammunition that can be shipped.

D.   Lock the Container, Keep the Key

As the rules stand today, TSA directs the passenger to keep the key to the lock, and if TSA desires to inspect the locked parcel, they will contact You. Airlines are pretty good in directing passengers where to wait until TSA makes this determination. If You cannot be located, the luggage containing the firearm will not be transported. Under federal law, it is illegal to flag a bag as containing a firearm. Nevertheless, it has occurred in the past.

An important legal right that You must understand is that federal law allows interstate transportation, including in checked baggage, of a firearm from any lawful place to any other place it would be lawful to possess. Nevertheless, in New York in the not-too-distant past, passengers with checked firearms were detained and threatened with confiscation of the firearms or arrest.

E.   Keep the Ammunition in Separate Hard Box

Ammunition transported in checked luggage is limited in quantity. It must be kept in a separate container, although this may be the same locked container as holds the firearms. A factory cardboard box in which the ammunition was shipped by the manufacturer is generally preferred and clearly marked as to what it contains.

Since ammunition is heavy, it may be cheaper to purchase it at the destination if it is a standard caliber and readily available.

These five (5) considerations, along with some of my personal insight as a frequent flyer with firearms, should aid in Your education about the process in order to make a meaningful decision if the benefit is worth the risk for flying with a checked handgun for reciprocal carry.

III. Airline Requirements

To be lawful, any firearm checked in luggage must follow the TSA's requirements along with any other specific requirements of the airline. However, by federal law, the airline is not allowed to mark the baggage as containing firearms. Firearms have been stolen and/or lost from checked luggage, so insurance may be an important consideration.

IV. Conclusion

Unloaded firearms may be lawfully checked in passenger baggage if packaged correctly and declared. The TSA has very specific directions on this that must be followed. Their site, along with that of any given airline, must be checked just before the time of transportation.

Chapter Eleven
Amtrak

I.   Introduction

On December 15, 2010, Amtrak began accepting reservations for transportation of firearms and ammunition between Amtrak trains within the United States that offer and have the capability to offer checked baggage. Not all train routes offer this service, so taking a firearm in checked baggage must be carefully investigated in advance.

II.   24-Hour-Notice Provision

A passenger transporting a firearm in checked luggage must notify Amtrak no later than 24 hours *before* departure by contacting Amtrak at 1-800-USA-RAIL. There is no provision for online reservation or notification of firearms for checked luggage. As with flights, the passenger must travel on the same train as the firearm in his or her checked baggage. [http://gunla.ws/amtrak]

III.   Firearms Enclosure Requirements, Generally

Amtrak's provisions go on to closely track those for airline checking. The firearms must be unloaded and in an approved, locked, hard-sided container not larger than 62" L x 17" W x 7" D. Likewise, the passenger must maintain the key or combination for the locked container, which may not exceed 50 lbs. in total.

IV.   Handgun Enclosure Requirements

As it relates to handguns, they may be contained in a smaller, but locked, hard-sided container and placed in a checked suitcase.

The case that the firearm came in when purchased may well be suitable for reciprocal carry.

V.   Ammunition Packaging Requirements

Any ammunition carried must be packed in the original manufacturer's cardboard box, or in a fiber, wood, or metal box specifically designed for carrying ammunition. The maximum amount of ammunition and containers housing it must not exceed 11 lbs. Firearms are not allowed in passenger cabins. Therefore, it may be the case that firearms may not be able to be checked if this feature or option is not allowed/available on the route.

For Readers considering this newer right or way to interstate transport a firearm, it is suggested he or she follow the link in this chapter for up-to-date information.

VI.   Conclusion

It is possible, consistent with Congress' directives to Amtrak and the federal right to interstate transportation, to check a handgun for reciprocal carry on certain Amtrak routes.

Chapter Twelve
Bus Lines

At present, there is no mechanism to lawfully transport a handgun by commercial bus line for reciprocal carry in other states. However, it is always advisable to check with the carrier, such as Greyhound [http://gunla.ws/greyhound] or bus line You will travel on, to see if their policies have changed.

Chapter Thirteen
Driving by Private Transportation

I.   Introduction

The federal provision to transport a handgun, allows You to transport such from any lawful place to any other in a private passenger vehicle. The major division in the law relates to vehicles that have separate compartments for passengers versus gear, like a trunk, and those vehicles that do not have an external trunk or compartment. Federal law guarantees You safe passage with firearms as long as You are transporting them to another state where they are legal, even if You have to pass through states where Your firearms would be illegal. This provision requires that You do not stop for an extended period of time in a state where Your firearms are illegal (such as staying overnight). The law is unclear on how long of a stop is ok (stopping for gas or restrooms is acceptable), but it is best to stop in these states as briefly as possible.

II.   Transportation in Trunk (if available)

For vehicles that have a separate compartment from the passenger area, the firearm must be unloaded, and neither the firearm, nor any ammunition being transported, can be readily accessible or directly accessible from the passenger compartment.

III.   Transportation in Certain Locked Container and Unloaded

In cases where there is not a separate space or compartment from the passenger area, the firearm must be unloaded, and the firearm and ammunition must be contained in a locked container other than the glove compartment or console. In states where handguns are sold to individuals who do not have a license to carry, there is a similar provision to transport the firearm from the dealer to his or her residence or in moving between residences.

To minimize the risk of unintended violation, there should be as much separation and indication as possible that the firearm (handgun for reciprocal carry) is not available to the occupants of the vehicle. Where it is unclear, as in hundreds of such cases, the occupants may face risk of arrest for carrying a handgun without a license.

IV.   Conclusion

Readers should take care, at least analytically, to make a distinction between the federal right to interstate transportation of a firearm from any lawful place to any other lawful place, and state rights to transport a firearm, a handgun in particular, from a place of purchase or in moving in a "secure wrapper." While the condition of the firearm (unloaded) and removed from access may be the same, failure to understand all distinctions may cause unexpected failure to comply with the controlling provision. In addition, it is important to be mindful of the culture and attitude towards firearms in the states You pass through. If stopped in anti-gun states like New York with firearms that are illegal there, You may be arrested and have Your guns confiscated despite the federal law. While it is unlikely that You would be convicted of a crime due to the federal safeguard, You may be greatly inconvenienced.

PART III: FEDERAL PROPERTY

Any seasoned defense attorney will tell You that there is a vast difference between ordinary state criminal acts and those charged under the federal system, both in terms of conviction rate (which is extraordinarily high in the 90%+ range at the federal level) and sentencing (most time under the Federal Sentencing Guidelines is served). Therefore, carrying a handgun onto federal property, while allowable in certain situations, must be properly executed. There are different rules, and these are broken down and addressed in the following chapters:

- **Chapter 14: Federal Property and Lands**
- **Chapter 15: Federal Buildings**
- **Chapter 16: National Parks and Wildlife Refuges**
- **Chapter 17: Federal Courts and Courthouses**

Chapter Fourteen
Federal Property and Lands

I. Introduction

As a general rule, firearms are prohibited in federal facilities, which by extension include federal property, at least to some degree. Different types of federal properties have different penal or other rules that might impact reciprocal carry (yes, there can be reciprocal carry on federal lands, such as National Parks). Understanding the character and nature of the properties and being able to determine the classification they fit into is the key to lawful compliance with reciprocal carry.

II. Definition

Most federal facilities sit on federal lands (which may be owned, leased, or rented). There is an open question as to where the lands begin and end relative to the federal facility, an example being National Parks discussed herein. Does the federal land begin/end at the building or parking lot? Clearly, within the federal facility, it is a criminal act to carry a handgun, and there is no provision made for state permits or reciprocity.

Under the U.S. Code, "federal facility" is defined:

"(g)(1) The term 'Federal facility' means a building or part thereof owned or leased by the Federal Government, where Federal employees are regularly present for the purpose of performing their official duties."

III.   Penal Provision

Under federal law, a person who knowingly possesses or causes to be present a firearm or other dangerous weapon at a federal facility, or attempts to do so, shall be fined and/or imprisoned for not more than one year. It is an enhanced crime and level of punishment if the firearm or dangerous weapon is used in the commission of a crime or if any person is killed as a result of violation of this provision.

This would inherently include a handgun carried in a state under reciprocity where federal property is located within a state. There is federal property in every state. There is one exception that might apply in the course of reciprocal carry, namely hunting. In fact, this same U.S. Code provision goes on to except the lawful carrying of firearms or other dangerous weapons in a Federal facility incident to hunting or other lawful purpose.

EX **Hunting Seasons vs. Other Times.** Why and how this gets complicated is explained by an example. Take a given parcel of land that is federal property. During hunting season, a non-resident may hunt on this parcel and otherwise lawfully carry throughout non-excluded places in the reciprocal state. However, when it is not hunting season, this is likely criminal trespass and violation of the federal prohibition on carrying on federal lands, unless it is a National Park or Wildlife Refuge and the state allows this as discussed below.

As should be apparent by review in the next section, it is sometimes very difficult to determine what constitutes a federal facility. There are thousands of such places in every state.

IV.   Conspicuous Posting

However, under the U.S. Code, it is required that notice be conspicuously posted at each public entrance to the federal facility that possession of firearms and dangerous weapons is prohibited. For this reason, a person may not be convicted of this offense if such notice is not posted, unless the defendant had actual notice of this prohibition.

V.   Conclusion

No firearms are allowed in federal facilities, at least by civilians. Therefore, the distinctions between handguns, long guns, and reciprocity agreements are not applicable. Firearms are barred. The rule is fuzzier as it relates to certain federal lands. The key is advanced thought, research and planning in order to stay compliant.

Chapter Fifteen
Federal Buildings

I.   Introduction

The Federal government owns or leases more than 3.2 billion square feet of space in more than 500,000 buildings in the U.S. that may be subject to the noted prohibition on firearms, including handguns carried by reciprocity. These buildings are located in every state. Carry is not permitted in such buildings.

II.   Common Examples of Offices

A number of large, and common, examples may apply to Readers of all walks of life, professions, and include, but are not limited to, the following:

- Centers for Disease Control and Prevention
- Department of Homeland Security
- Department of Commerce
- Department of Defense
- Department of Energy
- Department of the Interior
- Department of Justice
- Department of Labor
- Department of State
- Department of Transportation
- Department of Education
- Environmental Protection Agency
- Federal Bureau of Investigation
- Federal Communications Commission
- Federal Emergency Management Agency
- Federal Protective Service

- Government Printing Office
- General Services Administration
- Department of Health and Human Services
- Department of Housing and Urban Development
- National Aeronautics and Space Administration
- Securities and Exchanges Commission
- Social Security Administration
- Department of the Treasury
- Transportation Security Administration
- Department of Agriculture
- United States Marshals Service
- United States Postal Service
- Department of Veterans Affairs

This noted, however, a prudent Reader should take care not to merely associate the federal building office or building prohibition with formal offices; these only account for twenty-three (23%) percent of the total space.

III. Largest Categories

The penal-code ban on firearms also applies to the other seventy-seven (77%) percent of federal buildings, offices and properties. Namely, it is any owned or leased property where federal employees are regularly present for the purpose of performing their duties.

The twelve (12) common categories of federal property are as follows:

- Institutional prison
- All other
- Institutional other
- Industrial
- Post Office

- Institutional hospital
- Institutional school
- Research and development
- Storage
- Service
- Housing
- Office

In fact, the three (3) largest holders of owned and leased office space are the GSA, first with 292 million square feet; defense agencies, second with 191 million square feet; and the Post Office, third with 190 million square feet. Therefore, this is potentially a huge category that any licensee carrying a concealed handgun in his or her own state or a reciprocal state should be *very* aware of.

IV.   Conclusion

Even though a federal facility is on federal land in some fashion, no firearms at all are allowed in federal facilities. This is a black and white rule. On the other hand, some firearms, including a concealed handgun carried pursuant to a reciprocity agreement may be carried on *some* (certain National Parks) but *not all* federal lands (i.e., military base).

Chapter Sixteen
National Parks and Wildlife Refuges

I. Introduction

The complexity of making a lawful determination if a handgun may be carried with reciprocity, including on federal lands, and where the theoretical legal boundaries exist, is found in the example of U.S. National Parks and Wildlife Refuges located throughout the Country. Carry *may be* allowed in those places.

II. Change in the Law

Under the Credit Cardholders' Bill of Rights Act of 2009, effective February 22, 2010, federal law prevented any law, rule or regulation from prohibiting the possession of a firearm in such places. This law applies to all 551 units of the National Wild Refuge System, as well as to National Monuments, along with the 392 units of the National Parks System.

III. Status of Person

However, the individual must lawfully possess the firearm (i.e., be a "proper person") and be in compliance with any state law (i.e., "reciprocal") in which such a federal parcel is located. However, the U.S. Fish & Wildlife Service looks to state and local law in the parcel's locality to determine whether possession and carry is allowed. If the state does not allow it, despite this federal law, You cannot carry in these places even with reciprocity.

IV. Exception for Physical Offices

On top of this, the federal facilities regulations still apply to actual federal buildings. Thus, in National Parks and Wildlife Refuges, federal buildings in these places, which may range from rudimentary ranger stations to expansive visitors' centers, are excluded, and it is illegal to carry a handgun there even if You are in a reciprocal state and state law allows carry on these federal lands.

V.   Conclusion

Subject to state law allowing the right, a CCP may be used for carry at National Park and Wildlife Refuges. However, this *does not* include Federal facilities, which may range from a remote ranger station to a formal visitor's center (i.e., Grand Canyon). In these federal facilities, firearms, including handguns, are still prohibited, and it is a federal crime to carry there.

Chapter Seventeen
Federal Courts and Courthouses

Under federal law, a person who knowingly possesses and/or causes to be present a firearm or other dangerous weapon at a federal court facility, or attempts to do so, shall be fined and/or imprisoned for not more than two (2) years.

Most every state has a similar provision under state law for state and local courts. Unlike the rest of federal facilities, there is no exception for lawfully carrying a firearm or other dangerous weapons in a federal court facility incident to hunting or any other lawful purpose.

In addition to this criminal provision, federal courts also possess the inherent powers to regulate their affairs by contempt and other powers. This is specifically accounted for in the federal penal code ("FPC"). As such, any Reader should also be aware that violation of the FPC on firearms and dangerous weapons may be punishable by contempt as well.

Furthermore, the federal courts also have the power to promulgate rules or orders regulating, restricting or prohibiting the possession of weapons within any building housing such court or any of its proceedings, or upon any grounds appurtenant to such buildings.

PART IV: FEDERAL REGULATION

Aside from its property and federal facilities sited upon the locations, the Congress, as well as many of the states, has adopted strict criminal laws to protect more vulnerable segments of our society, such as school children and passengers and guests at airports or aircrafts. The penalties for violation are severe, and each is addressed in its own chapter:

- **Chapter 18: Schools and School Zones**
- **Chapter 19: Airports and Aircraft**

Chapter Eighteen
Schools and School Zones

I. Introduction

Because of the complexity of the federal rule, and the overlap with state provisions, Readers are provided with more analysis than in other places in the GLBS Guide. In light of recent school shootings, there may be a zero-tolerance policy for even minor mistakes or technical violations. The most restrictive, state or federal laws must be strictly followed.

II. Commerce Clause

In the statutory language of the U.S. Code, it specifically references firearms that move in interstate commerce. This comes from the Gun Control Act of 1968, and is the express means by which Congress is empowered with the authority to regulate firearms in the states and their school zones. This, with other areas of federal authority, endures because of movement of firearms in interstate commerce.

III. Definition of Terms

A precise definition of terms is necessary.

Under federal law, a "school zone" is comprised of the grounds of, or within a public, parochial or private school or within a distance of 1,000 feet from the grounds of such a school. The term "school" itself means a school that provides elementary or secondary education as specified under state law.

Although it could differ under state law, generally speaking, an "elementary school" means any combination of kindergarten and Grades One (1) through Eight (8). A "secondary school" means a high school. A "high school" is a school with any combination of Grades Nine (9) through Twelve (12).

Thus, depending upon the state law where You anticipate carrying a handgun under reciprocity it may be necessary to delve into the educational or criminal statutes to determine the exact scope and application of how these schools and grades are classified under the applicable state law.

IV. Penal Rule

The federal penal provisions that Congress adopted make it generally unlawful for any individual to possess a firearm that the individual knows, or has reasonable cause to believe, is in a school zone. Equally, it is unlawful for any person to knowingly, or with reckless disregard for the safety of others, to discharge, or attempt to discharge, a firearm at a place the individual knows is a school zone.

Thus, when carrying in a reciprocal state, this federal criminal law would apply, along with any state criminal rules. However, there are exceptions for licensees under this federal law if the state allows and affords such right.

V.   Penalties for Violation

A person who violates the school zone law under the FPC shall be fined, imprisoned for not more than five (5) years, or both.

VI.   Exceptions Allowing Carry

There are a number of logical, and necessary, exceptions to the federal Gun Free School Zone legislation regarding prohibition of firearms in school zones. These may well apply to You in carrying a handgun under reciprocity in another state.

The most likely to be applicable with reciprocal carry are set forth and discussed, as follows:

A.   Private Property

The FPC prohibition does not apply to the possession of a firearm on private property that is not a part of the school grounds.

HY **Home or Gun Store Across from School**. A home or gun store might be right across the street from a primary or secondary school. This private property is not encompassed within the FPC prohibition, thus carrying is permitted on such private property.

B.   License to Carry

Another exception to the school zone provision of the U.S. Code is if the person possessing the firearm is licensed by the state in which the school zone is located.

This applies as long as the laws related to licensing require that, before an individual obtains such a License, the law enforcement authorities of the state verify that the person is qualified under law to receive the license (i.e., "proper person," "good character and reputation," and "proper reason") and the general prohibition rule does not apply to possession of a firearm.

As a word of caution, some states that issue permits and have reciprocity agreements do not recognize a CCP as valid for carry on a school premises, with limitations. If that is the case, You are committing a criminal act, even though Congress has allowed states to make this exception.

Also, "schools" may be more defined differently under state law, with differing penal scope and regulation.

C.   Unloaded and Locked

A common state and federal provision relates to the need to transport weapons. The FPC has a similar provision. The general criminal rule does not apply to a firearm that is not loaded and locked in a container, or locked in a firearms rack that is on a motor vehicle.

This is the federal right to intrastate and interstate transportation provided by federal law addressed in other provisions of the GLBS Guide. Obviously, in reciprocal carry, a number of scenarios could cause this to be considered by Readers.

D.   School Program/Activity

Some schools have or host firearms safety courses or events. Such events are exempted from the criminal provisions prohibition. That is, the FPC does not apply to an individual and firearm for use in a program approved by a school in the school zone. Again, while limited, there are a few foreseeable situations where this might apply in the overall context of reciprocal carry in another state.

E.   Traversing Premises for Access to Hunting Lands

The final exception relates to lawful hunting and accessing

the hunting lands from school property. A person may carry a firearm that is unloaded and is possessed by the individual while traversing school premises for the purpose of gaining access to public or private lands open to hunting, if the entry on school premises is authorized by school authorities.

F.　Exception for Discharge

Again, consistent with the needs of schools, and balancing private property rights against Congress' right to regulate under the Commerce Clause, discharge of firearms are excepted in certain situations. This situation is a couple of steps removed from reciprocal carry, but given the diversity of Readers and what they do, this is briefly set forth.

The FPC's school zone prohibition does not preclude discharge of a firearm on private property that is not a part of the school grounds. Equally, it does not preclude discharge of a firearm as part of a program approved by a school in the school zone, by an individual who is participating in the program.

VII.　Colleges and Universities

Following the Virginia Tech shootings (the first incident), a National debate with respect to the student's right to carry handguns on campus began. In essence, this pitted college students against their institutions. In fact, there is a national student group called Students for Concealed Carry on Campus (SCCC).

As a general rule of thumb, however, almost all colleges and universities in the Nation have a strong, point-blank policy against possession of firearms on campus. There is no federal law, penal or otherwise, addressing this.

Thus, You have to look to state law to determine if there is such a civil or penal prohibition. However, Utah and Texas have laws allowing carry on campus.

VIII. Conclusion

Many states have their own rules covering schools and school zones. For this reason, it can easily trip up a CCP if federal law has an applicable exception to allow the carry of the handgun, but state law does not. In this case, carrying is still prohibited because it is illegal under state law. This is a very complicated area, and due diligence in researching and planning is required.

Chapter Nineteen
Airports and Aircraft

I.   Introduction

As a general rule, except for lawfully checking a firearm, including a handgun in checked baggage for interstate transportation to another jurisdiction with reciprocal carry, firearms are not allowed at airports. There are a number of licensees who fail to remember that they are still carrying a handgun and proceed to security (a controlled or sterile area) and run into all sorts of criminal trouble.

Because our society has expressed a zero-tolerance policy for firearms anywhere near the controlled areas of an airport or in the passenger cabin of aircraft, the very strict provisions are set forth in the GLBS Guide to help solidify the great risk this may create for Readers with an inattentive focus or hostile approach to TSA. In other words, more coverage is provided and beyond the somewhat narrower focus in other chapters.

Specifically, under the U.S. Code, there are a number of civil and/or criminal provisions for attempting to enter a controlled area of an airport or aircraft with a firearm or other restricted device. The central provision prohibiting the carrying of a firearm onto an aircraft is set forth, followed by excepted persons. Following that, other applicable provisions of the FPC are identified and briefly analyzed.

II.   Boarding Aircraft

Under this category, there are several potential criminal acts:

A person shall not when on, or attempting to get on, an aircraft in, or intended for operation in, air transportation or intrastate air transportation, having on or about the person a concealed dangerous weapon that is or would be accessible to the individual during flight.

A person shall not place, or attempt to place, a loaded firearm on the aircraft in property that is accessible to passengers in flight. A loaded firearm means a starter gun or weapon designed or converted to expel a projectile through an explosive, and that has a cartridge, a detonator or powder in the chamber, magazine, cylinder or clip.

A person shall not place, or attempt to place, on the aircraft an explosive or incendiary device. For a violation of these FPC provisions, the person shall be fined under Title 18, imprisoned for not more than ten (10) years, or both.

Where a person willfully and without regard for the safety of human life, or with reckless disregard for the safety of human life, violates these FPC provisions, he or she shall be fined under Title 18, imprisoned for not more than twenty (20) years, or both. If death results as a result of the commission of the crime, the person shall be imprisoned for any term of years or for life.

This FPC provision does not apply to an individual transporting an unloaded and disclosed firearm in checked luggage. If the interstate transportation to the reciprocal state is by commercial flight, this is likely the means by which the handgun will be transported.

III.   Entering Airport or Aircraft in Violation of Security Requirements

A person may not knowingly and willfully enter an airport area or aircraft that serves as an air carrier or foreign air carrier, in violation of security laws and regulations. While the *mens rea* (mental) element of this crime might not ultimately allow for a conviction, an "accident" will not simply be brushed aside. You would be arrested and the weapon confiscated at a minimum. In transitioning from reciprocal carry to interstate transport and back, it is easy to forget about the concealed weapon; those who carry on a daily basis do it without super-conscious awareness.

A person who enters a controlled area of an airport or aircraft under this general penal rule shall be fined under Title 18, imprisoned for not more than one (1) year, or both. However, if the person enters the controlled area of the airport or aircraft, with the intent to commit a felony under Federal or State law, he or she shall be fined under Title 18, imprisoned for not more than ten (10) years, or both.

IV. Interference with TSA or Other Screeners

Transporting firearms in checked luggage is a new and sometimes stressful event for travelers. Thus, if TSA inspects or otherwise inquires about the firearm (presumably a handgun for purposes of the GLBS Guide) be calm, cool and collected. Otherwise, it may appear suspicious and open the door for unnecessary criminal risks.

An individual, in an area within a commercial service airport in the U.S., who assaults a Federal, airport or air carrier employee who has security duties within the airport, interferes with the performance of the employee's duties, or lessens the employee's ability to perform those duties, commits a crime.

A person interfering with an airport's security personnel shall be fined under Title 18, imprisoned for not more than ten (10) years, or both. If the individual used a dangerous weapon in committing the assault or interference, the individual may be imprisoned for any term of years or life imprisonment.

V. Conclusion

Airports and aircraft are highly regulated and controlled in all regards. This includes introducing firearms into the mix. However, the interstate right to transportation of a firearm from any lawful place to any other, coupled with the fairly clear TSA requirements, makes this serious topic relatively easy to comply with, and has little ambiguity. Firearms are routinely checked in passenger baggage every day.

PART V: STATE, LOCAL: OTHER REGULATION

Areas where large numbers of people congregate have long been a focus of state-based penal laws. The driving policy or theory is unclear in some cases (perhaps it is the consumption of alcohol or the presence of young children). Nevertheless, there are a substantial number of similar categories that should raise questions in Your mind with each state.

Many of these are specifically set forth in the penal law in individual states that follow. However, some categories may be primarily regulated outside penal law, such as by private property rules or regulations or ordinances, which are typically classified as civil matters. These should still be determined and followed under any classification.

These suspected places and/or events where carry may be restricted or prohibited are addressed in the following chapters:

- **Chapter 20: Areas/Places and Events/Gatherings**
- **Chapter 21: State Administrative Agency Regulations**
- **Chapter 22: Local Ordinances**
- **Chapter 23: Private Property**

Chapter Twenty
Areas/Places and Events/Gatherings

I.   Introduction

With a CCP issued in Your state of residence or under/with carry on a non-resident license, certain areas and places or events and gatherings that should always be considered suspect and presumed to be excepted for lawful carry, unless Your research demonstrates otherwise.

EX **Native American Tribal Lands.** Take for example the fact that Native American reservations are essentially individual nations and have their own laws, rules and regulations regarding firearms. If You are going into a state that has tribal lands, but You will not be in or near those areas, there is likely no need to conduct further research. However, state-based preemption generally does not cover Tribal Lands, and it is possible that a CCP that is honored in the rest of the state will not be valid on Tribal Lands. The GLBS Guide is a working tool to access and evaluate proposed reciprocal carry in advance and also in more real-time than traditional methods would allow. This is the reason for the hyperlinks.

II.   Areas/Places

The most commonly regulated (penal, private property, or ordinance) areas and places are set forth. You should research the law of the given state to determine if these places are restricted with a CCP, or avoid them altogether.

■ Day care centers, including the parking lot

- Public and private schools ranging from K through 12, including the parking lot
- Colleges and universities
- Churches
- Sterile and secured areas of airports
- Passenger cabin of commercial aircraft
- Hospitals
- Jails, prisons, and penal institutions
- Courts and courthouses or places where court may be held
- Military bases
- Federal property
- Federal Offices, such as the Social Security offices or IRS offices
- State and local government offices and/or meetings
- Parks
- National Parks and Wildlife Refuges
- Nuclear and chemical facilities and depots
- Retail stores
- Places liquor is sold and/or served
- Financial institutions
- Private homes or businesses of others with a possessory interest
- State and federal ports, bonded warehouses, or free-trade-zone facilities
- Battered-women or abuse shelters
- Juvenile-delinquency or ward-of-the state facilities

III. Events and Gatherings

- Sports games
- Funerals and funeral processions
- Parades
- Fairs

- Political rallies
- Government meetings
- Hunting (which may have a whole set of requirements regarding firearms)
- Concerts or other mass gatherings or large events

IV.   Conclusion

A particular event or activity may bar a licensee from carrying under state penal law. This would apply to reciprocal carry. In addition, these regulations may or may not be criminal but civil and subject a licensee violating such a ban to expulsion from the event and confiscation of the firearm. This in turn could, at least under some states' licensing law, create a basis for revoking a CCP.

Chapter Twenty-One
State Administrative Agency Regulations

Most state legislatures pass and handle matters related to the statutory, substantive criminal law. However, with the balance of matters, they create administrative agencies to pass rules and regulations. These may include regulations on firearms, but typically they are not criminal. Instead, they prohibit firearms at certain places and events.

Failure of a licensee, including one carrying with reciprocity, may subject him or herself to ejection, confiscation, and fine, though typically the same are not criminal. Criminal laws have a constitutional dimension in that they must be on notice in order to be penal in nature. Most administrative rules are buried in complex administrative texts.

A prudent use of reciprocal carry is to consider this in advance. There are a number of places and events that overlap on a civil front with those criminal in nature. Some of the more common places related to carrying a handgun with reciprocity (usually stated in terms of firearms and no exception for licensees) are as follows:

- Taverns and places where alcoholic beverages are sold and/or consumed
- Casinos
- Horse-racing tracks
- Parks
- Nature reserves
- Waterways
- Maritime ports
- Nuclear and chemical plants

Chapter Twenty-Two
Local Ordinances

I.   Introduction

A key inquiry in each state, as addressed on a state-by-state basis in each state chapter, is whether there is state-based preemption. A common area for questions and confusion involves the ability of local units of government to regulate firearms and ammunition. Where it exists, an ordinance violation is generally a civil matter and subject to fine.

The NRA has taken on this fight as it relates to some of the over-reaching local firearms regulations and has prevailed with state preemption campaigns in a number of states. If there is state-based preemption, this means the state has specifically set forth in state law what areas local governments may regulate regarding firearms. This minimizes searching through these hard-to-find ordinances.

II.   State versus Local Unit Authority

A.   Traditional Approach

Under the traditional approach taken by state legislative bodies, local governments only possess the powers expressly given to it by the Legislature. For this reason, and generally speaking, unless a state statute gave a unit of local government specific authorization to regulate certain affairs, it cannot. A centralized government is usually preferred.

B.   Home Rule

The notion of home rule, local governments regulating their own affairs, runs through Western history. Some states have thus adopted the Home Rule Acts. The purpose or policy of Home Rule is to transfer to local governmental units all powers necessary or desirable in conducting their local affairs. In order to exercise its powers, and direct lawful acts and omissions, local government passes ordinances.

If Home Rule is the law, many political units have firearms ordinances. Be aware!

III.   Scope of Preemption

In most states where there is state-based preemption, the state government may still afford some authority to local government to regulate firearms. These allowances of power generally fall into one of a few categories:

- Discharge
- Zoning
- Property that local government owns or rents
- Distance of sales of firearms near schools

Thus, where there are exceptions in state-based preemption statutes, they must be understood and any ordinances on point determined and followed. In the few states where there is no state-based preemption, the ordinances may vary (and do) from one side of the street to the next. These states, assuming reciprocity exists, present unique challenges for licensees in locating and following local ordinances.

A comprehensive list of local ordinances is maintained by ATFE [http://gunla.ws/atf] but is subject to two significant limitations. First, the local government must have published its ordinance in the Federal Register [http://gunla.ws/fr] to get picked up and placed on the list. Second, the list is always a year or more behind; and, therefore, it may not include the most current changes.

In addition, a few private databases [http://gunla.ws/mcode] are searchable and contain local ordinances. Local ordinances are problematic for reciprocal carry.

IV.   Conclusion

Local ordinances are an area where there is potential conflict with rights withheld by the Legislature. In addition, local ordinances are difficult to access in an efficient manner. However, violation is civil in nature, not criminal. It is necessary to determine if there is state-level preemption. If so, the only areas that need to be researched, if any, are the exceptions for local government.

Where there is no state-level preemption, a serious risk-benefit analysis should be taken by a person anticipating reciprocal carry. In a narrow scope, it may be able to be researched with relative ease. Without this, the matter will be a time-consuming process.

Chapter Twenty-Three
Private Property

I.   Introduction

Under the laws of most states, a person who holds an interest in real property may regulate affairs on the land. This includes the carry or possession of firearms as a general rule. However, there are a number of carve-outs across the states. For instance, some states carve out exceptions for employees.

Unless the employer is excluded, the general variant of this legislation allows an employee to bring a firearm onto workplace property so long as it remains in his or her vehicle. If the GLBS Guide is gelling with Readers, it should seem apparent that this is not a foreseeable exception to most reciprocal carry.

On the other hand, some states have penal statutes on the books that prohibit a person, including a licensee, from carrying a firearm on the property if it is posted and/or required notification by the person in possession of the property. Failure to do so may be criminal and the property owner may direct the person to leave. A failure to leave may subject the licensee, including reciprocal licensee, to arrest for criminal trespass.

Thus, depending on the nature and circumstance of Your reciprocal carry, You may need to dig into state property law, criminal law (i.e., trespass), or ordinances adopted by units of government below the state level.

II.   Definition/Explanation of Key Concepts

While states will vary, there is some uniformity with regard to the definition and/or explanation of the key terms and concepts as follows:

A.   Real Property

Conceptually, as reflected in the general definition, there are two (2) types of property. The first is land, or real estate, which may be improved, which means it has a structure built upon it as a general matter.

B.   Personal Property

The other type of property is a tangible thing, such as a firearm itself. This Chapter's focus is real property, unimproved or improved: all of those public and private places not already addressed in the GLBS Guide. Personal property analysis thus stops with its understanding for purposes of this Chapter.

C.   Real Property Interests

1.   Deeded Property

Broadly, real-property interests are of two (2) types. The first is real property owned by a deed. An example is a personal family home. However, real property may be encumbered by a mortgage, whereby the lender holds a security interest in the property by legal interest in the loan. The property owner, by deed, owns the whole bundle of rights in the land, such as minerals in the ground, unless sold off, in perpetuity.

2.   Leased Property

The second type of real-property interests that a person or entity may possess is a leasehold estate in the property. Here, there is a written interest in the land given by the deed owner to the lessee for a period of time, which runs for a fixed number of years. Taking the family-home example just provided, if this home were leased out by the deed owner, there would be two (2) real estate interests in the same parcel of property. How the real property may be used by the lessee is specified by contract – the lease. This may be critical as it relates to firearms.

D.   Licensees and Invitees

It should be self-apparent that most places that Readers visit are not owned by him/her by a deed or lease. Assuming the area is not posted "No Trespassing," there is likely an express or implied license to visit.

Taking the example of a private home, the sidewalk to the front door is likely deemed an implied license to anyone to go up and ring the doorbell, although the occupant (deed holder or lessee) may subsequently revoke this implied license and ask him/her to leave. Failure to do so then constitutes trespass.

Equally, a public shopping mall and its signage and parking lot is an invitation to visit the property for shopping. However, the mall owner or tenant (lessee) may ultimately demand that the visitor leave. This revokes the right to be there. If the invitee fails to leave, the police may be called and the person may be arrested for trespass.

An event at a public or private place for which a ticket for entry is purchased is an express license, although the ticket holder may be an invitee. In fact, as a point of advanced learning, Readers should look at event tickets — in the fine print on the back, it will almost certainly relate that it is a license, revocable by the issuer at will.

This noted, the point of a licensee/invitee status in the context of real estate is that it merely confers a personal privilege to perform some act(s) on the land of another without conveying an interest in the land. A license to perform some act on real property of another is revocable by nature and unassignable. An invitee's status is similar in that he or she must leave if requested to do so and has no right in the real estate, although the landowner owes the invitee a higher duty of care.

III. Interplay of Landholder and Licensee or Invitee Rights to Possess Firearms

In any given circumstance of carry or possession of a firearm, the Reader must understand not only the prohibitions noted that might apply, but his/her status on real property otherwise. This will determine a lawful course of action.

An actual example from the Author's practice makes this point. Leases routinely have contractual paragraphs barring the lessee from having firearms in the premises. If the tenant or lessee is a retail gun store, that clause, if not revised, would ensure continuing breach and actionable conduct by lessor (who should not have invited this problem by including this in a lease) and the lessee whose livelihood is at hand.

This same provision becomes much more difficult to analyze if the lessee/tenant operates a different type of business, such as a retail sporting-goods store. Presumably, customers who come into the premises by implied license, may carry firearms. Is the lessee in violation of his/her lease in conducting the anticipated affairs of the retail operation?

On the other hand, some states regulate certain private property, such as having a law that prohibits an employer from barring an employee from maintaining a lawfully possessed firearm in his/her vehicle. These provisions may bring this very issue to the legal forefront. The Author has received an inquiry along these lines from a business that leases its facility.

The business' lease prohibits firearms on the premises, and it is a breach of the lease, exposing the employer to liability from the landlord, if it allows employees to maintain firearms in their vehicles. Yet if the business prohibits employees from such, the business is liable to the employees. This will be played out and decided through the courts at some point.

This noted, the deed owner and lessee may bargain for provisions of their lease through contractual negotiations. The implied/express licensees to the public/private facility must adhere to the terms that are imposed on them. These may include, exclude or be silent as to firearms. The licensee has no effective remedy other than refund of any admission price or civil rights matters if that be the case.

IV. Liability in Ability to Regulate Firearms on Real Property

How all of this plays out and why it matters is the ultimate end of firearms on and within any given (improved) real property: someone is shot and injured or killed. If the owner by deed and/or lease can prohibit firearms from ever being on the property, this risk is reduced or eliminated.

Where it is not possible, probable, or desired to regulate or prohibit firearms on private or public property, the parties can anticipate risks in contractual relations if that is at issue (a lease, such as in indemnity provision for the landlord), make more-adept contingency plans for a negligent discharge of a weapon or intentional shooting, and/or insure the risk. What is not said here, but may be operational, is a political position on firearms rights.

Ultimately, on public or private property, the lessor and lessee are free to bargain for and contract provisions for firearms. The implied or express licensee must adhere to the rules or regulations. In Indiana, the store Tuesday Morning posts a sign on its storefronts that firearms are prohibited there. Gander Mountain welcomes loaded handguns by licensees.

HY **One Set of Considerations of Many.** Carrying a firearm is a dynamic event and not one to be considered in a static environment. In the course of a day, a person may go into a sporting-goods store and purchase a handgun, already possessing a license. If this is in a strip mall, and the licensee walks to the next store, he or she may not lawfully enter, if the store posts that no firearms are allowed. This is a civil matter, but nonetheless, a breach of law. If the purchaser then leaves, parks and goes into the local middle school to pick up his/her child, parks in the school lot, and leaves the handgun in his/her car, this might be a crime under state law.

V.   Conclusion

Private property considerations, to the extent criminal for violation, are set forth in state criminal codes. However, there is a wide array of situations that may arise in reciprocal carry where a licensee may not carry on private property. These are set out in state property law, civil law, or contract law. Such are beyond the GLBS Guide but nonetheless a consideration for all reciprocal carry. This general discussion should provide a framework of how to make the queries and obtain sound legal direction.

PART VI: USE OF FORCE

As a general proposition, reciprocal carry inherently embodies the notion You may run into an unexpected situation where force may be necessary to protect life, limb and property. It seems so simple.

Make no mistake, however, that even an unquestionably justified use of force in Your state or a reciprocal state will have life-long implications; ask any who has been there, civilian, police officer, or soldier about Post-Traumatic Stress Disorder.

Unfortunately, the examples of the day that permeate the headlines anchor the extremes: a fully-justified use of deadly force, like the security guard who saves several school children from a homicidal shooter's rampage to the uninformed store owner who shoots and kills a shoplifter who refuses to stop.

The majority of cases–those not seen in the media–are the ones that are the closer legal calls. Even if the person is ultimately not criminally charged or civilly sued, it may be weeks, months, or even years (and thousands of dollars) before this is decided by a prosecutor or grand jury–later in criminal defense attorney fees or civil law suit defense before dismissal.

For this reason, the book briefly covers the thorny legal topic of the use of force. The lawful use of such force lies on a factual-legal continuum; if Your case happens to lie in between fully-justified self-defense to unjustified, it is likely You will have to defend Yourself in criminal and/or civil courts.

By way of refinement, the right to use force, such as to grab the hand of an unarmed assailant to keep them from hitting You to shooting or killing a person are conceptually, legally, and analytically different. The use of force must be proportional.

As You may imagine, all sorts of variables play into any use of force, which are well beyond the GLBS Guide, but worth noting for Your future research:

- Timing of use of force in response to illicit force (shooting a fleeing felon is probably criminal).
- Politics (after a major incident, such as a rash of car-jackings or murders) of the situation may make the police, prosecutor, judge or jury view the situation differently and more or less likely to prosecute.
- Gender or race differences (on the very same facts, a female's exercise of deadly force may be viewed differently than a male).
- Local and regional incongruities exist in how firearms and the use of force are viewed, which is apparent in the strict handgun control laws of New York City and Washington, D.C.

In the next three (3) chapters, some of the basic components of the use of force are discussed to help orient Your thinking with Your life events and the news of the day. Ultimately, the correct legal and moral decision must be made on the day *what if* becomes *what is* and You are involved in a (deadly) force situation.

One of the staple books everyone should consider is Massad Ayoob's *In the Gravest Extreme* [http://gunla.ws/massad]. The GLBS Guide unpacks force and illustrates the extraordinary consequence of use of force. There are no do overs and a mistake in judgment may well land You in jail for a long time and the loss of another's life, not to mention civil liability.

The Chapters that address Use of Force and its criminal and civil dimensions are the following:

- **Chapter 24: Criminal Law (Legal Justification to Violate the Law through Deadly Force)**
- **Chapter 25: Civil Liability**
- **Chapter 26: Wisdom from a Death-Penalty Qualified Criminal Defense Attorney**

Chapter Twenty-Four
Criminal Law (Legal Justification to Violate the Law through Deadly Force)

I. Introduction

Do You see, understand, and can identify the color red? Everyone does. However, if a car is parked that edges into the pink or orange portion of the red continuum, is it red, pink or orange? You know it when You see it! But faced with the choice of making this "call" in the split second when the car speeds by we may all agree to disagree.

The use of force in response and to repel or terminate illicit force, including deadly force, falls within a continuum–lawful to unlawful. However, this "call" is not so trivial. Where to start? Within any state, the answer is with the penal definition of deadly force.

This varies from place to place, and requires some of the terms within the definition to have definitions. As a general rule of thumb, illicit use of "deadly force" to which deadly force may be used in response includes the notion the "victim" is at risk of serious bodily injury or death. What rises to this level is place and fact sensitive.

Nevertheless, determining the legal definition of this term through statutes or cases is a proper place to start in any jurisdiction. Then the real factual or legal analysis begins. Are there other circumstances where (deadly) force may be applied? Yes. For the most part, a close look at the law in every state will reveal that deadly force may be lawfully–and a justification to what would otherwise be a crime equal to murder–applied in one of three situations.

II. Common Legal Justifications

As the definition of deadly force hints at, one justification to use force, sometimes including deadly force, is with the illicit acts of a criminal that causes bodily injury. Where deadly force is the response, the bodily injury generally has to be one serious in nature.

A. Serious Bodily Injury

The term "serious bodily injury" (SBI) is variously defined amongst the varying states. However, there are some significant commonalities to a criminal's application of force to You and Your situation that may justify the use of deadly force to protect. Although perhaps self-apparent, serious bodily injury is not injury that is trivial in nature.

HY **Slap to the Face**. The nature and circumstance of serious bodily injury is illustrated by the example of walking down the street and a random person begins lightly slapping You. The exercise of deadly force in response, such as by drawing a lawfully possessed handgun and shooting this person in response to stop the slaps would be unjustified because no matter how many times slapped, it is unlikely this will cause serious bodily injury. However, a very slight change in fact and the situation is not nearly as clear. A 90-pound female is punched in the face by a 400-pound man. When he starts to punch her the second time, is she justified in using deadly force in response? It depends.

Generally, serious bodily injury has several hallmarks: it involves the real risk of death, disfigurement, loss of consciousness, or permanent or long-term impairment of a limb or organ. Again, however, in any given case, a slight change in the facts may make a difference between whether the person exercising the deadly force in response to the illicit act is deemed a "hero" or is going to prison.

B.   Dwelling and Curtilage

In a departure from the justification to use (deadly) force in response to an illegal act, a special place is carved out in the law for one's home and in some cases, curtilage. Within any jurisdiction and set of jurors, the term may carry different meaning.

As a general notion, a person's dwelling carries in its meaning a place where a person would feel comfortable conducting the most intimate acts of life, including showering, dressing and the like. This is a dwelling and may be temporary in some cases, such as a hotel, or movable, as may be the case with an RV or travel trailer.

In some states, deadly force may be used to stop or repel an unlawful entry into one's dwelling. Nevertheless, the more removed the place is from the traditional notion of a dwelling, such as a home in a subdivision with the white picket fence and two children, the more likely the use of force is to be called into question.

HY **Hotel and/or Hotel Room.** A good example of what may be a dwelling (or not) is found in a hotel room. If a person is staying day by day or week-by-week, it is much more likely this place will be deemed a dwelling for this legal justification than a hotel room rented for a party. How this is legally characterized is what good lawyers address each day.

Curtilage is a more amorphous concept. This is an ancient term and refers to the necessary parts of the outside of a home that effectively sustain (by growing crops and raising livestock) its occupants. A small storehouse or pen of animals might as well be a part of the house because their theft or plunder would leave the family to starve in the winter months.

In the present day, the curtilage is narrowly defined to include the immediate environs on the outside of the home. However, for search and seizure purposes–when a search warrant is required or exigent circumstances, the courts typically provide more leeway to the curtilage. It is thus less likely any law enforcement activities leading to arrest would be suppressed as within the curtilage and need for a warrant.

C.   Forcible Felonies

One of the more vexing queries for the average citizen (i.e., a person who is not a lawyer or involved in law enforcement in some way) is to determine what felonies may be justification to use deadly force, and what felonies are not. As a technical matter, forcible felonies are those that have an element of bodily harm.

The distinction is best made by illustration. If You are in a bank and observe a fellow customer forging a check to cash, this *is not* a forcible felony. On the other hand, take the situation the pen the forger is using to obtain money he or she does not deserve is traded for a handgun to extract the money from the teller. This *is* a forcible felony.

More common examples of crimes that may have force as an element of the crime under state or federal law include the following:

- Kidnapping
- Car-jacking
- Burglary
- Rape
- Robbery
- Arson

It is important to note that not every state allows for the use of deadly force against every forcible felony. Some states only allow deadly force against certain forcible felonies, so it is important to know which forcible felonies count in Your state.

EX **Minor Property Crime.** Take the case of a motorist who is properly stopped for a red traffic signal. The car behind him, who has a driver who has a suspended license, and if caught again, will lose his right to obtain and hold a driver's license for life, bumps this stopped motorist. In a moment of panic, the suspended driver flees. The motorist who is just another lawful member of society, suspecting damage to his car, gives chase. Ultimately, when the fleeing driver does not stop, the pursuing driver rolls down his window and begins firing at the fleeing driver who hit his car. When the chase leads into a residential neighborhood, several parents who are outside to welcome their children from the school bus call 911 in a panic and relay a car is chasing another and shooting at it. The driver who is shooting is subsequently stopped by the police and charged with criminal recklessness. The incensed driver relays he is the victim. The outcome? The driver is charged and convicted of a Class D felony for criminal recklessness for this behavior. The tables thus turned from victim to perpetrator. This is an operating environment for a deadly force case. A slight change in factual developments may result in a turn of the tides.

III. Legal Dynamics

Confused? Do You think these three (3) justifications to use (deadly) force are less than clear? Consider this in the operational environment: A night. And being awakened from a dead sleep. The supreme value placed on human life–and taking it without justification–is such that there is another layer of complexity to contend with and consider in any force situation.

The variables are any good reason why deadly force should not be exercised, some of which are more or less rooted in community values and standards. Some of the most common are enumerated and analyzed:

A.   Proportionality

As the title suggests, the use of (deadly) force must be a proportional response. Thus, a corporate officer who observes an employee transmitting trade secrets and who responds by shooting and killing the employee is not taking a proportional response under the American notion of law.

Make no mistake this is a felony, but it is not one that has an element of the crime involving force. If this corporate officer responds to an alarm and the employee is breaking in or in the workplace stealing this data after hours this may change the legal analysis and justification.

Like punishment for a crime, the justification to use deadly force must be proportional and exercised in the cases where society places the taking of a life in response to a crime on par with the crime and/or justified: (1) serious bodily injury or death; (2) breaking into a dwelling and or attack within the curtilage; (3) forcible felony.

It should also be noted that proportionality takes into consideration the relative size/weight/strength of the parties. For instance, a 90-pound woman using force against a 250-pound male attacker would be more proportional than an NFL linebacker using deadly force against a small, unarmed female aggressor. Proportionality considers the amount of force used compared to the level of threat posed by an attacker. The size and strength of the aggressor, whether they're armed (and with what) are taken into account. The same aggressor would pose a greater threat to someone who is disabled, elderly, or otherwise incapable of resisting than they would pose to a strong, fit individual.

110

Here a proportional response, as a matter of law by societal value, may be the justification to use deadly force–namely to meet all of the elements of the crime for what would otherwise be a murder and be justified in doing so and not be criminally charged. In all states this varies.

B.   Immediacy

The variable of immediacy is one that trips up even sophisticated scholars in theoretical considerations of self-defense. Any of the circumstances noted where deadly force may be justified will expire with the passage of time. A homeowner who chases after the burglar and shoots him in the street in the back is unlikely to be legally justified to commit what would otherwise be a crime from manslaughter to murder.

The passage of time and the fact the burglar has already left and is outside the home and curtilage resets the justification clock to unjustified at some indeterminate point. At this threshold, the victim, if he or she exercises force, and deadly force in particular, becomes a criminal as well. The burglar may serve jail time for burglary. The murderer, well, will serve time for murder or a lesser included crime.

C.   Retreat

In some states, human life is held more sacred than the ordinary categories where self-defense, including deadly force, may be justified if the victim of the crime can retreat and fails to retreat to the wall. What this means is, if there is a safe way to leave or flee the crime, the victim must do so until he "hits a wall" or barrier where he or she can no longer safely do so. It is only at "the wall" that the justification to use deadly force becomes valid.

D.   Standing Your Ground

On the other hand, in a growing number of states, a victim does not have to retreat or take any action to avoid the crime being inflicted if it falls within one of the categories. In these cases, a victim who is attacked in any place they have a legal right to be (such as public areas) may use deadly force and be justified in doing so and standing his or her ground and not retreating. However, many of these statutory provisions also include the qualifier that the use of deadly force must be reasonable.

EX **Open Lands.** It is always difficult to set out an example that may overshadow the rule. However, with the "reasonableness" component of standing one's ground, if that is the law of a jurisdiction You find yourself within, an example, even if extreme, may help Your educational development. Take a "victim" sitting in his or her bedroom, on a sunny day, reading. The French doors to this room are open and face a level panoramic prairie. At this moment, an overweight intruder yielding a baseball bat barges into the room. Would it be reasonable for the physically fit homeowner to shoot and kill the intruder if he or she merely had to turn and run outside to avoid the situation? If retreat is required in this state, or even if one can stand their ground, is this reasonable? No.

IV.   Standard Response.

Over time, the stressors of life and death decisions have led to defaults to be engaged in where incomplete information is at hand. For police officers, these are known as standard operating procedures ("SOPs"). In the military, these are referred to as the rules of engagement ("ROEs"). This ensures the law is followed and the right decision made in most cases.

112

In the civilian world, where taking a life is taboo, no cognizable and generally understood and agreed upon set of rules or defaults exist. However, if You could have a frank and open discussion with a seasoned police officer, criminal defense attorney, or prosecutor, You would find indeed they could come up with a more or less agreeable set of such rules.

These, again, are defaults in any one given case, but could fail and lead to detention, arrest, and conviction. However, the person who plays the odds in any situation, including those that involve life and death (swerve and risk rolling the car, or hit the deer and risk intrusion into the passenger's compartment and being kicked to death) prevails more often than not.

So, what are these rules You have never heard any talk about, and if they exist, when and how do You use and apply any such rules in a post-deadly-force encounter:

> **Rule #1: Aggressor Stopped.** Is the aggressor actually out of play and no longer a risk? Or alternatively, does he or she have on body armor and may become re-engaged in a short period of time?

> **Rule #2: Situational Awareness/Control.** Are You completely cognizant of the environment? Are there other aggressors? Are You in control and command of the situation or is this unknown?

> **Rule #3: Contact EMS.** Have You contacted emergency services? This is the key to protecting Yourself and mitigating any future unnecessary harm to the former criminal, now injured and/or dying. However, You should take care to make no incriminating statements on recorded 911 calls. Relay facts: "Someone has been shot;" not, "I shot someone."

Rule #4: First Aid and/or Retreat. Should You provide aid or retreat? This depends. There are a number of civilians and LEOs whose after-deadly-force actions, such as calling EMS or rendering aid (being aware of blood-borne pathogens), have saved the lives of the criminal. On the other hand, if the risk field, the situation You find Yourself in is unknown, such as with multiple assailants, should You leave the immediate scene, yet be available to point EMS to the injured?

Rule #5: Compliance with LEO Commands. On balance, while making specific fact statements is not prudent, this is far different from failing to comply with lawful law enforcement commands, such as for identification? You must comply with law enforcement commands and directives, but not go so far as to make statements or give an account of what occurred.

Rule #6: Remain Silent and Demand Counsel. Resist human nature. The human experience is to explain acts or omissions. If You have exercised deadly force against an assailant, the correct way to proceed to a statistical legal certainty is to invoke the right to remain silent and demand an attorney, no matter what deal or leniency You are promised. The exercise of deadly force and its stress causes chemical changes in the body that impair the ability–Your ability–to make a complete and accurate statement.

V.   Conclusion.

Carrying a handgun, or any firearm for that fact, and the specter of self-defense is a subject of contemplation/preparation, not mere reaction at the time at hand. As the old adage goes, "You will default to the mean, not rise to the occasion." This could result in missing Your aggressor in an otherwise lawful (deadly) force situation and killing an innocent bystander and/or making a statement that is not accurate leading to Your arrest, prosecution, and incarceration: Only to be followed by a civil lawsuit.

Chapter Twenty-Five
Civil Liability

I.   Introduction

As old as time itself is the question of how to address a wrong inflicted upon another or society at large. Under the American legal system, many civil wrongs have a remedy in court by a monetary award and criminal acts, those against individuals and/or society, at least the significant crimes, may be redressed by incarceration under state or federal law in local, state or federal jails and prisons.

An unlawful use of deadly force by the criminal perpetrator or the "victim" who uses excessive or otherwise unjustified deadly force, may also result in a civil suit by the family of the former criminal assailant or victim who goes too far in self-defense, extinguishing the right to this criminal defense to what would otherwise be a crime.

II.   Insurance

One of the greatest urban legends or myths is that an unlawful use of deadly force will be covered for criminal defense costs and civil litigation costs and any judgment by insurance. In a narrow set of factual and legal circumstances, an insurer may provide a defense, which is paying the legal fees for the most part.

However, in most cases, intentional acts, such as intending to shoot someone, be it as a criminal in the name of excessive self-defense, are excluded from coverage. If this seems strange, think of it this way. If You see an arch-enemy driving down the street and decide to, and do, ram his or her car, this is criminal and an intentional act.

As such, it is very likely that Your auto insurer will deny the

116

coverage for an intentional-acts-exception in Your coverage. In the event You have the same facts, but inadvertently hit this car that happens to contain someone You do not like because of Your care in driving, this is negligence and most likely covered by auto insurance.

The same set of typical exceptions applies to homeowner's insurance and umbrella coverage. Thus, if You carry a handgun for self-defense, including under reciprocal licensing, and make a mistake in judgment, it is highly unlikely any general insurance You have will provide even the costs of a defense.

There are citizen-driven defense funds that may provide legal fees and You are well-advised to look into these just as You consider strengthening the right to keep and bear arms by supporting the NRA [http://gunla.ws/nra] or GOA [http://gunla.ws/goa]. The most known is the Armed Citizens Defense Fund [http://gunla.ws/acdf] administered by attorney Marty Hayes.

III.   Intersection of Criminal Defense and Civil Liability

The interaction between a prudent criminal defense, which likely includes exercising the right to remain silent in any allegation and criminal charge of excessive force (i.e., the affirmative defense of self-defense is extinguished), is often confronted with any potential insurance defense. This is where a skilled legal team may help.

Specifically, an insurer who agrees to pay Your defense costs under any potential policy coverage, almost certainly has a cooperation clause in the insurance contract. For this reason, to learn about how much to set aside in the event You lose the civil suit (assuming there is no reservation of rights) an insurer will want to take Your statement and talk with You about the deadly force encounter.

This is generally incompatible with a criminal defense strategy, where a seasoned criminal defense attorney will want You

117

to remain silent and have the state prove their case for a crime (excessive force charged from manslaughter to murder) beyond the very high standard of a reasonable doubt. The more You say, the easier it is for the state to prevail. Thus, You likely will not want to cooperate with any insurer.

But the failure to cooperate may result in denial of otherwise valid coverage. This is a delicate timing act a skilled attorney can help You with. As with making the determination to carry a gun and potentially engage in self-defense, this is also a matter to think about–in advance, not after the fact. If You are not willing to consider these situations, You might do well not to carry a gun at all.

IV.   Reservation of Rights

A term of art mentioned in the prior discussion is a "reservation of rights." This is a common term among those in the insurance and legal industry. Insurance is nothing more than a contract to cover certain risks between an insured and an insurer.

Because the events of daily life are not orderly, but disorderly and downright messy, many claims occur that despite the best written insurance contract, may not be able to be determined for coverage at least before a court trial.

As such, an insurer may issue a reservation of rights letter in cases where it is unclear whether the act or omission (such as justified force or unjustified force) is covered in that it is an intentional act or negligent act. With such a letter, an insurer may agree to vigorously defend You, but when and if a judge or jury decides it is intentional, the defense funds and payment of a claim would terminate under the reservation of rights letter.

A reservation of rights letter is thus a double-edged sword. It will provide the legal defense costs–but You had better prevail.

V. Burden of Proof

At this juncture, it may seem odd that You could prevail in a criminal case–alleging Your use of (deadly) force was excessive and not justified–and still face civil suit. This is because there is a policy in our legal system that it is better a guilty person go free than an innocent person be incarcerated. To ensure this is the case, there is a very high standard of proof in criminal cases–beyond a reasonable doubt (this is indeterminate but probably in the 90% range of guilt on a 1 to 100 scale).

In closer cases, the use of deadly force may not be charged at all. Where it is tried, a judge or jury may acquit the defendant, agreeing the use of (deadly) force was justified. However, a civil wrong has a lower burden of proof. For this reason, a person who is not charged or acquitted may still face a long and expensive civil suit from the "victim's" family.

The legal theory where death results is that the excessive use of deadly force (unjustified) led to the wrongful death of the now deceased perpetrator. It is possible that in close cases a criminal case may be avoided, but the civil suit proceeds and the un-charged person who exercised deadly force loses a civil case and has to pay monies for the civil tort of wrongful death.

This is the bewildering way the legal system works. It is less than perfect, but is optimal in light of self-remedy or the old way of shooting it out at sundown. Hopefully, this chapter provides You with the insight to carefully consider the choice to carry a gun and engage in reciprocal carry. This is half the battle.

VI. Conclusion

In the event You are involved in a deadly force incident, the criminal and civil liability chapters should provide You with a framework to utilize in any particular jurisdiction and circumstance: remain silent and retain a skilled attorney.

Chapter Twenty-Six
Wisdom from a Death-Penalty Qualified Criminal Defense Attorney

In reviewing this Section on deadly force, Vernon Lorenz, a seasoned criminal defense attorney who is death-penalty qualified, provided the Author with his sage advice and thoughts about self-defense in deadly force cases.

In many respects, these say it all.

- If a prosecutor reviews Your case and decides to charge You, Your self-defense claim is likely garbage.
- If You have a choice between shooting or any other option that allows You to walk away safe and sound, You should not shoot.
- If after shooting, You find yourself thinking, "I really stepped in it this time," Your favorite color had better be orange.
- If You see an escaping felon who has not challenged You (or does not even know You are there), wish him well on his journey.
- If You start a fight and You end it with deadly force on another person, You are in deep.
- If You shoot someone other than Piers Morgan, Your actions will be scrutinized thoroughly with an eye toward prosecution.
- If a person is threatening You with a birthday candle, a milk carton, or similar item, You cannot shoot.
- If You shoot out of anger or retribution (unless it is on an X-Box), You had better be able to run and catch Your bullet before it hits someone, or You are going to prison.
- If You shoot someone outside a dwelling, get a good

look at Your home because it may be a while before You see it again.

- If You are shooting by reacting, not because You are making a thoughtful choice, You had better get a copy of the yellow pages and look under "A" for attorneys.

There are rarely heroes in a deadly force encounter. And in time, even heroes are forgotten. Every single Reader's sole focus and desire should be to go home every night and enjoy their life. Take steps to actively avoid any deadly force scenario. Put an extra lock on the front door. Take a longer way home through a safer part of town. Just be aware and do not walk around with Your head hung low, screaming "make me a victim." Use Your brain.

PART VII: THE INDIVIDUAL STATES

The foregoing frames the somewhat bewildering array of considerations, when lawfully engaging in reciprocal carry in another state.

Primarily, the GLBS Guide is focused on determining reciprocity between states (whether there is a provision, and if so, how it applies), lawfully transporting the firearm to the reciprocal state, avoiding criminal violations along the way, and lawfully carrying the handgun in the reciprocal state.

The ease (or difficultly) in accomplishing this is determined by looking at four (4) variables in each state:

- State constitutional right to bear arms
- State-based reciprocity by the legislature
- Reciprocity agreement, if any
- State penal laws that apply to and do not except licensees

This is the format for each of the fifty (50) states. Hyperlinks are provided in analysis of each state as available to controlling statutory provisions and reciprocity tables for more research and considerations.

 # ALABAMA GUN LAWS

Introduction

What stands out about Alabama's criminal laws and how they impact carry of a handgun is their simplicity or lack of laws. There is a peculiar statutory prohibition on brass or steel Teflon-coated handgun ammunition, but a fair reading of the statutes indicate that it seeks to make unlawful handgun ammunition of types that would or is designed to penetrate a police officer's body armor. Open carry of handguns is legal in Alabama with a valid license to carry.

For orientation to reciprocal carry, the population is a little under five (5) million people. The states bordering Alabama are Tennessee to the north, Georgia to the east, Florida to the south, and Mississippi to the west.

A.   State Constitution

The Alabama constitution provides the right to keep and bear arms:

"That every citizen has a right to bear arms in defense of himself and that state." [http://gunla.ws/AL1]

B.   Scope of Preemption

In Alabama, there is strong state-level preemption on local government's ability to regulate firearms. This is addressed in two (2) statutory provisions that differentiate between handguns and other firearms. Generally speaking, the state alone maintains the right to pass criminal laws on and otherwise regulate firearms.

Alabama's firearm preemption provision is very precise:

(c) Except as otherwise provided in Act 2013 - 283 or as expressly authorized by a statute of this state, the Legislature hereby occupies and preempts the entire field of regulation in this state touching in any way upon firearms, ammunition, and firearm accessories to the complete exclusion of any order, ordinance, or rule promulgated or enforced by any political subdivision of this state. [http://gunla.ws/AL2]

Given Alabama's very limited authority bestowed upon local government, a person contemplating reciprocal carry, as an out-of-state licensee, should start by familiarizing himself/herself with the state criminal prohibitions relating to firearms. The state (not local) government makes the firearms law where the most severe penalties for violation lie, remembering the federal criminal prohibitions that apply in every state.

C.   Reciprocal Carry

By statute, Alabama has a clear reciprocity provision recognizing out-of-state licensees:

"A person licensed to carry a handgun in any state shall be authorized to carry a handgun in this state. This section shall apply to a license holder from another state only while the license holder is not a resident of this state. A license holder from another state shall carry the handgun in compliance with the laws of this state."

Alabama now has a reciprocity agreement with all states. In order for this to occur, the Alabama AG requires both states' licensing laws must be substantially similar. The most current, official Alabama reciprocal gun law chart is referenced by this hyperlink [http://gunla.ws/AL3].

D.   NFA Items

Alabama permits ownership of all NFA items, provided they are legally obtained pursuant to federal law. Hunting with suppressors is legal.

E.   Duty to Inform Officers

Alabama law does not specifically state that you have to present your Permit/License to a LEO immediately upon contact. It does say a Permit is required if you carry a pistol in a vehicle or concealed on your person. You would have to present it to an officer if they knew you had a pistol in your vehicle or concealed on your person as a Permit/License is required to carry in those instances. If you did not have a Permit/License you would be in violation of 13A-11-73. It is recommended You always carry your Permit/License.

F.   Possession at Work

An employer may not restrict the storage or transportation of a lawfully possessed pistol or ammunition in a privately-owned vehicle parked on public or private land, subject to certain restrictions: having a valid concealed weapon permit and the gun is out of sight. 40-12-134(b). The handgun must be unloaded, locked in container stored in the vehicle and out of reach of any occupants. An employer who believes an employee is a danger to themselves or others may ask if the employee has a firearm in their vehicle, and if so, may further inquire to make sure the firearm is being stored in accordance with the provisions above.

G.   Self-defense Laws.

Alabama has both Castle Doctrine and SYG laws. There is no duty to retreat when attacked in any place You have a legal right to be, and You may use deadly force in self-defense if You reasonably believe it is necessary to prevent death or SBI, to prevent kidnapping, robbery, burglary, or forcible rape, or to stop the unlawful & forcible entry into Your dwelling, residence, or occupied motor vehicle. [http://gunla.ws/AL4]

H.   Carrying Firearms in Vehicles

It is a crime to carry a concealed handgun in a vehicle without a license. An individual may carry a pistol without a permit on their land or business property owned by the individual. 13A-11-73(a). An individual may not carry a pistol on his person on a premises that is not his own and/or is merely under his control without a license.

Except as otherwise prohibited by law, a person legally permitted to possess a pistol, but who does not possess a valid concealed weapon permit, may possess an unloaded pistol in his or her motor vehicle if the pistol is locked in a compartment or container that is in or affixed securely to the vehicle and out of reach of the driver and any passenger in the vehicle. [http://gunla.ws/AL5]

I.   Carry in Restaurants That Serve Alcohol

Yes. Alabama currently has no laws prohibiting individuals who are otherwise lawfully allowed to carry a firearm from doing so in restaurants that serve alcohol.

J.   Criminal Provisions

A prudent person contemplating possessing a firearm in a state other than where they live, particularly with reciprocal handgun carry, should understand the other state's basic criminal laws. The top criminal acts relative to the state's penal orientation (highly complex and numerous in some densely populated areas to virtually nonexistent in some southern or western states) relating to firearms are set forth.

However, it is critical to remember every rule has exceptions that may or may not apply. And they may be contained in statutes, rules, regulations or cases. These too should be considered as necessary, remembering always that federal firearms law also applies in all states. In states that do not have complete state preemption, local laws must be followed. Finally, in states with Native Americans, their lands are subject to tribal laws and restrictions on firearms. A CCP is invalid in the following locations:

- Any place prohibited by federal law
- At public demonstrations, pickets, or protests
- A courthouse
- A jail/prison
- The Alabama statehouse
- A facility providing inpatient or custodial care of those with psychiatric, mental, or emotional disorders
- A building where a county commission or city council is currently having a meeting
- On the property of a public K-12 school
- At the facility of a sports game sponsored by a private or public elementary or secondary school, or any private or public post-secondary education institution, unless You have the permission of the person hosting the event
- At secured locations with restricted access and security

guards

- Discharging a firearm into a school, bus, building, train, automobile, aircraft, or watercraft is prohibited
- The sale and possession of handgun ammunition with Teflon-coated bullets made from brass or steel is prohibited, except for hollow points made from either brass or lead
- It is illegal to carry a rifle or shotgun walking cane

For a list of places where carrying firearms in prohibited, see: [http://gunla.ws/AL6]

K.   Other Considerations

In addition, always consider the other areas of restrictions relating to firearms and/or reciprocal carry, including, but not limited to the following:

- Federal property and law on airports and schools
- Common areas and places and events and gatherings
- Case law, local government ordinances, custom and practice, including those related to hunting and outdoor activities

For the entire collection of Alabama laws regarding firearms and weapons, see: [http://gunla.ws/AL7]

 **ALASKA GUN LAWS**

Introduction

A unique attribute to Alaska (and Hawaii) is they are not a part of the contiguous United States, which simplifies the questions of reciprocal carry or interstate transportation to reach Alaska. The most likely scenario in which a non-resident would carry in Alaska would be by flying into the state.

While Alaska is the largest state in the United States, its remote location and harsher climate keeps population lower than most large cities, with a little over 740,000 in total population. It has no shared boundaries with any other U.S. state, but all foreign boundaries.

A.   State Constitution

As it relates to firearms, the Alaska Constitution states:

"A well-regulated militia being necessary to the security of a free state, the right of the people to keep and bear arms shall not be infringed. The individual right to keep and bear arms shall not be denied or infringed by the state or political subdivision of the State." [http://gunla.ws/ak1]

B.   Scope of Preemption

Alaska's legislature has codified state-based firearms' preemption, but does give local government some authority consistent with home rule notions:

130

"The authority to regulate firearms is reserved to the state, and, except as specifically provided by statute, a municipality may not enact or enforce an ordinance regulating the possession, ownership, sale, transfer, use, carrying, transportation, licensing, taxation, or registration of firearms." [http://gunla.ws/ak2]

This preemption statute goes on to set forth and provide local governments with the limited ability to regulate, enact, and adopt laws regulating the discharge of firearms within city limits, or to ban firearms from certain restricted areas of government buildings.

Anchorage, Fairbanks, and Juneau all have some sort of local regulations, and posted regulation in the Federal Register may be found at the following hyperlink: [http://gunla.ws/atf]

C.   Reciprocal Carry

By statute in Alaska, anyone 21 or older may legally carry a firearm, and also carry it concealed, without having to have a state-issued permit. However, Alaskans must obtain a concealed carry permit for purposes of reciprocal carry.

Alaskan statutes direct that a person holding a valid permit to carry a concealed handgun from another state, or political subdivision of another state, is treated just as an Alaskan permittee (except for licenses from Idaho, which Alaska requires they be Enhanced). However, the legislature requires the Department of Public Safety to enter into reciprocity agreements with other states so that Alaskans are afforded the same rights to carry a handgun in other, reciprocal states.

Not all states have reciprocity with Alaska. Therefore, it is critical to verify the current status of reciprocity between the states in advance of this carry. Alaska's most current reciprocity information may be referenced online. [http://gunla.ws/ak3]

D.   Duty to Notify Police Officer

A person otherwise lawfully carrying a concealed handgun, commits an illegal act if he/she fails to immediately inform a peace officer that he/she is carrying a concealed handgun or fails to allow the officer to secure the weapon or fails to secure the weapon at the direction of the peace officer. It is a felony for a federal official or agent to enforce new restrictions on gun ownership. [http://gunla.ws/ek5t]

E.   Carrying Firearms in Vehicles

Alaska permits anyone who may legally possess a firearm to possess a firearm while operating a motor vehicle, or to store a firearm in a locked motor vehicle when it is parked.

An employer or its agent may, however, prohibit firearm possession within a secured restricted area, in a vehicle owned, leased, or rented by the employer or its agent, or in a parking lot owned or controlled by the employer within 300 feet of the secured restricted area.
[http://gunla.ws/ak4]

F.   Constitutional Carry

Alaska permits anyone who is at least 21 years old and may legally possess a firearm to carry a handgun without a permit, openly or concealed. [http://gunla.ws/ak5]

G.   NFA Items

Alaska permits the ownership of all NFA items, provided they are legally obtained pursuant to federal law. Hunting with suppressors is legal. CLEOs are required to sign an application for the transfer of any item regulated under the NFA within 30 days if the applicant is not prohibited by law from receiving it. [http://gunla.ws/zxat]

H.   Self-defense Laws

Alaska has both Castle Doctrine and SYG laws. There is no duty to retreat when attacked in any place You have a legal right to be, and You may use deadly force in self-defense if You reasonably believe it is necessary to prevent death or SBI, to prevent kidnapping, robbery, burglary, or forcible rape, or to stop the unlawful & forcible entry into Your dwelling, residence, or occupied motor vehicle. [http://gunla.ws/ak6]

I.   Criminal Provisions

There is no prohibition against carrying a handgun concealed or open, even without a license, so long as the prohibited behaviors regarding the carry are respected:

- The person is 21 years or older
- The person is eligible to own or possess a handgun under state and federal laws
- The firearm is legal

Note: Alaska's laws do not apply to federal property, offices, installations, or places under federal jurisdiction. Such places can include national parks, military bases, federal court buildings, space rented by federal offices, airports, or airport terminal areas. Please consult with the appropriate federal agency before deciding if weapon carry or concealed carry is permitted.

The owners or management of facilities, including such places as hospitals, universities, gymnasiums, or private property, may restrict or deny concealed carry on their premises. Failure to comply while on their property could violate trespass statutes.

A prudent person contemplating possessing a firearm in a state other than where they live should understand the other state's basic criminal laws.

The top criminal acts relative to the state's penal orientation relating to firearms are set forth. It is critical, however, to remember every rule has exceptions that may or may not apply. And they may be contained in statutes, rules, regulations or cases. These too should be considered, as necessary, remembering always federal firearms law also applies in all states. In states that do not have complete state preemption, local laws must be followed. In states with Native American lands, additional tribal laws and restrictions on firearms apply.

[http://gunla.ws/ak7]

Under Alaska law, a license to carry a handgun does not permit carry in any of the following places or circumstances:

- Anywhere prohibited by federal law
- Aboard a commercial or charter aircraft
- An area of an airport to which access is controlled by the inspection of persons and property
- A courthouse
- A domestic violence or sexual assault shelter
- A child care center (except for a private residence being used as such)
- In or on school property, property being used by a school for a school function, or a school bus (except for possession inside a motor vehicle being used to transport another to or from a school or school function). Note that You may have a firearm in the parking lot of a school as long as You are at least 21, not a student, and the firearm is unloaded and locked in Your vehicle
- In the private residence of another, unless You have their permission

■ It is illegal to carry a firearm or have possession of it in Your occupied motor vehicle while under the influence of alcohol or drugs

J.   Carry in Restaurants That Serve Alcohol

No. In Alaska, a person commits the crime of misconduct involving weapons in the fifth degree if the person knowingly possesses a loaded firearm in any place where intoxicating liquor is sold for consumption on the premises. You are prohibited from carrying while consuming alcohol or while under the influence of alcohol. [http://gunla.ws/0y25]

K.   Do "No Gun Signs" Have the Force of Law?

Yes. If a property or establishment has a "No Guns" sign or the person in lawful possession communicates to you that guns are not allowed, you are prohibited from carrying on the property or into the establishment. Failure to obey such signs or verbal warnings constitutes trespass. [http://gunla.ws/cqnp]

L.   Open Carry

Open carry is legal in Alaska. Individuals who are legally allowed to possess a firearm may open carry without a permit/license. Places as listed in the "Criminal Provisions" above apply to those who open carry. The minimum age for open carry is 21.

M.   Other Considerations

In addition, always consider the other areas of restrictions relating to firearms and/or reciprocal carry, including, but not limited to the following:

- Military bases
- Native American reservations
- Correctional facilities/courts
- Federal buildings
- Local government limitations
- National parks and wildlife refuges
- Hunting rules and regulations

For a list of places where carrying a firearm is prohibited, see: [http://gunla.ws/ak8]

ARIZONA GUN LAWS

Introduction

Tracing its roots back to Western days and ranching, Arizona is one of a few states where open carry of a handgun is allowed without a license, unless there is a sign posted that clearly limits the possession of weapons on the licensed premises or a property owner verbally informs You to that effect. Arizona is a constitutional carry state whereby a resident may carry a handgun without a license unless otherwise prohibited. Indeed, anyone spending much time in Arizona will observe this practice, particularly in less-urbanized areas and in particular in the desert.

Arizona is a large state. However, approximately only fifteen (15%) percent of land is privately owned. Most is public forest or land owned by the state trust, or Native American reservations.

The state has about 6,900,000 residents, and is located in the Southwest. It is bordered to the north by Utah, to the east by New Mexico, and to the west by California and Nevada, after crossing the Colorado River. It also shares an international boundary with Mexico. As a general rule, handguns are prohibited in Mexico.

A.   State Constitution

Regarding the right to bear arms, the Arizona Constitution states:

"The right of the individual citizen to bear arms in defense of himself or the State shall not be impaired, but nothing in this section shall be construed as authorizing individuals or

137

corporations to organize, maintain, or employ an armed body of men." [http://gunla.ws/saz1]

B.   Scope of Preemption

Arizona generally withholds or preempts local units of government from regulating firearms by statute, as follows:

(A) "Except as provided in subsection C of this section, a political subdivision of this state shall not enact any ordinance, rule or tax relating to the transportation, possession, carrying, sale, transfer or use of firearms or ammunition or any firearm or ammunition components in this state…" [http://gunla.ws/saz2]

(C) "A political subdivision of this state shall not require or maintain a record in any form, whether permanent or temporary, including a list, log, or database, of any of the following:

> 1. Any identifying information of a person who purchases or exchanges a weapon, who leave a weapon for repair or sale on contingent or who leave a weapon in temporary storage at any public establishment or public event.
> 2. Any identifying information of a person who sells or transfers a firearm, unless the person is a federally licensed firearms dealer
> 3. The description, including the serial number, of a weapon that is purchased, sold, transferred, exchanged, left for repair or sale on consignment or left in temporary storage at any public establishment or public event." [http://gunla.ws/saz3]

However, there is some regulation of firearms by local government that a person carrying or possessing or using a firearm must be aware of to avoid running afoul of the law. The categories where local government may regulate are set forth:

- Imposing tax on income from the sale, lease or rental of firearms or ammunition like other tangible personal property
- Prohibiting minors from possessing firearms without proper supervision
- Restricting use of land by zoning, including firearms' businesses
- Regulating employees or contractors of the unit of government who are acting within the course and scope of employment or contract.
  [http://gunla.ws/saz4]

Most recently, Arizona enacted a law that prevents localities from requiring background checks for private gun sales. [http://gunla.ws/m7ub] It is also important to note that state preemption does NOT apply to Indian Reservations, which are allowed to adopt their own gun laws, which are often stricter than Arizona state law.

C.   Reciprocal Carry

You must be at least 21 years old to apply for a permit to carry, or to carry a concealed firearm without a permit. However, You only need to be 18 to possess or open carry a handgun.

Arizona recognizes all other states' valid permits, except Vermont, providing the following conditions are met:

"shall recognize a concealed weapon, firearm or handgun permit or license that is issued by another state or a political subdivision of another state if both: 1. The permit or license is recognized as valid in the issuing state. 2. The permit or license holder is all of the following: (a) Legally present in this state. (b) Not legally prohibited from possessing a firearm in this state." [http://gunla.ws/saz5]

However, a person with a permit or license from another state may not carry in Arizona if the person is:

"under twenty-one years of age or is under indictment for, or has been convicted of, a felony offense in any jurisdiction, unless that conviction is expunged, set aside or vacated or the person's rights have been restored and the person is currently not a prohibited possessor under state or federal law." [http://gunla.ws/saz6]

Some states do not require a license to carry or have not entered into a written agreement and are not reciprocal. Anyone contemplating carry in Arizona should follow this hyperlink to the Arizona Department of Public Safety and verify with their Reciprocal and Recognition Agreement at the time of the proposed reciprocal carry in Arizona. Arizona's most current reciprocity table may be referenced by this hyperlink. [http://gunla.ws/az1]

Note: Arizona will only honor Idaho Enhanced Permits and will not honor the Idaho Standard Permit.

D.   Constitutional Carry

Arizona allows anyone who is at least 21 years old and not prohibited from owning firearms to carry a concealed firearm without a permit. This is not limited to Arizona residents, meaning residents of other states may carry in Arizona even without reciprocity. In addition, anyone who is at least 18 years old and not prohibited from owning firearms may possess and open carry a handgun, but they cannot carry it concealed until they turn 21. It should be noted that a CCP is required in order to carry in a bar. [http://gunla.ws/az2]

E. NFA Items

Arizona permits ownership of all NFA items, provided they are legally obtained pursuant to federal law. Hunting with suppressors is legal. CLEOs are required to sign an application for the transfer of any item regulated under the NFA within 60 days if the applicant is not prohibited by law from receiving it. [http://gunla.ws/hww3] & [http://gunla.ws/kbpg]

F. Carrying Firearms in Vehicles

Anyone who is legally allowed to possess a firearm may openly carry a loaded firearm in a vehicle whether in a holster, case, compartment, or in plain view. Adults between the age of 18 and 21 may openly carry a loaded or unloaded firearm in a vehicle only if it is in plain view. Property owners cannot prohibit people from keeping a firearm in their locked vehicle, or in a locked compartment of a motorcycle, so long as the firearm is not visible from outside. [http://gunla.ws/az3]

G. Duty to Inform Officers

Arizona does not require individuals to inform a LEO of a permit or license to carry immediately upon contact, but if an Officer asks about a weapon, by law, an answer must be supplied. However, You do not need to disclose the existence of the weapon if it is contained in a visible case, holster, scabbard, pack, or luggage; or if it is in a storage compartment, map pocket, trunk, or glove compartment. [http://gunla.ws/az4]

H. Private "No Gun" signs

It is illegal to carry on any private property or private establishment where the owner or any other person having lawful control over the property has given reasonable notice forbidding the carrying of deadly weapons or firearms. Failure to obey a properly posted sign or the verbal instructions of the property owner or those who represent constitutes trespass.

I. Firearms in Establishments that serve Alcohol

There are restrictions governing the carrying of firearms in establishments that hold a liquor license. Unless the business has a properly posted sign banning carrying firearms on the premises, it is generally lawful for people with a CCP to carry into the establishment. The sign must be located in a conspicuous location and be displayed right next to the liquor license in order to be valid and enforceable. It is illegal to consume alcohol while carrying a firearm. Note that You must have a valid CCP in order to carry in these establishments; constitutional carry doesn't allow You to carry in establishments that serve alcohol, and open carry is also illegal there. The prohibition against carrying guns in establishments with liquor licenses does not apply to guests staying at hotels or motels that serve alcohol. [http://gunla.ws/az5]

J. Self-defense Laws

Arizona has both Castle Doctrine and SYG laws. There is no duty to retreat when attacked in any place You have a legal right to be, and You may use deadly force in self-defense if You reasonably believe it is imminently necessary to prevent death or SBI, kidnapping, robbery, burglary, forcible rape, aggravated assault, or arson of an occupied building. [http://gunla.ws/az6]

142

K. Firearms on Native American Reservations

Native American reservations cover more than 25% of Arizona's landmass, and may have more restrictive gun laws than the rest of the state. State preemption laws do not apply to Tribal reservations. Many tribes such as the Navajo have laws prohibiting the carrying of firearms (especially without a permit), and often seize firearms found during traffic stops, particularly if they are loaded and accessible to the driver. You must present proof of ownership in order to have a seized gun returned to You. Tribal areas still subject to the federal safe passage provision of FOPA, meaning guns must be stored unloaded and out of reach of the driver, such as in the trunk. It is recommended that You store guns unloaded and out of reach when traveling through tribal areas to avoid the possibility of having Your firearm confiscated. [http://gunla.ws/az7]

L. Criminal Provisions

A prudent person contemplating possessing a firearm in a state other than where they live should understand the other state's basic criminal laws. The top criminal acts relative to Arizona's penal orientation, relating to firearms, are set forth below.

Under Arizona law, a license to carry a handgun does not permit carry in any of the following places or circumstances:

- Anywhere prohibited by Federal law
- In a polling place on an election day
- At a nuclear or hydroelectric power station
- The secured area of an airport
- At a jail or prison
- In or on school property, property being used by a school for a school function, or a school bus. Firearms may be stored in a vehicle parked in a school parking lot as long

as the firearm is unloaded, not visible from outside the vehicle, and the vehicle is locked.

- At a public establishment or event after the sponsor or operator of the establishment/event asks You to remove Your weapon and place it in a temporary secure location. If the sponsor of an establishment or event asks You to remove Your firearm, they must provide You with a secure location to store it and allow You to retrieve the firearm immediately upon exiting the event. [http://gunla.ws/saz8]

M.   Other Considerations

In addition, always consider the other areas of restrictions relating to firearms and/or reciprocal carry, including, but not limited to the following:

- Military bases
- Native American reservations
- Correctional facilitics/courts
- Federal buildings
- Local government limitations
- National parks and wildlife refuges
- Hunting rules and regulations

For a list of places where carrying a firearm is prohibited, see: [http://gunla.ws/az8]

N.   Open Carry

Open carry is legal in Arizona. Places as listed in the "Criminal Provisions" above apply to those who open carry. The minimum age for open carry is 18.

ARKANSAS GUN LAWS

Introduction

A unique aspect of Arkansas concealed carry law is that the Arkansas State Police maintain a fairly comprehensive list of places carry is accepted with a CCP. In most states, assembling this information, if it can be readily obtained, is a tedious job. Arkansas is a constitutional carry state, meaning that anyone legally allowed to possess a handgun may carry it open or concealed without a license.

Arkansas population is just under 3,000,000. Arkansas shares its southern border with Louisiana, and its northern border with Missouri. To the east it borders with Tennessee and Mississippi. Its western borders are with Texas and Oklahoma.

A.   State Constitution

Regarding the right to bear arms, the Arkansas Constitution states:

"The citizens of this state shall have the right to keep and bear arms for their common defense." [http://gunla.ws/ar1]

B.   Scope of Preemption

The controlling language of Arkansas preemption statutes is set forth as follows:

"(a) As used in this section, 'local unit of government' means a city, town, or county.

(b)(1)(A) A local unit of government shall not enact any ordinance or regulation pertaining to, or regulate in any manner, the ownership, transfer, transportation, carrying, or possession of firearms, ammunition for firearms, or components for firearms, except as otherwise provided in state or federal law. (B) This shall not prevent the enactment of an ordinance regulating or forbidding the unsafe discharge of a firearm." [http://gunla.ws/ar2]

C.   Reciprocal Carry

By statute, Arkansas will recognize another state's license to carry if that state recognizes Arkansas license:

"(a) Any person in possession of a valid license issued by another state to carry a concealed handgun issued to the person by another state is entitled to the privileges and subject to the restrictions prescribed by this subchapter if the state that issued the license to carry a concealed handgun recognizes a license to carry a concealed handgun issued under this subchapter.

(b) The Director of the Department of Arkansas State Police shall: (1) Make a determination as to which states' licenses to carry concealed handguns will be recognized in Arkansas and provide that list to every law enforcement agency within the state; and (2) Revise the list from time to time and provide the revised list to every law enforcement agency in this state."

Since there is no national carry license, as with the other states, some states are reciprocal with Arkansas and some are not. Anyone contemplating reciprocal carry should check with the official list maintained by the Arkansas State Police at the point in time the reciprocal carry is to occur. States add *and* delete states with reciprocity agreements over time. Arkansas's most current reciprocity information may be referenced by this hyperlink [http://gunla.ws/ah8a].

D.   Duty to Inform Officers

Yes. If You are in possession of a handgun, when a LEO asks for identification You must also notify the LEO that You have a CCP and that You have a handgun in Your possession. [http://gunla.ws/75t3]

E.   NFA Items

Arkansas permits ownership of all NFA items, provided they are legally obtained pursuant to federal law. Hunting with suppressors is legal. MGs may not have ammunition .30 inches (7.63 mm) or larger unless the gun is registered to an ammunition corporation. CLEOs are required to sign an application for the transfer of any item regulated under the NFA within 15 days if the applicant is not prohibited by law from receiving it. [http://gunla.ws/nb7m] & [http://gunla.ws/ucks]

F.   Carrying Firearms in Vehicles

Arkansas forbids the carrying of a handgun in Your vehicle unless You have a valid permit to carry, are on Your own property, are a licensed security guard acting in the course of Your duties, You are driving to or from a hunting area with the intent of hunting with a handgun, or You are a prosecuting attorney with valid authorization. [http://gunla.ws/ar3]

G. Self-defense Laws

Arkansas has a Castle Doctrine law but no SYG law. There is no duty to retreat when attacked in Your home or curtilage, but there is a duty to retreat in all other places. You may use deadly force in self-defense if You reasonably believe it is necessary to prevent imminent death or SBI, a forcible felony, or an act as part of pattern of domestic abuse that is imminently endangering Your life or about to victimize You. [http://gunla.ws/ar4]

H. Constitutional Carry

As of 8/16/13, Arkansas permits anyone who is at least 21 years old and not prohibited from owning a firearm to carry a handgun without a permit, openly or concealed. However, Arkansans must obtain a concealed carry permit for purposes of reciprocal carry. [http://gunla.ws/ar5]

I. Do "No Gun Signs" Have the Force of Law?

Yes. If a property or establishment has a "No Guns" sign or the person in lawful possession communicates to you that guns are not allowed, you are prohibited from carrying on the property or into the establishment. Failure to obey such signs or verbal warnings constitutes trespass. [http://gunla.ws/1f88]

J. Carry in Restaurants That Serve Alcohol

Yes, You may carry in a restaurant that serves alcohol. Places like Fridays or Chili's unless posted with "No Gun Signs." This does not include a bar or the bar area of a restaurant. You are prohibited from carrying while you consume alcohol or are under the influence of alcohol. [http://gunla.ws/widm]

K.   Criminal Provisions

Under Arkansas law, a license to carry a handgun does not permit the licensee to carry in any of the following places or circumstances, no matter if it was issued by Arkansas or a state with a current reciprocity agreement with Arkansas:

- Any police station, sheriff's station, or Department of Arkansas State Police Station
- Any Arkansas Highway Police Division of the Arkansas State Highway and Transportation Department facility
- Any building of the Arkansas State Highway and Transportation or onto grounds adjacent to any building of the Arkansas State Highway and Transportation Department. However, this does not extend to rest areas or weight stations of the Arkansas State Highway and Transportation Department.
- Any detention facility, prison, or jail
- Any courthouse or courtroom
- Any polling place (unless You have 8 hours of handgun training and an enhanced permit)
- Any meeting place of the governing body of any governmental entity
- A meeting of the General Assembly or a committee of the General Assembly
- Any state office (unless You have 8 hours of handgun training and an enhanced permit)
- Any athletic event (unless You have 8 hours of handgun training and an enhanced permit)

- Any portion of an establishment, except restaurants, licensed to dispense alcoholic beverages for consumption on the premises
- Any school, college, or university campus building or event, unless for the purpose of participating in an authorized firearms-related activity (except at state colleges and You have 8 hours of handgun training and an enhanced permit)
- Inside the passenger terminal of any airport, except that no person is prohibited from carrying any legal firearm into the passenger terminal if the firearm is encased for shipment for purposes of checking the firearm as baggage to be lawfully transported on any aircraft
- Any church or other place of worship
- Any place where a parade or demonstration requiring a permit is being held, and the licensee is a participant in the parade or demonstration
- There is no duty to retreat when attacked in Your home or residence, and You may use deadly force in self-defense if You reasonably fear You are in danger of death of serious bodily injury.
- Any licensee entering a private home must notify the occupant that the licensee is carrying a concealed handgun

In addition, as with all other states, there may be other sources of law impacting reciprocal carry that should be considered as a part of the research, and where CCPs are commonly not accepted for carry, including, but not limited to the following:

- Military bases
- Native American reservations
- Correctional facilities/courts

150

- Federal buildings
- Local government limitations
- National parks and wildlife refuges
- State hunting rules and regulations

For a list of places where carrying firearms is prohibited, see: [http://gunla.ws/ar6]

Note: Arkansas recently passed Act 562 which expands their concealed carry law to allow those with an enhanced permit and eight hours of handgun training to carry a concealed handgun at state colleges, airports, polling places, athletic events, most state offices and the state Capitol. [http://gunla.ws/uame]

L.   Open Carry

A recent Arkansas AG's Opinion addresses open carry and states that if a person does not have the intent to "attempt to unlawfully employ a handgun . . . as a weapon against [another]," he or she may "possess a handgun . . . on or about his or her person, in a vehicle occupied by him or her, or otherwise readily available for use" without violating Ark. Code § 5-73-120(a). However, this is still subject to the specified restrictions in the "Criminal Provisions" above.

To view the Arkansas AG's Opinion, see: [http://gunla.ws/7gsi]

CALIFORNIA GUN LAWS

Introduction

As it relates to all firearms, California is unique in its use of state-based preemption. California has used preemption to ensure the strictest of firearms regulation; it has even preempted regulation of 'look-alike' guns.

California has the largest population in the U.S. with over 38,000,000 residents. To the north, it shares a border with Oregon. To the east (across the Colorado River), it borders with Nevada and Arizona. Its southern border is shared with Mexico, which generally prohibits private possession and carry of handguns. The balance of the state is coastal on the Pacific Ocean.

A.   State Constitution

California does not have a constitutional provision for the right to bear arms. California's constitution can be accessed/reviewed in full online. [http://gunla.ws/ca1]

B.   Scope of Preemption

The controlling language of the California's preemption statute is set forth as follows:

> "It is the intention of the legislature to occupy the whole field of regulation of the registration or licensing of commercially manufactured firearms as encompassed by the provisions of the Penal Code, and such provisions shall

be exclusive of all local regulations, relating to registration or licensing of commercially manufactured firearms, by any political subdivision as defined in Section 1721 of the Labor Code."

However, despite this law, some localities in California (such as San Francisco and Los Angeles) have enacted ordinances regulating ammunition, magazines, gun stores, and some firearms. [http://gunla.ws/ca2]

C. Reciprocal Carry

California does not recognize permits from any other state.

Recent Court Case: On 6/9/16 the 9th Circuit Court of Appeals upheld California's "may issue" policy which requires people applying for concealed carry permits to show "good cause" in order to obtain the permit, and grants local authorities discretion in deciding whether or not to issue them. In its decision, the court specifically said that the Second Amendment does not protect a right of the general public to carry concealed weapons.

D. Criminal Provisions

Under California law, it is a crime to carry a concealed firearm, with limited exceptions:

"A person is guilty of carrying a concealed firearm when the person does any of the following: (1) Carries concealed within any vehicle that is under the person's control or direction any pistol, revolver, or other firearm capable of being concealed upon the person. (2) Carries concealed upon the person any pistol, revolver, or other firearm capable of being concealed upon the person."

[http://gunla.ws/ca3]

The above provision does not apply to:

- Any peace officer (listed in Penal Code 830.1 or 830.2)
- Any other duly appointed peace officer
- Any honorably retired peace officer (listed in Penal Code 830.5)
- Any other honorably retired peace officer who, during the course and scope of employment as a peace officer, was authorized to, and did, carry a firearm
- Any full-time paid peace officer of another state or the federal government who is carrying out official duties while in California
- Any person summoned by any of these officers to assist in making arrests or preserving the peace while the person is actually engaged in assisting that officer

E.   Firearm Safety Certificate

Individuals wishing to purchase any firearm are required to take and pass a written test on firearm safety.

F.   Storage of Firearms in Homes with Prohibited Persons

Any gun owner residing with an individual who is prohibited from owning firearms to either keep the firearm in a locked device or carry the firearm on his/her person. Firearm owners may be criminally liable for storage of a firearm in a place where it is reasonably knowable by a person prohibited from possessing firearms.

G.   Carrying Firearms in Vehicles

California allows people who are legally allowed to possess firearms but do not have a carry permit to carry them in their vehicle so long as the firearm is unloaded and sealed in a locked compartment such as the trunk, or in a locked container such as a safe. These restrictions do not apply to people who hold a valid carry permit. [http://gunla.ws/ca4]

H.   High-Capacity Magazine Ban

California bans the sale, transfer, and possession of high-capacity magazines. High-capacity magazines are defined as magazines capable of holding more than ten (10) rounds. There are two exceptions to this: internal tube/helical magazines for .22 firearms and internal tube/helical magazines for lever action guns aren't considered "high-capacity" magazines even if they can hold >10 rounds, and are therefore legal. Firearm owners are prohibited from using "conversion kits" to manufacture high-capacity ammunition magazines. This includes assembling the parts of the magazine. Firearms owners are also prohibited from importing, transferring or selling high-capacity magazines to people within CA, but can legally sell or transfer the magazines to someone outside of CA. Possession of high-capacity magazines is prohibited from a new law that took effect on 7/1/17. This new law completely bans the possession of all high-capacity magazines, with no grandfather exemption for magazines that were previously owned legally. Anyone in possession of a high-capacity magazine is required to dispose of them. There are four ways a person can legally dispose of these magazines: destroy them, surrender them to a law enforcement agency, sell them to a licensed FFL, or remove them from the state. Note that law enforcement agencies will not compensate You for the cost of any large capacity magazines surrendered to them, so selling the magazines out of state is the only way to recoup some of their value.

I. Duty to Inform Officers

Some counties in California do not require individuals to inform a LEO of a permit or license to carry but if an Officer asks about a weapon, by law, an answer must be supplied.

J. NFA Items

California permits ownership of all NFA items except for suppressors and pen guns (a type of AOW) provided they are legally obtained pursuant to federal law and additional regulations imposed by CA. A special permit from the CA DOJ is required to own a MG, and these are rarely granted. Short-barrel rifles and shotguns are only legal if they qualify as a Curio & Relic. In addition, NFA items must also comply with CA's Assault Weapons Ban. [http://gunla.ws/8779]

K. Waiting Period

California requires a ten (10) day waiting period before purchasing a firearm. This ten (10) day waiting period applies to all persons even if you have previously and/or recently purchased a firearm. There are a few exceptions (firearms dealers, those with special weapons permits, curio and relic collectors, and peace officers) as listed here [http://gunla.ws/ca10]. The California legislature may adopt new rules for the waiting period in future. [http://gunla.ws/9xif]

L.   Universal Background Checks

Background checks are mandatory for all firearm sales, and transfers between private parties must go through a licensed dealer. [http://gunla.ws/lxlx]

M.   Loans of Guns are Now Subject to Background Checks

A new law treats loaning a firearm to anyone other than immediate family (spouse, parent, child, grandparent, grandchild, or sibling) as a transfer, meaning that it would have to go through a licensed dealer and the recipient would have to undergo a background check and 10 day waiting period. This would make it a crime to let a friend shoot Your gun at the range or take it hunting unless they completed a background check and waiting period.

N.   Background Checks for Ammunition Sales

A new law requires all sales of ammunition to go through a licensed ammunition vendor, who would be required to conduct a background check on the purchaser and keep records of every sale of ammo for two years. Internet sales of ammunition would have to be sent to a licensed ammunition vendor and picked up in person, much like online sales of firearms. The requirement for all sales to go through vendors takes effect on 1/1/18, and the requirement for vendor record keeping and background checks takes effect on 7/1/19.

EXCEPTIONS to ammo restrictions:

Certain transactions will not be subject to the new restrictions, and will not have to go through a licensed dealer or background check. You can sell 50 rounds per month to immediate family members, or give (without compensation) any amount of ammunition to family or friends without having to follow the new restrictions.

O.   Penalty for Falsely Reporting a Gun as Stolen

It is now a misdemeanor to falsely report a gun as lost or stolen to the police when You know such report to be false. Furthermore, anyone convicted of making such a false report is banned from owning guns for 10 years after being convicted.

P.   Mental Health Prohibitions

An individual who communicates to a licensed psychotherapist a serious threat of physical violence against a reasonably identifiable victim is restricted from possessing a firearm for five (5) years following the psychotherapist's reporting of the threat within 24 hours.

"A person is guilty of carrying a loaded firearm when the person carries a loaded firearm on the person or in a vehicle while in any public place or on any public street in an incorporated city or in any public place or on any public street in a prohibited area of unincorporated territory." Penal Code 25850(a). [http://gunla.ws/ca5]

Note: California defines permissible types of guns. Laws defining guns and which types are permissible within the state can be found online. [http://gunla.ws/30500]

Q.   Gun Restraining Orders

Family members can ask a judge to issue a temporary order seizing someone's firearms for up to 21 days if the judge believes that person poses a danger to themselves or others.

R.   Self-defense Laws

California has a form of Castle Doctrine, but does not have SYG. According to California laws, the use of deadly force is justified when all four of the following conditions are met: (1) the use of deadly force is used against a person who is not a resident of the home; (2) the person using the deadly force in their home reasonably believed they or another person was in immediate danger of SBI or killed; (3) the person using the deadly force believed that it was the only way to stop that imminent danger; and (4) they used no more force than was necessary to stop the threat. [http://gunla.ws/a1iu]

S.   Ban on .50 Caliber Rifles

Centerfire rifles chambered in the caliber .50 BMG are generally illegal to own, unless they were owned prior to 12/31/04 and registered by 4/30/06.

T.   Assault Weapons Ban

California has an extensive "Assault Weapons Ban" (AWB) which bans possession and sale of firearms that are deemed "assault weapons," unless they are legally registered (see below). "Assault Weapons" are defined in two ways, either being specified by name, or by possessing certain features. California recently expanded their definition of an "assault weapon" to include all semi-automatic rifles having a pistol grip and a button to release a magazine. Assault weapons are divided into 3 categories: Category 1 are those that were named in the original AWB of '89, Category 2 are those that were listed in the second AWB of '99, and Category 3 are those that were defined based on features they possess. Category 1 and 2 assault weapons are banned by name (i.e., AR15, AK47), and a complete list of them can be found at the hyperlink below. Category 3 defines "assault weapons" as semi auto centerfire guns capable of accepting a detachable magazine, that also possess one of the following features:

(A) A pistol grip that protrudes conspicuously beneath the action of the weapon
(B) A thumbhole stock
(C) A folding or telescoping stock
(D) A grenade launcher or flare launcher
(E) A flash suppressor
(F) A forward pistol grip
(G) A semi auto rifle with an overall length under 30"

Many manufacturers made special "California legal" rifles that avoided using prohibited features so as not to be considered Assault Weapons. One main feature of CA legal assault weapons using an inset magazine release that required a tool to activate (generally the tip of a bullet) as opposed to a normal mag release, as this was not a detachable magazine and were therefore exempt from the AWB. However, a new law taking effect on 7/1/17 puts an end to this by expanding the definition of assault weapons to include firearms with these "bullet buttons" as prohibited assault weapons. Many "California Legal" rifles will be affected by this new law, and must either be registered as assault weapons or disposed of. All "assault weapons" must be registered prior to January 1, 2018. Assault weapons not registered prior to January 1, 2018 must be turned in to local law enforcement for destruction. [http://gunla.ws/ca7] & [http://gunla.ws/ca8]

U.   Registering Assault Weapons

There is a way to legally own firearms classified as "Assault Weapons" in California, and that is if they were registered with the state prior to a certain date. California generally does not allow You to register new Assault Weapons, so only those that were registered at the appropriate time were grandfathered in. The period during which Assault Weapons could have been registered are as follows:

- **Category 1 AW:** must have been owned by 12/31/1991 and registered by 03/31/1992
- **Category 2 AW:** must have been owned by 08/16/2000 and registered by 01/23/2001
- **Category 3 AW:** must have been owned by 12/31/1999 and registered by 12/31/2000

Note that registration only allows You to retain possession of a firearm You already owned, You may not sell or transfer an assault weapon to any other CA resident even if it is registered. Also note that registered Category 3 Assault Weapons can be delisted as assault weapons (and therefore legally transferred) if they are modified to remove the prohibited features and comply with the AWB.

Registration will be opened again for "California Legal" rifles that will be affected by the newest ban on assault weapons. These firearms that will now be classified as assault weapons must have been owned before 12/31/16 and must be registered before 1/1/18 in order to remain legal. There is a $20 fee to register them.

For a list of places where carrying firearms is prohibited, see: [http://gunla.ws/ca9]

V.   Do "No Gun Signs" Have the Force of Law?

No. "No Firearm" signs in California do not have the force of law unless they are posted on property that is specifically mentioned in State Law as being off limits to those with a permit/license to carry. However, as a possessor with a real property interest, a retailer, has the right to limit, and qualify the right to enter the property, subject to not carrying a handgun. It would be improper to enter, and the licensee would be subject to ejection for possession of a handgun thereat. Failure to leave once requested would subject the licensee to arrest for criminal trespass.

W.   Carry in Restaurants That Serve Alcohol

Yes. There is no law stating it is illegal except the California application states that you are prohibited from carrying a concealed weapon into bars. You can carry in a restaurant that serves alcohol. Places like Fridays or Chili's unless they have a "No Gun Sign," then it is suggested that You not carry into the establishment. This does not include a bar or the bar area of a restaurant. You can carry your firearm into a restaurant that serves alcohol, but you are prohibited from consuming alcohol while carrying a firearm.

X.   Other Prohibitions

While carrying a concealed firearm, You are prohibited from:

- Consuming any alcoholic beverage
- Being under the influence of any medication or drug; whether prescribed or not
- Refuse to show the license or surrender the concealed weapon to any LEO upon demand
- Unjustifiably displaying a concealed weapon
- Carrying a concealed weapon not listed on the permit

- Carrying a concealed weapon at times or circumstances other than those specified in the permit

COLORADO GUN LAWS

Introduction

Colorado has an interesting history as it relates to firearms. The right is clear and express in their constitution, but qualified, which states "nothing herein contained shall be construed to justify the practice of carrying concealed weapons." However, other law sets forth that open carry is allowed and sets forth licensing provisions for concealed carry. With a population of about 5,348,000, Colorado is bordered to the north by Wyoming, to the northeast by Nebraska, to the east by Kansas, to the south by Oklahoma and New Mexico, and to the west by Utah.

A.   State Constitution

Regarding the right to bear arms, the Colorado Constitution states:

> "The right of no person to keep and bear arms in defense of his home, person and property, or in aid of the civil power when thereto legally summoned, shall be called in question; but nothing herein contained shall be construed to justify the practice of carrying concealed weapons."
> [http://gunla.ws/co1]

B.   Scope of Preemption

The controlling language of the Colorado preemption

statute is set forth as follows:

> "...the general assembly concludes that:
> (a) The regulation of firearms is a matter of statewide concern;
> (b) It is necessary to provide statewide laws concerning the possession and ownership of a firearm to ensure that law-abiding persons are not unfairly placed in the position of unknowingly committing crimes involving firearms." 29-11.7-101 (2).
>
> (2)(a) "...the general assembly concludes that the carrying of weapons in private automobiles or other private means of conveyance for hunting or for lawful protection of a person's or another's person or property while traveling into, through, or within, a municipal, county, or city and county jurisdiction, regardless of the number of times the person stops in a jurisdiction, is a matter of statewide concern and is not an offense.
> (b) Notwithstanding any other provision of law, no municipality, county, or city and county shall have the authority to enact or enforce any ordinance or resolution that would restrict a person's ability to travel with a weapon in a private automobile or other private means of conveyance for hunting or for lawful protection of a person's or another's person or property while traveling into, through, or within, a municipal, county, or city and county jurisdiction, regardless of the number of times the person stops in a jurisdiction." 18-12-105.6 [http://gunla.ws/co2]

Note: "Open Carry" - A local government may enact an ordinance, regulation, or other law that prohibits the open carrying of a firearm in a building or specific area within the local government's jurisdiction. If a local government enacts an ordinance, regulation, or other law that prohibits the open carrying of a firearm in a building or specific area, the local government shall post signs at the public entrances to the building or specific area informing persons that the open carrying of firearms is prohibited in the building or specific area. 29-11.7-104

C.   Reciprocal Carry

By statute, Colorado will recognize another state's license to carry if that state recognizes Colorado's license:

"(1) A permit to carry a concealed handgun or a concealed weapon that is issued by a state that recognizes the validity of permits issued pursuant to this part 2 shall be valid in this state in all respects as a permit issued pursuant to this part 2 if the permit is issued to a person who is: (a) Twenty-one years of age or older; and (b)(I) A resident of the state that issued the permit, as demonstrated by the address stated on a valid picture identification that is issued by the state that issued the permit and is carried by the permit holder; or (II) A resident of Colorado for no more than ninety days, as determined by the date of issuance on a valid picture identification issued by Colorado and carried by the permit holder. (2) For purposes of this section, a "valid picture identification" means a driver's license or a state identification issued in lieu of a driver's license."

Since there is no national carry license: some states are reciprocal with Colorado, some are not. Anyone contemplating reciprocal carry should check with the official list maintained by the Colorado State Police at the point in time the reciprocal carry is to occur. Colorado's most current reciprocity information may be referenced online. [http://gunla.ws/co3]

D.   Open Carry

Colorado allows the open carry of firearms without a permit, however local governments can restrict or ban open carry. The city of Denver does not allow open carry.

E.   High-Capacity Magazine Ban

Colorado bans the sale, transfer, and possession of magazines capable of holding more than fifteen (15) rounds. Internal tube/helical magazines for .22 firearms and internal tube/helical magazines for lever action guns are not considered high-capacity magazines, even if capable of holding more than 15 rounds. High-capacity magazines that were legally owned before 7/1/13 are grandfathered in and may be kept and used, but not sold or transferred. [http://gunla.ws/d226]

F.   Universal Background Checks

Colorado requires that all firearm sales, even between private parties, go through a FFL who must conduct a background check. For a private party transfer, You must get approval of the transfer from the Colorado Bureau of Investigation. Transfers of antique firearms, bona-fide gifts or loans from immediate family members, and transfers to estate executors or trustees are exempt. Temporary transfers are strictly regulated. [http://gunla.ws/8b16]

G.   Duty to Inform Officers

Colorado does not require individuals to inform a LEO of a permit or license to carry but if an Officer asks about a weapon, by law, an answer must be supplied. You must carry Your permit, together with valid photo identification, at all times that you are in actual possession of a concealed handgun. You must produce both documents upon demand by a LEO. [http://gunla.ws/51b9]

H. Carrying Firearms in Vehicles

Colorado allows anyone who may legally own a firearm to carry a concealed firearm in an automobile or other form of private conveyance, even without a permit. If carrying a long gun, there cannot be a round in the chamber. [http://gunla.ws/co4]

I. NFA Items

Colorado permits ownership of all NFA items, provided they are legally obtained pursuant to federal law. Hunting with suppressors is currently legal.

J. Self-defense Laws

Colorado has a Castle Doctrine but no SYG law. There is no duty to retreat when attacked in a dwelling (it doesn't have to be Your dwelling, as long as You have permission to be there), and You may use deadly force in self-defense against someone who unlawfully enters that dwelling, if You reasonably believe the intruder has or is about to commit a crime in the dwelling in addition to unlawful entry, or the intruder intends to commit a crime against person or property in addition to unlawful entry, or that the intruder intends to use force (however slight) against an occupant of the dwelling. [http://gunla.ws/co5]

K. Criminal Provisions

Under Colorado law, a license to carry a handgun does not permit carry in any of the following places or circumstances, no matter if it was issued by Colorado or if carry is pursuant to a

168

reciprocity agreement with Colorado:

- Failure to obtain a background check during the purchase of a firearm at a gun show commits a class 1 misdemeanor and shall be punished as provided in section 18-1.3-501, C.R.S. A gun show promoter shall arrange for the services of one or more licensed gun dealers on the premises of the gun show to obtain the background checks. If any part of a firearm transaction takes place at a gun show, no firearm shall be transferred unless a background check has been obtained by a licensed gun dealer
- A place where carrying firearms is prohibited by federal law
- A public building at which security personnel regularly screen for weapons upon entry
- The property of a public elementary, middle, junior high or high school, unless it is the permittee's vehicle. If the permittee is not inside the vehicle, the handgun must be in a compartment in the vehicle and the vehicle must be locked
- Possession of firearm within Motor Vehicle: It is unlawful for any person, except a person authorized by law or by the division, to possess or have under his control any firearm, other than a pistol or revolver, in or on any motor vehicle unless the chamber of such firearm is unloaded. Any person in possession or in control of a rifle or shotgun in a motor vehicle shall allow any peace officer, as defined in section 33-1-102 (32), who is empowered and acting under the authority granted in section 33-6-101 to enforce articles 1 to 6 of this title to inspect the chamber of any rifle or shotgun in the motor vehicle. For the purposes of this section, a "muzzle-loader" shall be considered unloaded if it is not

primed, and, for such purpose, "primed" means having a percussion cap on the nipple or flint in the striker and powder in the flash pan. Any person who violates this section is guilty of a misdemeanor and, upon conviction thereof, shall be punished by a fine of fifty ($50.00) dollars and an assessment of fifteen license suspension points.

[http://gunla.ws/9cy5]

For a list of places where carrying firearms is prohibited, see: [http://gunla.ws/co6]

L. Do "No Gun Signs" Have the Force of Law?

No. "No Firearm" signs in Colorado do not have the force of law unless they are posted on property that is specifically mentioned in State Law as being off limits to those with a permit/license to carry. However, as a possessor with a real property interest, a retailer, has the right to limit, and qualify the right to enter the property, subject to not carrying a handgun. It would be improper to enter, and the licensee would be subject to ejection for possession of a handgun thereat. Failure to leave once requested would subject the licensee to arrest for criminal trespass.

M. Carry in Restaurants That Serve Alcohol

Yes. There is no law stating it is illegal. You can carry in a restaurant that serves alcohol. Places like Fridays or Chili's unless they have a "No Gun Sign," then it is suggested that You not carry into the establishment. This does not include a bar or the bar area of a restaurant. You can carry your firearm into a restaurant that serves alcohol, but you are prohibited from consuming alcohol while carrying a firearm.

170

 # CONNECTICUT GUN LAWS

Introduction

A point of much debate with professionals in the industry and individuals with CCPs is whether concealed carry should be the standard. The rationale behind this is two-fold. First, some tactical advantage may be lost in self-defense if the handgun is observed in advance by a would-be criminal.

Secondly, the question is whether this disturbs the public generally. An official firearms board in Connecticut has taken the position a firearm should be carried in a way to ensure it is concealed to avoid alarming the people who would see it. This statement of official policy is more or less a custom in many states. Even still, open carry is legal in Connecticut with a valid license to carry.

Despite its tiny size, Connecticut has a dense population of 3,600,400 people. It borders Long Island Sound on the south. On the west, Connecticut borders New York State. To the north it borders Massachusetts, with Rhode Island to the east.

A.   State Constitution

Regarding the right to bear arms, the Connecticut Constitution states:

"Every citizen has a right to bear arms in defense of himself and the state." [http://gunla.ws/ct1]

B.   Scope of Preemption

Connecticut state statutes preempt local firearm regulation in two areas: firearm sales and hunting regulation. Connecticut Courts have not considered whether the legislature has demonstrated the intent to occupy areas of firearm regulation in other areas. CGS §§ 29-28 to -32; *State v. Brennan* (3 Conn. Cir. Ct. 413, 216 A.2d 294 (1965)) and *Kaluszka v. East Hartford* (60 Conn. App. 749 (2000)). [http://gunla.ws/ct2]

C.   Reciprocal Carry

By statute, Connecticut does not honor any other state's carry permit, but instead requires holders of out of state carry permits to apply for a permit to carry in Connecticut:

> "Any bona fide resident of the United States having no bona fide residence or place of business within the jurisdiction of any local authority in the state, but who has a permit or license to carry a pistol or revolver issued by the authority of another state or subdivision of the United States, may apply directly to the Commissioner of Public Safety for a permit to carry a pistol or revolver in this state." 28-29(f).

Connecticut's most current reciprocity information may be referenced online. [http://gunla.ws/ct3]

D.   Duty to Inform Officers

Connecticut does not require individuals to inform a LEO of a permit or license to carry but if an Officer asks about a weapon, by law, an answer must be supplied. You must carry Your permit, together with valid photo identification, at all times that you are in actual possession of a concealed handgun. You must produce both documents upon demand by a LEO. [http://gunla.ws/i8vo]

172

E.   Self-defense Laws

Connecticut has a Castle Doctrine law but no SYG law. There is no duty to retreat when attacked on any property You own, control, or have permission to be on, and You may use deadly force in self-defense if You reasonably believe it is imminently necessary to prevent death or SBI, kidnapping, an attempt by the intruder to commit arson or another violent crime, or to the extent necessary stop the unlawful & forcible entry into the property. [http://gunla.ws/ct4]

F.   Criminal Provisions

To obtain a firearm in Connecticut a person must be a Connecticut resident of at least 21 years of age and a background check is now required whether purchase is online, in person, or at a gun show. A license to carry a handgun does not permit carry in any of the following places or circumstances:

- On school grounds, including the real property of a private or public elementary or secondary school, or a school-sponsored event
- Some federal properties and buildings with fixed security checkpoints such as courthouses.
- SBR, SBS, destructive devices, and suppressors are prohibited unless they were purchased before 10/1/93, or comply with the state assault weapons ban
- MGs are prohibited unless purchased and registered with the state before 1/1/14

For a list of places where carrying firearms is prohibited, see: [http://gunla.ws/ct5]

G.   Permit required to purchase Firearms and

Ammunition

You must obtain a permit in order to purchase firearms or ammunition in Connecticut. Separate permits are required to purchase handguns, long guns, and ammunition. Applicants must complete a safety training course, pass a background check, and have clean mental health records in order to obtain a permit to purchase. Purchase permits are valid for five years, and there is no limit to the number of firearms or ammunition that may be purchased by valid permit holders. Background checks are required for all firearm sales. You must be at least 18 years old to apply for a long gun or ammunition purchase permit, and 21 years old to apply for a handgun purchase permit. [http://gunla.ws/ksnm]

H.   Waiting Period

Connecticut does not impose a waiting period on firearm purchases or transfers. However, a purchaser or transferee must obtain a permit or certificate prior to receiving a firearm. [http://gunla.ws/in8v]

I.   High-Capacity Magazine Ban

High-capacity magazines are defined as magazines capable of holding more than ten (10) rounds. There are two exceptions to this: tube/helical magazines for .22 firearms (even if detachable) and internal tube/helical magazines for lever action guns aren't considered "large capacity" magazines even if they can hold >10 rounds, and are therefore legal. The transfer, sale, and possession of high-capacity magazines within the state is prohibited, subject to the following exception.

High-capacity magazines that were lawfully possessed before 4/4/13 were grandfathered in as long as their owners

174

registered them with the state before 1/1/14. People who registered high-capacity magazines prior to 1/1/14 may continue to possess them, but may not sell or transfer them within the state. In addition, it is illegal to possess a high-capacity magazine (even if registered) that is loaded with more than 10 rounds, except at the owners' residence or at a licensed shooting range. Even if one possesses a permit to carry and has registered magazines, it is illegal to have them loaded with more than 10 rounds in public. [http://gunla.ws/ju7t]

J.   Assault Weapons Ban

It is illegal to possess an assault weapon, unless it was possessed before October 1, 1993 or the individual received a certificate of possession from the Connecticut State Police prior to July of 1994. Assault weapons may not be sold or transferred to any person other than a licensed gun dealer or any individual who is going to relinquish it to the police. [http://gunla.ws/4gu3]

Theft of a lawfully possessed assault weapon must be reported within 72 hours by the person who possesses the title:

"An "Assault Weapon" is defined as: Any selective-fire firearm capable of fully automatic, semiautomatic or burst fire at the option of the user or any of the following specified semiautomatic firearms listed on the Connecticut Commissioner of Service and Public Protection. The term "assault weapon" does not include any firearm modified to render it permanently inoperable." [http://gunla.ws/7gcr]

The definition and list of assault weapons may be found at: [http://gunla.ws/ct6]

K.   Carrying Firearms in Vehicles

175

It is generally illegal to transport a firearm in a vehicle in Connecticut without a carry permit. The exception is that an unloaded handgun may be transported, provided the firearm (and ammunition) is inside a locked container or not accessible from the passenger compartment, and You must be transporting the gun: to Your home or place of business, to or from a repair shop, to or from a competition, or when transporting Your household goods from one place to another. [http://gunla.ws/ct7]

L.   NFA Items

Connecticut permits ownership of all NFA items provided they are legally obtained pursuant to federal law, but imposes additional regulations. Select-fire MGs are prohibited, meaning they must only be capable of fully-automatic fire and not semi-automatic, (can be set only to "safe" or "auto", not "semi" or "burst"). Non-selective fire MGs may be transferred to another resident within Connecticut. MGs are legal if purchased and registered with the state before January 1, 2014. NFA items must comply with the state assault weapons ban, unless they were owned prior to 8/1/93. Hunting with suppressors is legal. [http://gunla.ws/ufky]

M.   Carry in Restaurants That Serve Alcohol

Yes. There is no law stating it is illegal. You can carry in a restaurant that serves alcohol. Places like Fridays or Chili's unless they have a "No Gun Sign," then You are prohibited from carrying into the establishment. This does not include a bar or the bar area of a restaurant. You can carry your firearm into a restaurant that serves alcohol, but you are prohibited from consuming alcohol while carrying a firearm.

N.   Do "No Gun Signs" Have the Force of Law?

Yes. If a property or establishment has a "No Guns" sign or the person in lawful possession communicates to you that guns are not allowed, you are prohibited from carrying on the property or into the establishment. Failure to obey such signs or verbal warnings constitutes trespass. [http://gunla.ws/0ts7]

DELAWARE
GUN LAWS

Introduction

Delaware is situated on the Atlantic Coast. It is surrounded on the south and west by Maryland, and bordered to the east by New Jersey. Pennsylvania is found just to the north. Delaware is a small state in area, with a population of about 934,000 total. It is divided into three counties, two of which are agricultural, and one of which is industrial. Open carry is legal in Delaware even without a license to carry.

A.   State Constitution

Regarding the right to bear arms, the Delaware Constitution states:

"A person has the right to keep and bear arms for the defense of self, family, home and State, and for hunting and recreational use." [http://gunla.ws/de1]

B.   Scope of Preemption

The controlling language of the Delaware preemption statute is set forth as follows:

"The county governments shall enact no law or regulation prohibiting, restricting or licensing the ownership, transfer, possession, or transportation of firearms or components of firearms or ammunition except that the discharge of a firearm may be regulated; provided any law, ordinance or regulation incorporates the justification defenses as found in Title 11 of the Delaware Code." [http://gunla.ws/de2] Title 11: [http://gunla.ws/de3]

C.   Reciprocal Carry

By statute, Delaware will recognize another state's license to carry if that state recognizes Delaware's license:

"Notwithstanding any other provision of this Code to the contrary, the State of Delaware shall give full faith and credit and shall otherwise honor and give full force and effect to all licenses/permits issued to the citizens of other states where those issuing states also give full faith and credit and otherwise honor the licenses issued by the State of Delaware pursuant to this section and where those licenses/permits are issued by authority pursuant to state law and which afford a reasonably similar degree of protection as is provided by licensure in Delaware..."

Delaware's most up-to-date reciprocity agreement can be viewed online. [http://gunla.ws/7t7m]

D.   Criminal Provisions

Under Delaware law, a license to carry a handgun is not valid in any of the following places or circumstances, whether it is issued by Delaware, or a person is carrying pursuant to reciprocity between his or her state of license and Delaware:

- Federal Buildings
- State approved "SLOTS"

- Courthouses, police stations, prisons and detention facilities
- State and National Forests and State Parks (in state parks, firearms are allowed for hunting only, no concealed carry)
- Wildlife Management Areas
- Shooting from any motor vehicle, motor or sail boat or while riding in or upon any piece of farm machinery. Discharge of a firearm within 15 yards of a public road, nor across a public road.

For a list of places where carrying firearms is prohibited, see: [http://gunla.ws/de4]

E.   NFA Items

The only NFA items that may be owned in Delaware are SBRs and AOWs. The city of Wilmington prohibits possession of SBRs within city limits. MGs, suppressors, DDs and SBSs are prohibited for non-LEO individuals. [http://gunla.ws/kxb1]

F.   Duty to Inform Officers

Delaware does not require individuals to inform a LEO of a permit or license to carry but if an Officer asks about a weapon, by law, an answer must be supplied. You must carry a valid photo identification at all times that you are in actual possession of a concealed handgun. You must produce identification upon demand by a LEO.

G.   Carrying Firearms in Vehicles

Delaware requires a permit in order to carry a concealed firearm in a vehicle. People without a permit may carry a handgun in their vehicle so long as it is in plain view and can be seen from outside the vehicle, such as on the dashboard or passenger seat. [http://gunla.ws/de5] & [http://gunla.ws/x1er]

H.   Universal Background Checks

Background checks are mandatory for all firearm sales, and transfers between private parties, except between family members, must go through a licensed dealer. This does not apply to holders of a valid Delaware carry license. [http://gunla.ws/huly]

I.   Self-defense Laws.

Delaware has modified form of Castle Doctrine but no SYG law. There is no duty to retreat when attacked in Your dwelling or place of work, and You may use deadly force in self-defense if You reasonably believe it is imminently necessary to prevent death or SBI, kidnapping, or rape. [http://gunla.ws/de6]

J.   Carry in Restaurants That Serve Alcohol

Yes. There is no law stating it is illegal. You can carry in a restaurant that serves alcohol. Places like Fridays or Chili's unless they have a "No Gun Sign," then it is suggested that you not carry into the establishment. This does not include a bar or the bar area of a restaurant. You can carry your firearm into a restaurant that serves alcohol, but you are prohibited from consuming alcohol while carrying a firearm.

K.   Do "No Gun Signs" Have the Force of Law?

No. "No Firearm" signs in Delaware do not have the force of law unless they are posted on property that is specifically mentioned in State Law as being off limits to those with a permit/license to carry. However, as a possessor with a real property interest, a retailer, has the right to limit, and qualify the right to enter the property, subject to not carrying a handgun. It would be improper to enter, and the licensee would be subject to ejection for possession of a handgun thereat. Failure to leave once requested would subject the licensee to arrest for criminal trespass.

L.   Open Carry

Open carry without a permit is legal in Delaware. Places as listed in the "Criminal Provisions" section above apply to those who open carry. The minimum age for open carry is 18.

 # DISTRICT OF COLUMBIA GUN LAWS

Introduction

Perhaps no other state (district) has shaped our thinking about firearms, and handguns in particular, more than Washington, D.C. It was just 2008, when SCOTUS determined that the right to keep and bear arms set forth in the Second Amendment was an individual right, not a collective right. The district is just 68 square miles and has about 680,000 residents. It is bordered by Maryland to the southeast, northeast and northwest. Virginia shares its border to the southwest.

A.   State Constitution

Washington D.C. does not have a constitutional provision for the right to bear arms.

B.   Scope of Preemption

Washington D.C. does not have a preemption statute, however the code states otherwise:

> "The Council of the District of Columbia is hereby authorized and empowered to make, and the Mayor of the District of Columbia is hereby authorized and empowered to enforce, all such usual and reasonable police regulations, in addition to those already made under §§ 1-303.01 to 1-

303.03 as the Council may deem necessary for the regulation of firearms, projectiles, explosives, or weapons of any kind in the District of Columbia."

C.   Reciprocal Carry

Washington D.C. will not recognize another state's license to carry a firearm, however, per the D.C. Official Code § 22-4504:

"(a) No person shall carry within the District of Columbia either openly or concealed on or about their person, a pistol, or any deadly or dangerous weapon capable of being so concealed. Whoever violates this section shall be punished as provided in § 22-4515, except that:

(1) A person who violates this section by carrying a pistol or any deadly or dangerous weapon, in a place other than the person's dwelling place, place of business, or on other land possessed by the person, shall be fined not more than $ 5,000 or imprisoned for not more than 5 years, or both; or (2) If the violation of this section occurs after a person has been convicted in the District of Columbia of a violation of this section or of a felony, either in the District of Columbia or another jurisdiction, the person shall be fined not more than $ 10,000 or imprisoned for not more than 10 years, or both.

(a-1) Except as otherwise permitted by law, no person shall carry within the District of Columbia a rifle or shotgun. A person who violates this subsection shall be subject to the criminal penalties set forth in subsection (a)(1) and (2) of this section."

There are exceptions for legally registered firearms and authority to carry a firearm in certain places and for certain purposes. D.C. Official Code § 22-4504.01.

"Notwithstanding any other law, a person holding a valid registration for a firearm may carry the firearm:

Within the registrant's home;
While it is being used for lawful recreational purposes;
While it is kept at the registrant's place of business; or
While it is being transported for a lawful purpose as expressly authorized by District or federal statute and in accordance with the requirements of that statute.

VI. Transporting Firearms
District transport law:

§ 22-4504.02. Lawful transportation of firearms.

(a) Any person who is not otherwise prohibited by the law from transporting, shipping, or receiving a firearm shall be permitted to transport a firearm for any lawful purpose from any place where he may lawfully possess and carry the firearm [see § 22-4504.01, above] to any other place where he may lawfully possess and carry the firearm if the firearm is transported in accordance with this section.
(b)(1) If the transportation of the firearm is by a vehicle, the firearm shall be unloaded, and neither the firearm nor any ammunition being transported shall be readily accessible or directly accessible from the passenger compartment of the transporting vehicle.
(2) If the transporting vehicle does not have a compartment separate from the driver's compartment, the firearm or ammunition shall be contained in a locked container other

than the glove compartment or console, and the firearm shall be unloaded.

(c) If the transportation of the firearm is in a manner other than in a vehicle, the firearm shall be:

(1) Unloaded;

(2) Inside a locked container; and

(3) Separate from any ammunition."

Washington D.C.'s most current reciprocity information may be referenced online. [http://gunla.ws/dc1]

D.   Duty to Inform Officers

Yes. Washington, D.C. requires a licensee to possess the license and registration certificate for the pistol being carried. If a LEO initiates an investigative stop of a licensee carrying a pistol, the licensee must immediately disclose to the LEO that he or she is carrying a concealed pistol and present the license and registration certificate. [http://gunla.ws/idlt]

E.   Criminal Provisions

Under Washington D.C.'s law, a license to carry a handgun does not permit carry in any of the following places or circumstances, whether it is issued in Washington D.C., or carry is pursuant to a reciprocity agreement with his/her state of license:

- No person or organization in the District shall possess or control any firearm, unless the person or organization holds a valid registration certificate for the firearm
- Anyone carrying a firearm registered with the District of Columbia shall keep such firearm in his possession unloaded and either disassembled or secured by a

trigger lock, gun safe, locked box, or other similar device

- Any area within 1,000 feet of a public or private school, including:
  - A day care center
  - An elementary school
  - A vocational school
  - A secondary school
  - A college
  - A junior college
  - A university
- A public swimming pool
- A video arcade
- A hospital, or an office where medical or mental health services are the primary services provided
- A polling place while voting is occurring
- A public transportation vehicle, including the Metrorail transit system and its stations
- A stadium or arena
- A youth center
- A public library
- In and around public housing as defined in section 3(1) of the United States Housing Act of 1937, approved August 22, 1974 (88 Stat. 654; 42 U.S.C. § 1437a(b))
- In or around housing that is owned, operated, or financially assisted by the District of Columbia Housing Authority
- No person shall keep or have in his or her possession any firearm:
  - Any assault style rifle
  - If convicted in any court of a crime punishable for a term of 1 year or more
  - If not licensed under § 22-4510 to sell weapons
  - Is a fugitive from justice

- Is addicted to any controlled substance as defined in § 48-901.02(4)
- Is subject to a court order that restrains the person from assaulting, harassing, stalking, or threatening any other person named in the order; and requires the person to relinquish possession of any firearms
- If convicted of a drug offense or making threats to commit bodily harm within the last five years.
- Has been convicted of an intrafamily offense, as defined in § 16-1001, or a substantially similar offense in another jurisdiction.

- Any property under the control of the District of Columbia which the District has prohibited or restricted carrying of a firearm
- Any private property where the owner has prohibited the carrying of a firearm
- One *may* transport a firearm, provided that:
    - For any lawful purpose from any place where he or she may lawfully possess and carry the firearm to any other place where he/she may lawfully possess and carry the firearm
    - If the transportation of the firearm is by a vehicle, the firearm shall be unloaded, and neither the firearm nor any ammunition being transported shall be readily accessible or directly accessible from the passenger compartment of the transporting vehicle (i.e. in a trunk)

For a list of places where carrying firearms is prohibited, see: [http://gunla.ws/dc2]

F.   NFA Items

All NFA items are prohibited in Washington D.C.

G.   Self-defense Laws.

Washington D.C. does not have a Castle Doctrine or SYG law. There is a duty to retreat when attacked, and You may use deadly force in self-defense only as a last resort, if retreating is impossible or cannot be done safely.

H.   Carrying Firearms in Vehicles

Washington D.C. prohibits carrying firearms in vehicles without a permit unless the firearm is unloaded, stored separately from ammunition, and neither the firearm nor ammunition are accessible from the passenger compartment. [http://gunla.ws/k1sx]

I.   Universal Background Checks

Background checks are mandatory for all firearm sales, and transfers between private parties, except between family members, must go through a licensed dealer. This only applies to sales made within the District of Columbia. Sales made by District of Columbia firearms owners outside of the District of Columbia must only conform to that state's transfer law. [http://gunla.ws/3y8t]

J.   High-Capacity Magazine Ban

The intrastate manufacture, sale, and possession of magazines capable of holding more than ten (10) rounds is prohibited. [http://gunla.ws/at9e]

K.   Waiting Period

Washington D.C. imposes a ten (10) day waiting period before purchasing a firearm.

L.   Do "No Gun Signs" Have the Force of Law?

Yes. If a property or establishment has a "No Guns" sign or the person in lawful possession communicates to you that guns are not allowed, you are prohibited from carrying on the property or into the establishment. Failure to obey such signs or verbal warnings constitutes trespass. [http://gunla.ws/jdan]

M.   Carry in Restaurants That Serve Alcohol

Yes. D.C. law states you cannot carry in a place that serves alcohol but gives exemptions to places that hold a Class C/R or D/R license. These are restaurant licenses for food and beverages with spirits, beer and wine allowed for sale on the premises for consumption. D.C. forbids a licensed carrier from consuming or being under the influence when carrying.

N.   Open Carry

Open carry is illegal in the District of Columbia.
Note: On July 25, 2017, the U.S. Court of Appeals for the District of Columbia issued a permanent injunction stopping the local Washington, D.C. government from denying people the right to carry concealed handguns in the nation's capital unless they could convince local officials they had a special and compelling need to protect themselves (the 'good reason' requirement). However, the decision was put on hold to allow D.C. to appeal. D.C. filed its appeal for rehearing on August 24, 2017. A decision from the rehearing is currently pending. [http://gunla.ws/m46h]

 **FLORIDA GUN LAWS**

Introduction

As it relates to reciprocal carry, Florida has a well-developed and maintained non-resident license program. Florida resident and non-resident licenses are well regarded both in terms of training and materials. Florida has approximately 19,000,000 residents, and spans over two (2) time zones. It shares its northern border with Alabama and Georgia.

A.   State Constitution

Regarding the right to bear arms, the Florida Constitution states:

"(a) The right of the people to keep and bear arms in defense of themselves and of the lawful authority of the state shall not be infringed, except that the manner of bearing arms may be regulated by law." [http://gunla.ws/FL1]

B.   Scope of Preemption

The controlling language of the Florida preemption statute is set forth as follows:

"Except as expressly provided by the State Constitution or general law, the Legislature hereby declares that it is occupying the whole field of regulation of firearms and ammunition, including the purchase, sale, transfer, taxation, manufacture, ownership, possession, storage, and transportation thereof, to the exclusion of all existing and future county, city, town, or municipal ordinances or any administrative regulations or rules adopted by local or state government relating thereto. Any such existing ordinances, rules, or regulations are hereby declared null and void." [http://gunla.ws/FL2]

C.   Reciprocal Carry

By statute, Florida will recognize another state's license to carry:

"(1) A resident of the United States who is a nonresident of Florida may carry a concealed weapon or concealed firearm while in this state if the nonresident: (a) Is 21 years of age or older; and (b) Has in his or her immediate possession a valid license to carry a concealed weapon or concealed firearm issued to the nonresident in his or her state of residence. (2) A nonresident is subject to the same laws and restrictions with respect to carrying a concealed weapon or concealed firearm as a resident of Florida who is so licensed." [http://gunla.ws/FL3]

D.   Duty to Inform Officers

Florida does not require individuals to inform a LEO of a permit or license to carry but if an Officer asks about a weapon, by law, an answer must be supplied. You must carry your license, together with valid identification, at all times in which You are in actual possession of a concealed weapon or firearm and must display both the license and proper identification upon demand by a LEO. [http://gunla.ws/wv34]

E.   NFA Items

Florida permits ownership of all NFA items, except DDs, provided they are legally obtained pursuant to federal law. Hunting with suppressors is legal. Making, possessing, throwing, projecting, or discharging any destructive device, or any attempt to do so is a felony in Florida. [http://gunla.ws/crro]

F.   Carrying Firearms in Vehicles

Florida allows carrying of long guns in vehicles without a permit. Handguns may only be carried without a permit if they are not readily accessible to the driver, such as being in a locked container or in the trunk. [http://gunla.ws/FL4]

G.   Self-defense Laws.

Florida has both Castle Doctrine and SYG laws. There is no duty to retreat when attacked in any place You have a legal right to be, and You may use deadly force in self-defense if You reasonably believe it is imminently necessary to prevent death or SBI, or to stop the unlawful & forcible entry into Your dwelling, residence, or occupied motor vehicle. [http://gunla.ws/FL5]

H.   Waiting Period

Florida imposes a three (3) day waiting period, which does not count weekend or holidays, before purchasing a firearm. This waiting period is waived for holders of a valid Florida license to carry. Holders of a valid Florida license to carry are also exempt from state background checks, but not federal ones. Florida does not require a waiting period for the purchase of long guns (rifle/shotgun). [http://gunla.ws/d22w]

I. Criminal Provisions

A license to carry a handgun is not valid in any of the following places or circumstances, whether it is issued by Florida, or a person is carrying pursuant to a reciprocity agreement between his or her state of license and Florida:

- A firearm must be stored in a locked container with a trigger lock so as to be unattainable to a minor under the age of 18
- A person carrying a weapon should not exhibit the weapon in a rude, careless, angry, or threatening manner, unless in self-defense
- A person carrying a weapon should not exhibit the weapon on public or private school grounds or facilities, a school bus, a school bus stop, at school-sanctioned activities, or within 1,000 feet of school property or any professional athletic event
- Discharge of a firearm in a public place, or on a public road, including from inside a vehicle (within 1,000 feet of any person), unless in self-defense
- Use a firearm (have it readily accessible and loaded) while under the influence of alcohol, controlled, or chemical substance, which impairs a person's normal faculties.
- An individual shall not carry a firearm if they habitually use alcohol or other substances to impair his or her normal functions

For a list of places where carrying a firearm is prohibited, see: [http://gunla.ws/FL7]

J. Do "No Gun Signs" Have the Force of Law?

No. "No Firearm" signs in Florida do not have the force of law unless they are posted on property that is specifically mentioned in state law as being off limits to those with a permit/license to carry. However, as a possessor with a real property interest, a retailer, has the right to limit, and qualify the right to enter the property, subject to not carrying a handgun. It would be improper to enter, and the licensee would be subject to ejection for possession of a handgun thereat. Failure to leave once requested would subject the licensee to criminal charges.

K. Carry in Restaurants That Serve Alcohol

Yes. There is no law stating it is illegal. You can carry in a restaurant that serves alcohol. Places like Fridays or Chili's unless they have a "No Gun Sign," then it is suggested that You not carry into the establishment. This does not include a bar or the bar area of a restaurant. You are prohibited from consuming alcohol while carrying a firearm. [http://gunla.ws/dodq]

L. Open Carry of Firearm

Open carry is generally not legal in Florida. Exceptions include in the home, place of work, hunting, fishing, camping, or while practice shooting and while traveling to and from those activities. Florida recently decriminalized the temporary exposure of a firearm by concealed firearms license holders, protecting them from being arrested and charged with a crime for the temporary and open exposure of a firearm.
[http://gunla.ws/rvh2] & [http://gunla.ws/awak]

Florida's laws on weapons and firearms may be accessed here:
[http://gunla.ws/FL6]

 **GEORGIA GUN LAWS**

Introduction

Georgia is in the southeastern part of the United States, with a state population of about 10,000,000 people. It shares borders to the north with Tennessee and North Carolina. To the east, Georgia is bounded by South Carolina and the Atlantic Ocean. The southern border is shared with Florida, with Alabama framing Georgia's western border. Open Carry is legal in Georgia with a valid license to carry.

A. State Constitution

Regarding the right to bear arms, the Georgia Constitution states:

"The right of the people to keep and bear arms shall not be infringed, but the General Assembly shall have power to prescribe the manner in which arms may be borne."
[http://gunla.ws/ga1]

B. Scope of Preemption

The controlling language of the Georgia preemption statute is set forth as follows:

"...no county or municipal corporation, by zoning or by ordinance, or resolution, nor any agency, board, department, commission, or authority of this state, other than the General Assembly, by rule or regulation shall regulate in any manner: (A) gun shows; (B) the possession, ownership, transport, carrying, transfer, sale, purchase, licensing, or registration of firearms or other weapons or components of firearms or other weapons; (C) firearms dealers; or (D) dealers in components of firearms or other weapons." [http://gunla.ws/ga2]

C. Reciprocal Carry

By statute, Georgia will recognize another state's license to carry if that state recognizes Georgia's license:

"Any person licensed to carry a handgun or weapon in any other state whose laws recognize and give effect to a license issued pursuant to this part shall be authorized to carry a weapon in this state, but only while the licensee is not a resident of this state; provided, however, that such licensee shall carry the weapon in compliance with the laws of this state."

Anyone contemplating reciprocal carry should check with the official list maintained by the Georgia Department of Public Safety. [http://gunla.ws/ga3]

D. NFA Items

Georgia permits ownership of all NFA items, provided they are legally obtained pursuant to federal law. Hunting with suppressors is legal.

E. Carrying Firearms in Vehicles

Georgia allows anyone who is legally allowed to possess firearms to carry them in their vehicles, without a permit. In the case of long guns, the firearm must either be unloaded or plainly visible from outside the vehicle if loaded. In the case of handguns, they must be unloaded and enclosed in a case. If You do not have a permit/license honored in Georgia, You can only carry a firearm in Your own vehicle. If You are riding in a vehicle that is not Yours, You must have permission of the person who has legal control of the vehicle. [http://gunla.ws/ga4]

F. Duty to Inform

No. Georgia does not require individuals to inform a LEO of a permit or license to carry immediately on contact, but if an Officer asks about a weapon, by law, an answer must be supplied. You must carry your license, together with valid identification, at all times in which You are in actual possession of a firearm and must display both the license and proper identification upon demand by a LEO. [http://gunla.ws/18bl]

G. Self-defense Laws

Georgia has both Castle Doctrine and SYG laws. There is no duty to retreat when attacked in any place You have a legal right to be, and You may use deadly force in self-defense if You reasonably believe it is imminently necessary to prevent death or SBI, the commission of a forcible felony, or to stop the unlawful & forcible entry into Your dwelling, residence, or occupied motor vehicle. [http://gunla.ws/pfnu]

H.   Criminal Provisions

Under Georgia law, a license to carry a handgun does not permit carry in any of the following places or circumstances, no matter if it is issued by Georgia, or carry is pursuant to a reciprocity agreement between his/her state of license and Georgia:

- Any place prohibited by federal law
- A government building that has a metal detector at each public entrance, or security guards screening visitors
- A courthouse
- A jail/prison
- A place of worship, unless the leader of the congregation permits the carrying of weapons by license holders
- A bar, unless the owner of the establishment permits the carrying of weapons by license holders
- Within a private or public school safety zone, school building, school function, school property, school bus, or other transportation furnished by a school, unless authorized to by the school board, or while picking up or dropping off their child
    - Teachers or other school personnel who are authorized to possess or carry weapons on the premises may do so provided the weapon is in a locked compartment of an automobile or in a locked firearms container.
    - Concealed carry of a handgun is permitted on Georgia's public college campuses if You have a CCP
- On the premises of a nuclear facility
- Discharge a firearm while under the influence of alcohol or drugs

For a list of places where carrying firearms is prohibited, see: [http://gunla.ws/ga6]

I. Do "No Gun Signs" Have the Force of Law?

No. "No Firearm" signs in Georgia do not have the force of law unless they are posted on property that is specifically mentioned in state law as being off limits to those with a permit/license to carry. However, as a possessor with a real property interest, a retailer, has the right to limit, and qualify the right to enter the property, subject to not carrying a handgun. It would be improper to enter, and the licensee would be subject to ejection for possession of a handgun thereat. Failure to leave once requested would subject the licensee to arrest for criminal trespass.

J. Carry in Restaurants That Serve Alcohol

Yes. There is no law stating it is illegal. You can carry in a restaurant that serves alcohol. Places like Fridays or Chili's unless they have a "No Gun Sign," then it is suggested that you not carry into the establishment. This does not include a bar or the bar area of a restaurant. You can carry Your firearm into a restaurant that serves alcohol, but you are prohibited from consuming alcohol while carrying a firearm. [http://gunla.ws/yu2d]

K. Open Carry

Open carry is legal in Georgia but you must have a valid CCP to open carry. Places listed in the "Criminal Provisions" above apply to those who open carry. In Georgia it is not against the law for You to possess a firearm without a valid weapon carry license inside Your home, motor vehicle or place of business. [http://gunla.ws/3nu2]

Note: A comprehensive gun law was passed in 2014 that, among other things, prohibits the police and National Guard from disarming citizens during a State of Emergency, prohibits public housing from banning guns on their premises, allows the use of suppressors while hunting, allows felons to use deadly force in self-defense, and allows license holders to carry firearms in unsecured areas of airports, but not to take them through security.

HAWAII GUN LAWS

Introduction

Like Alaska, Hawaii is unique in that it shares no borders with any other U.S. states. It is most unique in that it has only water boundaries and the entire state is a series of islands. Hawaii has, perhaps, the most restrictive gun laws out of all the United States. It is very important to be fully versed and aware of the laws in this state before traveling there. The four (4) major islands are Hawaii, Honolulu, Kauai, and Maui. The total population is about 1,400,000. Open carry is legal in Hawaii with a valid license to carry, but carry licenses are very difficult to obtain in Hawaii.

A. State Constitution

Regarding the right to bear arms, the Hawaii Constitution states:

> "A well regulated militia being necessary to the security of a free state, the right of the people to keep and bear arms shall not be infringed." [http://gunla.ws/hi1]

B. Scope of Preemption

Hawaii does not appear to have a specific preemption statute.

C. Reciprocal Carry

By statute, Hawaii does not have a reciprocal carry statute. Hawaii requires an application for a license to carry to be submitted and approved by the Chief of Police where there is an established necessity (including fear of injury to one's person or property). There is no provision for persons with carry licenses from other states. Additionally, even permits issued in the state of Hawaii are only good within the county of issuance.

"In an exceptional case, when an applicant shows reason to fear injury to the applicant's person or property, the chief of police of the appropriate county may grant a license to an applicant who is a citizen of the United States of the age of twenty-one years or more or to a duly accredited official representative of a foreign nation of the age of twenty-one years or more to carry a pistol or revolver and ammunition therefore concealed on the person within the county where the license is granted. Where the urgency or the need has been sufficiently indicated, the respective chief of police may grant to an applicant of good moral character who is a citizen of the United States of the age of twenty-one years or more, is engaged in the protection of life and property, and is not prohibited under section 134-7 from the ownership or possession of a firearm, a license to carry a pistol or revolver and ammunition therefore unconcealed on the person within the county where the license is granted. The chief of police of the appropriate county, or the chief's designated representative, shall perform an inquiry on an applicant by using the National Instant Criminal Background Check System, to include a check of the Immigration and Customs Enforcement databases where the applicant is not a citizen of the United States, before any determination to grant a license is made. Unless renewed,

the license shall expire one year from the date of issue."
[http://gunla.ws/hi2]

D.   NFA Items

MGs, SBRs, SBSs, and suppressors are prohibited for non-
LEO individuals. Certain DDs and AOWs are allowed with proper
tax stamp and NFA paperwork from the ATF(E).

E.   Carrying Firearms in Vehicles

Hawaii generally bans carrying firearms in vehicles without
a carry permit. Hawaii permits the open carrying of a long gun in a
motor vehicle, but only if traveling to and from hunting or target
shooting locations with a valid hunting license. Handguns may only
be carried with a permit. [http://gunla.ws/edah]

F.   Self-defense Laws

Hawaii has a Castle Doctrine but no SYG law. You do not
have a duty to retreat if attacked in Your dwelling or place of work.
You have a duty to retreat if attacked in public, and if You can
retreat safely by surrendering possession of property to someone
robbing You or by complying with their demands, You must do so
before resorting to deadly force. You may use deadly force in self-
defense only if You cannot retreat or are attacked in Your dwelling,
and if You reasonably believe it is imminently necessary to prevent
death or SBI, kidnapping, rape, or forcible sodomy.
[http://gunla.ws/hi3]

G.   Waiting Period

There is a fourteen (14) day waiting period after application
before a permit to purchase a firearm will be issued.

[http://gunla.ws/eqkw]

H.   High-Capacity Magazine Ban

Hawaii prohibits the intrastate manufacture, sale, and possession of magazines that can be inserted into a pistol and are capable of holding more than ten (10) rounds. Members of organizations are exempt from the pistol magazine limit at places of target shooting. [http://gunla.ws/9mnb]

I.   Universal Background Checks

Every sale or transfer of firearms, even by private parties, is required to go through an FFL to conduct a background check. [http://gunla.ws/6y3t]

J.   Duty to Inform

No. Hawaii does not require individuals to inform a LEO of a permit or license to carry but if an Officer asks about a weapon, by law, an answer must be supplied. You must have a valid identification at all times in which You are in actual possession of a firearm and must display proper identification upon demand of a LEO.

K.   Criminal Provisions

Under Hawaii law, it is a crime to possess a firearm by gift, purchase, inheritance or to transport a firearm unless it has first been registered with a local official:

"Every person arriving in the State who brings or by any other manner causes to be brought into the State a firearm of any description, whether usable or unusable, serviceable or unserviceable, modern or antique, shall register the firearm within three days after arrival of the person or of the firearm, whichever arrives later, with the chief of police of the county of the person's place of business or, if there is no place of business, the person's residence or, if there is neither a place of business nor residence, the person's place of sojourn." [http://gunla.ws/hi2]

- A permit is required in order to purchase a firearm, and You must pass a background check to obtain this permit.

For a list of places where carrying firearms is prohibited, see: [http://gunla.ws/hi4]

L.   Do "No Gun Signs" Have the Force of Law?

Yes. If a property or establishment has a "No Guns" sign or the person in lawful possession communicates to you that guns are not allowed, you are prohibited from carrying on the property or into the establishment. Failure to obey such signs or verbal warnings constitutes trespass. [http://gunla.ws/14wl]

M.   Carry in Restaurants That Serve Alcohol

Yes. There is no law stating it is illegal. You can carry in a restaurant that serves alcohol. Places like Fridays or Chili's unless they have a "No Gun Sign," then You are prohibited from carrying into the establishment. This does not include a bar or the bar area of a restaurant. You can carry Your firearm into a restaurant that serves alcohol, but you are prohibited from consuming alcohol while carrying a firearm.

N.   Open Carry

Open carry is illegal in Hawaii. A firearm may only be openly carried when hunting with a pistol and You must possess the proper license while doing so.

IDAHO
GUN
LAWS

Introduction

Idaho is located in the Rocky Mountains in the northwest United States. It has a little over 1,600,000 residents. At the northernmost portion, Idaho has a short boundary with British Columbia, Canada. The other states it borders are Montana and Wyoming to the east. Utah and Nevada bound it in the south. Oregon and Washington are the states that make up its western boundary. Open carry is legal in Idaho even without a license to carry.

A.   State Constitution

Regarding the right to bear arms, the Idaho Constitution states:

> "The people have the right to keep and bear arms, which right shall not be abridged; but this provision shall not prevent the passage of laws to govern the carrying of weapons concealed on the person nor prevent passage of legislation providing minimum sentences for crimes committed while in possession of a firearm, nor prevent the passage of legislation providing penalties for the possession of firearms by a convicted felon, nor prevent the passage of any legislation punishing the use of a firearm. No law shall impose licensure, registration or special taxation on the ownership or possession of firearms or ammunition. Nor shall any law permit the confiscation of firearms, except those actually used in the commission of a felony."

[http://gunla.ws/id1]

B. Scope of Preemption

The controlling language of the Idaho preemption statute is set forth as follows:

> "Except as expressly authorized by state statute, no county, city, agency, board or any other political subdivision of this state may adopt or enforce any law, rule, regulation, or ordinance which regulates in any manner the sale, acquisition, transfer, ownership, possession, transportation, carrying or storage of firearms or any element relating to firearms and components thereof, including ammunition." [http://gunla.ws/id2]

C. Reciprocal Carry

Idaho will recognize another state's license to carry if the licensee has it in his or her physical possession:

> "The requirement to secure a license to carry a concealed weapon under this section shall not apply to the following persons: (g) Any person who has a valid permit from a state or local law enforcement agency or court authorizing him to carry a concealed weapon. A permit issued in another state will only be considered valid if the permit is in the licensee's physical possession." [http://gunla.ws/id3]

D. NFA Items

Idaho permits ownership of all NFA items, provided they are legally obtained pursuant to federal law. Hunting with suppressors is legal.

E.   Carrying Firearms in Vehicles

Idaho allows anyone who is legally allowed to possess firearms to carry them openly in a motor vehicle without a permit. Someone without a permit may carry a long gun, but handguns may not be carried concealed within city limits unless they are either disassembled or unloaded and secured in a locked container. [http://gunla.ws/id4]

F.   Self-defense Laws

Idaho has a Castle Doctrine but no SYG law. There is no duty to retreat when attacked in Your dwelling or place of work, and You may use deadly force in self-defense if You reasonably believe it is imminently necessary to prevent death or SBI, a forcible felony, or to stop the unlawful & forcible entry into Your dwelling by someone who intends to commit violence against an occupant of that dwelling. Idaho requires that deadly force in the defense of others be used as a last resort. You must, in good faith have endeavored to decline any further struggle before using deadly force. [http://gunla.ws/pdxq]

G.   Constitutional Carry

As of 6/1/16, Idaho permits Idaho residents who are at least 21 years old and not legally prohibited from owning firearms to carry a handgun without a permit, openly or concealed. Note that it was already legal for Idaho residents who are at least 18 years old and not legally prohibited from owning firearms to open carry a handgun, or to carry a concealed handgun as long as You are outside of city limits. The new law allows permitless concealed carry within city limits by Idaho residents who are at least 21, which had previously required a permit. [http://gunla.ws/id6]

210

H. Duty to Inform

No. Idaho does not require individuals to inform a LEO of a permit or license to carry but if an Officer asks about a weapon, by law, an answer must be supplied. You must have a valid identification at all times in which You are in actual possession of a concealed weapon or firearm and must display proper identification upon demand by a LEO.

I. Criminal Provisions

Under Idaho law, a license to carry a handgun does not permit carry in any of the following places or circumstances:

- Discharge any firearm from or across a public highway
- Carry a concealed weapon when intoxicated or under the influence of an intoxicating drink or drug. People can carry weapons in bars, so long as they do not drink.
- Carry a concealed weapon in a courthouse, a juvenile detention facility, or a jail
- Carry a concealed weapon in a public or private school
- Possess a firearm while on school property, including stadiums or other structures on school grounds, at a school sponsored activity, or on school provided transportation, regardless of location
- Possess a firearm negligently or carelessly where the actions would result in discharge and injury to an individual
- The Board of Regents of the University of Idaho, the Boards of Trustees of the state colleges and universities, the Board of Professional-Technical Education and the Boards of Trustees of each of the community colleges have the authority to prescribe rules and regulations

relating to firearms regarding their respective properties.

For a list of places where carrying firearms is prohibited, see: [http://gunla.ws/id7]

J.   Do "No Gun Signs" Have the Force of Law?

No. "No Firearm" signs in Idaho do not have the force of law unless they are posted on property that is specifically mentioned in state law as being off limits to those with a permit/license to carry. However, as a possessor with a real property interest, a retailer, has the right to limit, and qualify the right to enter the property, subject to not carrying a handgun. It would be improper to enter, and the licensee would be subject to ejection for possession of a handgun thereat. Failure to leave once requested would subject the licensee to arrest for criminal trespass.

K.   Carry in Restaurants That Serve Alcohol

Yes. You are allowed to carry into any establishment that serves alcohol, including bars. You are prohibited from carrying while you consume alcohol or are under the influence of alcohol.

L.   Open Carry

Open carry is legal in Idaho. Places listed in the "Criminal Provisions" above apply to those who open carry. You may carry openly without a permit in a vehicle or on foot.

 # ILLINOIS
GUN
LAWS

Introduction

Ironically, Chicago, Illinois, with famously strict gun laws, including a (prior) ban on private possession of handguns, served as the basis for SCOTUS' 2010 decision in *McDonald v. City of Chicago* that Second Amendment applies to the states through the Fourteenth Amendment.

On July 9, 2013 Illinois became the last state in the country to allow citizens of the state the right to carry concealed weapons. Possession of the permit is granted to those who are 21 or older and who pass a 16-hour training course. Applicants may be denied a permit if the law enforcement agency finds reasonable suspicion that the applicant is a danger to themselves or others.

Illinois has water boundaries with other states, in some cases further complicating an interstate transportation and/or reciprocal carry analysis. To the north, Illinois borders Wisconsin, although the boundary line lies in Lake Michigan. Illinois' eastern border with Indiana is within Lake Michigan and the Wabash and Ohio Rivers. The Ohio River is the southern border with Kentucky. The western border with Missouri and Iowa is the Mississippi River.

A.   State Constitution

Regarding the right to bear arms, the Illinois Constitution states:

"Subject only to the police power, the right of the individual citizen to keep and bear arms shall not be infringed."
[http://gunla.ws/IL1]

B. Scope of Preemption

Illinois does have a preemption statute that states under Section 90:

"The regulation, licensing, possession, registration, and transportation of handguns and ammunition for handguns by licensees are exclusive powers and functions of the State. Any ordinance or regulation, or portion thereof, enacted on or before the effective date of this Act that purports to impose regulations or restrictions on licensees or handguns and ammunition for handguns in a manner inconsistent with this Act shall be invalid in its application to licensees under this Act on the effective date of this Act. This Section is a denial and limitation of home rule powers and functions under subsection (h) of Section 6 of Article VII of the Illinois Constitution." [http://gunla.ws/IL2]

It is imperative to check local cities and municipality's ordinances regarding the carrying of a firearm, concealed or unconcealed. Handguns have been banned in some municipalities in Illinois and certain cities require registration of firearms (e.g., Chicago) while others do not. The Director of State Police compiles and provides these ordinances to the public free of charge.

C.   Reciprocal Carry

Illinois does not have an explicit reciprocity statute and restricts the possession of a firearm by law. However, it will recognize a nonresident's right to carry a firearm in some circumstances:

Section 40. Non-resident license applications.
"(a) For the purposes of this Section, "non-resident" means a person who has not resided within this State for more than 30 days and resides in another state or territory.
(b) The Department shall by rule allow for non-resident license applications from any state or territory of the United States with laws related to firearm ownership, possession, and carrying, that are substantially similar to the requirements to obtain a license under this Act.
(c) A resident of a state or territory approved by the Department under subsection (b) of this Section may apply for a non-resident license. The applicant shall apply to the Department and must meet all of the qualifications established in Section 25 of this Act, except for the Illinois residency requirement in item (xiv) of paragraph (2) of subsection (a) of Section 4 of the Firearm Owners Identification Card Act. The applicant shall submit:
(1) The application and documentation required under Section 30 of this Act and the applicable fee;
(2) a notarized document stating that the applicant: (A) is eligible under federal law and the laws of his or her state or territory of residence to own or possess a firearm; (B) if applicable, has a license or permit to carry a firearm or concealed firearm issued by his or her state or territory of residence and attach a copy of the license or permit to the application; (C) understands Illinois laws pertaining to the possession and transport of firearms, and (D) acknowledges that the applicant is subject to the jurisdiction of the Department and Illinois courts for any violation of this Act; and

(3) a photocopy of any certificates or other evidence of compliance with the training requirements under Section 75 of this Act; and

(4) a head and shoulder color photograph in a size specified by the Department taken within the 30 days preceding the date of the application.

(d) In lieu of an Illinois driver's license or Illinois identification card, a non-resident applicant shall provide similar documentation from his or her state or territory of residence. In lieu of a valid Firearm Owner's Identification Card, the applicant shall submit documentation and information required by the Department to obtain a Firearm Owner's Identification Card, including an affidavit that the non-resident meets the mental health standards to obtain a firearm under Illinois law, and the Department shall ensure that the applicant would meet the eligibility criteria to obtain a Firearm Owner's Identification card if he or she was a resident of this State.

(e) Nothing in this Act shall prohibit a non-resident from transporting a concealed firearm within his or her vehicle in Illinois, if the concealed firearm remains within his or her vehicle and the non-resident: (1) is not prohibited from owning or possessing a firearm under federal law; (2) is eligible to carry a firearm in public under the laws of his or her state or territory of residence; and (3) is not in possession of a license under this Act. If the non-resident leaves his or her vehicle unattended, he or she shall store the firearm within a locked vehicle or locked container within the vehicle in accordance with subsection (b) of Section 65 of this Act." [http://gunla.ws/IL2]

Currently, Illinois only issues Illinois Non-Resident permits to residents of Arkansas, Mississippi, Texas and Virginia. Non-residents must complete 16 hours of Concealed Carry firearms training provided by an ISP approved instructor. [http://gunla.ws/4x0t]

D. Duty to Inform Officers

Illinois does not require individuals to inform a LEO of a permit or license to carry but if an Officer asks about a weapon, by law, an answer must be supplied. You are required to possess a license at all times You carry a concealed weapon and must present your license to a LEO upon their request. LEOs or emergency services personnel may secure Your firearm during the duration of the contact if they determine that it is necessary for their safety. [http://gunla.ws/x00j]

E. NFA Items

The only NFA items legal in Illinois are AOWs and SBR. You must possess a Curio & Relic license in order to purchase/manufacture/own a SBR or be a member of a bona fide military reenactment group. The rifle itself does not have to qualify as a Curio & Relic. AOWs and large-bore DDs allowed with proper approval and tax stamp from ATF(E). [http://gunla.ws/v5y7]

F. Private Sales Background Checks

The seller must verify the buyer's FOID with the Illinois State Police and must keep a record of the sale for at least ten years. [http://gunla.ws/nwfq]

G. Carrying Firearms in Vehicles

Illinois generally prohibits carrying firearms in vehicles without a carry permit. People who possess a FOID card but not a carry permit may transport firearms in their vehicle only if the firearm is unloaded and secured in a locked container, or otherwise not immediately accessible. [http://gunla.ws/IL3]

H.   Self-defense Laws

Illinois has a Castle Doctrine but no SYG law. There is no duty to retreat when attacked in Your dwelling, and You may use deadly force in self-defense if You reasonably believe it is necessary to prevent imminent death, SBI, or the commission of a forcible felony. Deadly force may also be used if to stop the unlawful & forcible entry into Your dwelling or residence if the entry is violent and You reasonably believe the intruder intends to commit violence against an occupant of the dwelling, or if the intruder intends to commit a felony within the dwelling. Anyone who is justified in using force in self-defense has civil immunity from lawsuits relating to said use of force by the intruder, their family, or their estate. [http://gunla.ws/dv7f]

I.   Criminal Provisions

To obtain a firearm in Illinois an individual must first obtain a Firearms Owner's Identification Card (FOID), which requires passing a background check. It is *required* for any person to purchase a gun or ammunition and it is unlawful to possess any firearm or ammunition without a valid FOID. There is a 24-hour waiting period before buying a rifle or shotgun, and 72-hour waiting period before buying a handgun.

A licensee may carry a loaded or unloaded concealed firearm, fully concealed or partially concealed, in the individual's vehicle whether loaded or unloaded and concealed. [http://gunla.ws/IL2]

■ A licensee must possess a license at all times while carrying a firearm except on the licensee's land or in one's abode or fixed place of business or in the land of another as an invitee with that person's permission

- Assault weapons are banned in certain counties and cities
- Cook county imposes a $25 tax on gun sales
- Magazine restrictions are valid in certain cities

Under Illinois law, a licensee shall not knowingly carry a handgun in any of the following places or circumstances, whether the license was issued by Illinois, or the person is carrying pursuant to a reciprocity agreement between his or her state of license and Illinois.

- Any location that firearms are prohibited from under federal law
- Any building, property and parking under control of a public or private elementary or secondary school, pre-school or child care facility
- Any property, including parking areas and sidewalks of a private community college, college or university
- Any property under the control of an officer of the executive or legislative branch of government, except bikeway or trail in a park regulated by the Department of Natural Resources
- Any building designated for court purposes or under control of a unit of local government
- Any area under the control of an adult or juvenile detention or correctional institution, prison or jail
- Any area under the control of a public or private hospital or hospital affiliate, mental health facility, or nursing home
- Any form of transportation paid for, in part or whole, with public funds and any building under the control of a public transportation facility paid for, in part or whole, with public funds
- Any area owned or leased by a gaming facility

- Any stadium arena or parking area including collegiate or professional sporting events
- Any library land
- Any amusement park, zoo, or museum
- Any area under the control of an airport
- Firearms are not allowed to be stored inside a vehicle while it is located on the street, driveway, parking area, building or facility of a nuclear energy, storage weapons or development site
- Any public gathering, excluding a place where showing, demonstration or lecture involving the exhibition of unloaded firearms is conducted
- On any public street, alley, or other public lands/parks/playgrounds, on one's own land, abode, or fixed place of business)
- A firearm being transported must be either:
  - Broken down in a non-functioning state
  - Not immediately accessible; or
  - Unloaded and enclosed in a case, firearm carrying box, shipping box, or other container

For a list of places where carrying a firearm is prohibited, see: [http://gunla.ws/IL5]

J.   Do "No Gun Signs" Have the Force of Law?

Yes. If a property or establishment has a "No Guns" sign or the person in lawful possession communicates to you that guns are not allowed, You are prohibited from carrying on the property or into the establishment. Failure to obey such signs or verbal warnings constitutes trespass. [http://gunla.ws/qvq8]

K. Carry in Restaurants That Serve Alcohol

Yes, unless posted. You are prohibited from carrying a firearm into restaurants or bars that receive more than 50% of their revenue from the sale of alcohol. Restaurants and Bars in Illinois are required to post this information in a conspicuous location at their establishment. [http://gunla.ws/hdrs]

L. Open Carry

Open carry is not legal in Illinois. You must have an Illinois permit to carry a firearm. A handgun carried on or about a person with an Illinois permit to carry must be concealed from view of the public or on or about a person within a vehicle. [http://gunla.ws/0mez]

M. Chicago and Laser Sights

In Chicago it is illegal to possess, display for sale, sell, or otherwise transfer any laser sight accessory, or a firearm silencer or muffler. LEOs and members of the armed forces are exempt from this law. Any such items will be seized and forfeited to the city.

Any owner of record of any motor vehicle that contains an assault weapon, a laser sight accessory, or firearm silencer or muffler is subject to a $2,000 fine, or a $3,000 fine if the violation occurs within 500 feet of a public park or elementary or secondary school. Any such vehicle is subject to seizure and impoundment at the owner's expense. [http://gunla.ws/jn5z]

 # INDIANA GUN LAWS

Introduction

The State of Indiana stands out on the topic of reciprocal carry in two (2) ways. First, a statutory reciprocity scheme recognizes all other states' licenses to carry a handgun, except Vermont.

Second, Indiana was the first state to adopt a lifetime license to carry. Upon initial application or renewal, a person may pay additional fees and obtain a lifetime license to carry a handgun. So long has he/she remains a "proper person," the license remains valid for life and no renewal is required. Open carry is legal in Indiana with a valid license to carry.

For orientation purposes in reciprocal carry or interstate transportation, Indiana is bordered on the north by Michigan, on the east by Ohio and on the west by Illinois. The Ohio River physically separates Indiana from the State of Kentucky.

A.   State Constitution

Regarding the right to bear arms, the Indiana Constitution states:

"The people shall have a right to bear arms, for the defense of themselves and the State." [http://gunla.ws/in1]

B.   Scope of Preemption

Generally, no unit of government may regulate in any manner the ownership, possession, sale, transfer, or transportation of firearms or ammunition. [http://gunla.ws/in2]

C.   Reciprocal Carry

By statute, Indiana will recognize another state's license to carry:

"Licenses to carry handguns, issued by other states or foreign countries, will be recognized according to the terms thereof but only while the holders are not residents of Indiana."

Indiana's most current reciprocity information may be referenced online. [http://gunla.ws/in3]

D.   Duty to Inform Officers

Indiana does not require individuals to inform a LEO of a permit or license to carry but if an Officer asks about a weapon, by law, an answer must be supplied. Unless You are carrying in Your dwelling or fixed place of business, You must possess a permit in order to carry a firearm. [http://gunla.ws/oih1]

E.   Carrying Firearms in Vehicles

Indiana permits anyone who is legally allowed to own a gun to carry a long gun in their vehicle, without a permit. Someone without a permit may only carry a handgun if it is unloaded, not readily accessible, and secured in a case, AND the vehicle is owned, leased, rented, or otherwise legally controlled by the person carrying the handgun. [http://gunla.ws/in4]

F.   NFA Items

Indiana permits the ownership of all NFA items, provided they are legally owned pursuant to federal law. Suppressors may also be used while hunting. CLEOs are required to sign an application for the transfer of any item regulated under the NFA within 15 days if the applicant is not prohibited by law from receiving it. [http://gunla.ws/6va3] & [http://gunla.ws/fw7m]

G.   Self-defense Laws.

Indiana has both Castle Doctrine and SYG laws. There is no duty to retreat when attacked in any place You have a legal right to be. You may also use reasonable force to arrest or prevent the escape of a person who has just committed a felony. You may use deadly force in defense of yourself or others if You reasonably believe it is necessary to prevent imminent death, SBI, the commission of a forcible felony, or to stop the unlawful & forcible entry into Your dwelling, residence, occupied motor vehicle, or to prevent the hijacking of an airplane while in flight.

In addition, a law passed in 2012 expands the castle doctrine to allow the use of force against public servants (such as LEO) if You reasonably believe it is necessary to:

(1) protect the person or a third person from what the person reasonably believes to be the imminent use of unlawful force;

(2) prevent or terminate the public servant's unlawful entry of or attack on the person's dwelling, curtilage, or occupied motor vehicle; or

(3) prevent or terminate the public servant's unlawful trespass on or criminal interference with property lawfully in the person's possession, lawfully in possession of a member of the person's immediate family, or belonging to a person whose property the person has authority to protect.

This law allows the use of deadly force if necessary to prevent death or SBI if You reasonably believe the public servant is either acting unlawfully or not engaged in executing their official duties.

NOTE: Despite the above law, it is extremely inadvisable to use force against the police, and doing so will almost certainly result in You being prosecuted (even if You aren't convicted), or may cause the police officer to shoot You. Determining whether or not the actions of LEO are lawful is usually a complex legal question that requires careful deliberation by lawyers and does not lend itself well to snap decisions made in the heat of the moment. If You use force against a public servant whose actions turn out to be lawful, You can expect to be charged with resisting arrest, assault on a police officer, or a number of other serious felonies. The safest and most prudent course of action will almost always be to cooperate with the LEO and challenge their actions in court later. [http://gunla.ws/in5] & [http://gunla.ws/in6]

A recent court case, *Cupello v. State*, applied the Indiana law authorizing the use of force against public servants, and overturned a man's conviction for battery against a police officer on the grounds of self-defense. In that case, an off-duty cop stuck his foot in the doorway of an apartment while questioning the occupant, and the occupant slammed the door on the cop, hitting his foot. The court ruled that slamming the door was a reasonable use of force to terminate an unlawful entry into the dwelling. *Cupello v. State*, 27 N.E.3d 1122, 1129 (Ind. Ct. App. 2015) [http://gunla.ws/in7]

H.   Age to Purchase Handguns and Carry Permit

You only need to be 18 to purchase a handgun or handgun ammunition from a private party in Indiana. In addition, the minimum age for obtaining an Indiana carry permit is 18. Indiana is a shall issue state, and offers both 4 year and lifetime carry permits.

As of July 1, 2017, persons who are: (1) at least 18 years old; (2) protected by a protection order; (3) have applied for a license; and (4) are not prohibited from possessing a handgun may carry a handgun without a license for 60 days from the date of the protection order being issued. [http://gunla.ws/e85z]

I.   Private Transfers

Indiana has few laws regulating the private transfer of firearms between two Indiana residents, and these laws only address the private sale of handguns, not long guns. Private transfers are not subject to background checks. Indiana prohibits selling handguns to people under 18 (except transfers from parents/guardians to their children). It is illegal to sell or transfer a handgun to anyone You know is prohibited from owning a handgun or intends to use the firearm in the commission of a crime, but You do not have a duty to conduct an inquiry or actively investigate whether the prospective buyer is a prohibited person. Private transfers are the only way for people under 21 to legally obtain handguns. When selling a firearm to a private party, You should ask for identification to show that the purchaser is a resident of Indiana. An Indiana CCP is the best form of ID because it also shows that the purchaser is not a prohibited person.

J.   Out of State Firearm Purchases

Indiana residents may purchase long guns from an FFL in any state and take the firearm back to Indiana without having to ship it to an FFL located in Indiana, so long as the state of purchase allows sales to people from out of state. If You buy a handgun from an FFL or any firearm from a private party in another state, that firearm must be shipped to an Indiana FFL for pick up. Indiana allows residents of other states to purchase long guns from an Indiana FFL.

K.   Firearms at Work

Most employers are not allowed to adopt or enforce policies that forbid employees from keeping firearms and ammunition in their vehicle, even on the employer's premises. Holders of a CCP have the right to store guns in their cars without fear of punishment, so long as the firearm is locked in the trunk, in the glove box of a locked vehicle, or stored out of sight within a locked vehicle. Employers may still ban guns from the property of child care centers, domestic violence shelters, college campuses, or secured locations.

Employees are permitted to store firearms in their personal vehicles parked at correctional facilities. Additionally, licensed state employees are permitted to carry a handgun within the state capitol building. [http://gunla.ws/in8] & [http://gunla.ws/7909]

L.   Criminal Provisions

Under Indiana law, a license to carry a handgun does not permit carry in any of the following places or circumstances:

- Knowingly or intentionally pointing a firearm at another
- Aboard a commercial or charter aircraft

- An area of an airport to which access is controlled by the inspection of persons and property
- In or on school property, property being used by a school for a school function, or a school bus (except for possession inside a motor vehicle being used to transport another to or from a school or school function)
- Discharge of a firearm in a park, where not designated for hunting or firearm sport
- Inside a Riverboat Casino or shipping port. 130 IAC 4-1-10
- Firearms must be locked in a vehicle during the Annual State Fair. 80 IAC 4-4-4
- Any building that contains a courtroom, but the restriction does not apply to areas of the building occupied by residential tenants or private businesses

For a list of places where carrying a firearm is forbidden, see: [http://gunla.ws/in9]

M.   Do "No Gun Signs" Have the Force of Law?

No. "No Firearm" signs in Indiana do not have the force of law unless they are posted on property that is specifically mentioned in State Law as being off limits to those with a permit/license to carry. However, as a possessor with a real property interest, a retailer, has the right to limit, and qualify the right to enter the property, subject to not carrying a handgun. It would be improper to enter, and the licensee would be subject to ejection for possession of a handgun thereat. Failure to leave once requested would subject the licensee to arrest for criminal trespass.

N.   Carry in Restaurants That Serve Alcohol

Yes. There is no law stating it is illegal. You can carry in a restaurant that serves alcohol. Places like Fridays or Chili's unless they have a "No Gun Sign," then You are prohibited from carrying into the establishment. This does not include a bar or the bar area of a restaurant. You can carry your firearm into a restaurant that serves alcohol, but you are prohibited from consuming alcohol while carrying a firearm.

O.   Open Carry

Open carry is legal in Indiana but You must have a valid permit/license to open carry. Places listed in the "Criminal Provisions" above apply to those who open carry.

In May 2017, the Indiana Supreme Court ruled that detaining an individual based solely upon their possession of a handgun (in order to verify that they are licensed) violates the Fourth Amendment absent any other reasonable articulable suspicion of a crime being committed.
[http://gunla.ws/3iuv] & [http://gunla.ws/dlz9]

IOWA
GUN
LAWS

Introduction

Iowa is somewhat unique in the firearms realm because it does not have direct constitutional provision to keep and bear arms. However, it has a robust firearms culture and does recognize out-of-state licenses for carry in Iowa. It also has a nonprofessional permit to carry weapons that is granted after completion of certain requirements. Open carry is legal in Iowa with a valid license to carry.

Iowa is geographically oriented in the north-central portion of the U.S. It is bordered on the north by Minnesota, to the east by Wisconsin and Illinois (across the Mississippi River), to the south by Missouri, and to the west by Nebraska (across the Missouri River) and South Dakota.

A.   State Constitution

Regarding the right to bear arms, the Iowa Constitution does not explicitly state that there is a right to bear arms, however it does state that there are certain inalienable rights, which include:

"defending life and liberty, acquiring, possessing and protecting property, and pursuing and obtaining safety and happiness." [http://gunla.ws/mlkw]

B.   Scope of Preemption

The controlling language of the Iowa preemption statute is

set forth as follows:

"A political subdivision of the state shall not enact an ordinance regulating the ownership, possession, legal transfer, lawful transportation, registration, or licensing of firearms when the ownership, possession, transfer, or transportation is otherwise lawful under the laws of this state." [http://gunla.ws/ia1]

C.   Reciprocal Carry

By statute, Iowa will recognize another state's license to carry:

"A valid permit or license issued by another state to any nonresident of this state shall be considered to be a valid permit or license to carry weapons issued pursuant to this chapter." [http://gunla.ws/ia2]

D.   NFA Items

In Iowa you can use a Gun Trust or NFA Trust to own MGs, AOW, DD, SBS, and SBR. Although Title II weapons are permitted in the state, their ownership, except for suppressors, is severely limited. As of March 31, 2016, suppressors are legal and may be used for hunting. As of April 13, 2017, SBR and SBS are legal.

For a complete list of ownership limitations on NFA items, see: [http://gunla.ws/x748]

E.   Carrying Firearms in Vehicles

Iowa generally prohibits carrying firearms in vehicles without a permit, unless they are unloaded and secured in a locked container or in a compartment of the vehicle not readily accessible (such as the trunk). When a motor home is used a residence (parked) or place of business (parked), no permit is required. When it is being used as transportation, the firearm must be properly stored. [http://gunla.ws/ia3]

F.   Self-defense Laws

Iowa has a Castle Doctrine but no SYG law. There is no duty to retreat when in Your home or place of business. You may use force, including deadly force, in defense of yourself or others if You reasonably believe it is necessary to prevent imminent death, SBI, or the commission of a forcible felony. [http://gunla.ws/ia4]

G.   Duty to Inform

No. Iowa does not require individuals to inform a LEO of a permit or license to carry immediately upon contact, but if an Officer asks about a weapon, by law, an answer must be supplied. Unless You are carrying in Your dwelling or fixed place of business, You must possess Your permit in order to carry Your firearm. Failing to provide your permit is a misdemeanor offense. [http://gunla.ws/zfbf]

H.   Criminal Provisions

Under Iowa law, a license to carry a handgun is not valid in any of the following places or circumstances:

- Carry or possess in a "weapons-free zone," which include: within 1,000 feet of the property of a public or private elementary or secondary school, the property of a public park (except those designated as a hunting area)
- No firearms allowed on a school bus

- Possession or carrying while intoxicated
- Intentional discharge of a firearm in a reckless manner
- Iowa requires a permit to purchase a handgun. A permit may be applied for through local law enforcement, are issued in three (3) days, and are valid for one (1) year. Permits to purchase are not required by holders of a valid Iowa license to carry.
- Lists of people who have licenses to carry or purchase firearms are now private and not publicly available
- People with carry permits may carry a loaded handgun (open or concealed) while operating an ATV or snowmobile on other people's property, so long as the gun is secured in a holster. It is unlawful to discharge a firearm from an ATV or snowmobile, You must dismount first.

Iowa has no statues prohibiting the possession of firearms in the following locations, although administrative regulations may apply:

- Parks
- Hospitals
- Places of worship
- Sports arenas
- Polling places

For a list of places where carrying a firearm is forbidden, see: [http://gunla.ws/ia5]

I.   Do "No Gun Signs" Have the Force of Law?

No. "No Firearm" signs in Iowa do not have the force of law unless they are posted on property that is specifically mentioned in State Law as being off limits to those with a permit/license to carry. However, as a possessor with a real property interest, a retailer, has the right to limit, and qualify the right to enter the property, subject to not carrying a handgun. It would be improper to enter, and the licensee would be subject to ejection for possession of a handgun threat. Failure to leave once requested would subject the licensee to arrest for criminal trespass.

J.   Carry in Restaurants That Serve Alcohol

Yes. There is no law stating it is illegal. You can carry in a restaurant that serves alcohol or in a bar. If the restaurant or bar has a "No Gun Sign," then it is suggested that you not enter the establishment. You can carry your firearm into a restaurant that serves alcohol or a bar, but you are prohibited from consuming alcohol while carrying a firearm.

K.   Open Carry (Without a Valid Permit/License)

Open carry is legal in Iowa, but with many restrictions. You must have a valid permit to carry a loaded handgun. Open carry in Incorporated areas is illegal without a valid permit/license. Places listed in the "Criminal Provisions" above apply to those who open carry. [http://gunla.ws/izr8]

 # KANSAS
GUN
LAWS

Introduction

Kansas' population is just shy of 3,000,000 residents. It is centered in the continental U.S. It has four (4) neat and clear (almost straight) borders. Nebraska is its neighbor to the north. To the east is Missouri, with Oklahoma to the south. Kansas shares its western border with Colorado.

A.   State Constitution

Regarding the right to bear arms, the Kansas Constitution states:

> "The people have the right to bear arms for their defense and security; but standing armies in time of peace, are dangerous to liberty, and shall not be tolerated, and the military shall be in strict subordination to the civil power." [http://gunla.ws/ks1]

B.   Scope of Preemption

The controlling language of the Kansas preemption statute is set forth as follows:

> "No city or county shall adopt any ordinance, resolution or regulation, and no agent of any city or county shall take any administrative action, governing the purchase, transfer,

ownership, storage or transporting of firearms or ammunition, or any component or combination thereof." [http://gunla.ws/ks2]

C.   Reciprocal Carry

By statute, Kansas will recognize another state's license to carry if that state recognizes Kansas's license:

"A valid license, issued by any other state or the District of Columbia, to carry concealed weapons shall be recognized as valid in this state, but only while the holder is not a resident of Kansas, if the attorney general determines that standards for issuance of such license or permit by such state or district are equal to or greater than the standards imposed by this act."

By statute, Kansas residents 21 or older may legally carry a concealed firearm, without having to have a state-issued permit. However, Kansans must obtain a concealed carry permit for purposes of reciprocal carry. Anyone contemplating reciprocal carry should check with the official list maintained by the Kansas AG at the point in time the reciprocal carry is to occur. Reference the Kansas reciprocity agreements here: [http://gunla.ws/ks3]

D.   Constitutional Carry

As of 7/1/15, Kansas permits any resident of Kansas who is at least 21 years old and not prohibited from owning a firearm to carry a handgun without a permit, openly or concealed. [http://gunla.ws/ks4]

E.   Duty to Inform Officers

Kansas does not require Kansas residents to inform a LEO of a permit or license to carry. If an Officer asks a non-resident about a weapon, by law, an answer must be supplied. With permitless carry you do not have to have a permit/license to carry in Kansas as long as you can legally possess the firearm.

F.   NFA Items

SBS and MGs must be registered under the NFA. However, a personal firearm, a firearm accessory or ammunition that is owned or manufactured commercially or privately in Kansas and that remains within the borders of Kansas is not subject to any federal law. Suppressors that are manufactured in Kansas and remain within the borders of Kansas are not subject to any federal law, including the NFA. A firearm manufactured in Kansas must have the words "Made in Kansas" clearly stamped on a central metallic part, such as the receiver or frame.

CLEOs are required to sign an application for the transfer of any item regulated under the NFA within 15 days if the applicant is not prohibited by law from receiving it. [http://gunla.ws/n72f] & [http://gunla.ws/53sh]

G.   Carrying Firearms in Vehicles

Kansas has no laws regulating the manner of carrying firearms in vehicles, so anyone who is legally allowed to possess firearms may carry them in vehicles without a permit, concealed or openly. Anyone who is 21 years of age who can legally possess a handgun can carry it concealed or openly in Kansas without any type of permit/license, both in a vehicle and on foot. [http://gunla.ws/e8ce]

H.   Self-defense Laws

Kansas has both Castle Doctrine and SYG laws. There is no duty to retreat from any place You have a legal right to be. You may use force, including deadly force, in defense of yourself or others if You reasonably believe it is necessary to prevent imminent death, SBI, the commission of a forcible felony, or to stop the unlawful & forcible entry into Your dwelling, residence, or occupied motor vehicle if You reasonably believe it is necessary to prevent imminent death or SBI as a result of the unlawful entry. [http://gunla.ws/vdgu] & [http://gunla.ws/l8u2]

I.   Criminal Provisions

Under Kansas law, a license to carry a handgun does not permit carry in any of the following places or circumstances:

- Within the governor's residence
- Any private or public building (not including a parking lot adjacent thereto) that chooses to restrict carry, and has posted with AG approved signage for the prohibition
- An individual may be charged with trespass to an area if an area has an AG approved sign stating no firearms and the individual does not leave when asked to
- Preschools, elementary schools and middle schools whether public or private with AG approval
- In the Docking state office building
- Within 500 feet of the Landon state office building
- Within the Judicial center, or any other state-owned or leased building
- Secure areas of a jail, correctional facility or law enforcement agency
- In a county courthouse

- While under the influence of alcohol, or drugs, or both
- State government employees with valid carry permits may now carry while on the job, and public (but not private) employers may not prohibit their employees from carrying on the job. This provision does NOT affect existing bans on carrying weapons in sensitive places such as courthouses or the state capitol.

You may conceal carry in any public area of state and municipal buildings. This encompasses carrying at public universities. [http://gunla.ws/s0ij]

For a list of places where carrying a firearm is forbidden, see: [http://gunla.ws/ks6]

J.   Do "No Gun Signs" Have the Force of Law?

No. "No Firearm" signs in Kansas do not have the force of law unless they are posted on property that is specifically mentioned in State Law as being off limits to those with a permit/license to carry. However, as a possessor with a real property interest, a retailer, has the right to limit, and qualify the right to enter the property, subject to not carrying a handgun. It would be improper to enter, and the licensee would be subject to ejection for possession of a handgun thereat. Failure to leave once requested would subject the licensee to arrest for criminal trespass. [http://gunla.ws/1xe6]

K.   Carry in Restaurants That Serve Alcohol

Yes. There is no law stating it is illegal. You can carry in a restaurant that serves alcohol or in a bar. If the restaurant or bar has a "No Gun Sign," then it is suggested that you not enter the establishment. You can carry your firearm into a restaurant that serves alcohol or a bar, but you are prohibited from consuming alcohol while carrying a firearm. [http://gunla.ws/x2bi]

L.   Open Carry

Open carry is legal for those without a valid permit/license. The state preempts all local firearm laws in the state. The minimum age for open carry is 18. Places listed in the "Criminal Provisions" above apply to those who open carry. [http://gunla.ws/s7nf]

 # KENTUCKY GUN LAWS

Introduction

Kentucky is also located in the heart of the United States. Kentucky has a population of approximately 4,400,000 residents. The long north boundary of Kentucky is the Ohio River and the states of Illinois, Indiana and Ohio. The eastern border is West Virginia and Virginia. The southern border is Tennessee, and to the west is Missouri. Open carry is legal in Kentucky even without a valid license to carry. By statute, Kentucky allows residents of other states to purchase firearms in Kentucky, and allows Kentucky residents to purchase firearms in other states, provided such sales comply with federal law.

A.   State Constitution

Regarding the right to bear arms, the Kentucky Constitution states:

"All men are, by nature, free and equal, and have certain inherent and inalienable rights, among which may be reckoned: ... 7) The right to bear arms in defense of themselves and of the State, subject to the power of the General Assembly to enact laws to prevent persons from carrying concealed weapons." [http://gunla.ws/ky1]

B.   Scope of Preemption

The controlling language of the Kentucky preemption statute is set forth as follows:

> "No city, county or urban-county government may occupy any part of the field of regulation of the transfer, ownership, possession, carrying or transportation of firearms, ammunition, or components of firearms or combination thereof."

Kentucky allows the following entities to restrict concealed carry: (1) postsecondary educational institutions; and (2) any unit of government within the state in buildings that it owns, leases, or occupies – however, concealed carry is allowed in highway rest areas, public housing, and private dwellings.

[http://gunla.ws/ky2] & [http://gunla.ws/6vya]

C.   Reciprocal Carry

By statute, Kentucky will recognize another state's license to carry if that state recognizes Kentucky's license:

> "A person who is not a resident of Kentucky and who has a valid license issued by another state of the United States to carry a concealed deadly weapon in that state may, subject to provisions of Kentucky law, carry a concealed deadly weapon in Kentucky, and his or her license shall be considered as valid in Kentucky." [http://gunla.ws/ky3]

Since there is no national carry license, as with the other states, some states are reciprocal with Kentucky and some are not. Anyone contemplating reciprocal carry should check with the official list maintained by the Kentucky State Police at the point in time the reciprocal carry is to occur. Reference Kentucky's reciprocity agreements here: [http://gunla.ws/s5rh]

242

D.   Duty to Inform Officers

Kentucky does not require individuals to inform a LEO of a permit or license to carry but if an Officer asks about a weapon, by law, an answer must be supplied. You must carry Your license at all times You are carrying a concealed firearm and You must display Your license upon request of a LEO. [http://gunla.ws/g01p]

E.   NFA Items

Kentucky permits ownership of all NFA items, provided they are legally obtained pursuant to federal law. Hunting with suppressors is legal. CLEOs are required to sign an application for the transfer of any item regulated under the NFA within 15 days if the applicant is not prohibited by law from receiving it. [http://gunla.ws/0h3j]

F.   Carrying Firearms in Vehicles

Kentucky permits anyone who is legally allowed to possess a firearm to carry it without a permit in any closed container or compartment built into the vehicle, such as the glove compartment, center console, or seat pocket. [http://gunla.ws/ky3]

G.   Self-defense Laws

Kentucky has both Castle Doctrine and SYG laws. There is no duty to retreat from any place You have a legal right to be. You may use force, including deadly force, in defense of yourself or others if You reasonably believe it is necessary to prevent imminent death, SBI, the commission of a forcible felony, or to stop the unlawful & forcible entry into a dwelling, residence, or occupied motor vehicle. [http://gunla.ws/ky4]

H.   Criminal Provisions

Under Kentucky law, a license to carry a handgun is not valid in any of the following places or circumstances, whether it was issued by Kentucky, or a person is carrying pursuant to a reciprocity between his or her state of license and Kentucky:

- Any police station or sheriff's office
- A detention facility, prison or jail
- The portion of an establishment licensed to dispense alcohol for consumption on the premises, where that part of the establishment is primarily devoted to such purpose
- A courthouse, solely occupied by the Court of Justice courtroom, or court proceeding
- A school, including elementary, secondary, or day-care facility
- Any part of an airport subject to inspection of persons and property
- Firearms may be carried openly, but not concealed, in most public buildings, including the state capitol, libraries, courthouses, and public busses
- Zoos and parks may not ban concealed carry on their premises
- Firefighters with valid carry permits can carry on the job
- Universities may ban the carrying of weapons on their premises
- The law does not prohibit the owners of private land to exclude individuals carrying firearms. Failure to leave private land when asked could result in criminal trespass charges [http://gunla.ws/s5rh]
- Any place prohibited by federal law

For a list of places where carrying a firearm is prohibited, see: [http://gunla.ws/ky5]

I.   Do "No Gun Signs" Have the Force of Law?

No. "No Firearm" signs in Kentucky do not have the force of law unless they are posted on property that is specifically mentioned in state law as being off limits to those with a permit/license to carry. However, as a possessor with a real property interest, a retailer, has the right to limit, and qualify the right to enter the property, subject to not carrying a handgun. It would be improper to enter, and the licensee would be subject to ejection for possession of a handgun thereat. Failure to leave once requested would subject the licensee to arrest for criminal trespass. [http://gunla.ws/9sdo]

J.   Carry in Restaurants That Serve Alcohol

Yes. You can carry in a restaurant that serves alcohol. Places like Fridays or Chili's unless they have a "No Gun Sign," then it is suggested that you not carry in the establishment. This does not include a bar or the bar area of a restaurant. You can carry your firearm into a restaurant that serves alcohol, but you are prohibited from consuming alcohol while carrying a firearm. [http://gunla.ws/xw3o]

K.   Open Carry

Open carry is legal in Kentucky. You may carry openly without a permit/license. The state preempts all local firearm laws in the state. The minimum age for open carry is 18. Places listed in the "Criminal Provisions" above apply to those who open carry. [http://gunla.ws/y2oo]

 # LOUISIANA
GUN LAWS

Introduction

Louisiana is in the deep south of the United States. The state is notable for the confiscation of lawfully owned firearms in the aftermath of Hurricane Katrina. This confiscation precipitated the passage by Congress of the Stafford Act, which prohibits any law enforcement agency receiving federal funds from confiscating lawfully possessed firearms in the time of declared emergency or disaster. Starting August 1, 2013, Louisiana began issuing lifetime conceal and carry permits to its residents. Open carry is generally legal in Louisiana even without a permit to carry, but may be restricted in some localities.

Louisiana is bordered by Arkansas on the north and the Gulf of Mexico to the south. Mississippi borders Louisiana on the east, and Texas is its western border. Louisiana has a population of about 4,600,000 people.

A.   State Constitution

Regarding the right to bear arms, the Louisiana Constitution states:

> "The right of each citizen to keep and bear arms is fundamental and shall not be infringed. Any restriction on this right shall be subject to strict scrutiny." [http://gunla.ws/w6s6]

B.   Scope of Preemption

The controlling language of the Louisiana preemption statute is set forth as follows:

"No governing authority of a political subdivision shall enact after July 15, 1985, any ordinance or regulation more restrictive than state law concerning in any way the sale, purchase, possession, ownership, transfer, transportation, license, or registration of firearms, ammunition, or components of firearms or ammunition; however, this Section shall not apply to the levy and collection of sales and use taxes, license fees and taxes and permit fees, nor shall it affect the authority of political subdivisions to prohibit the possession of a weapon or firearm in certain commercial establishments and public buildings."
[http://gunla.ws/la1]

C.   Reciprocal Carry

By statute, Louisiana will recognize another state's license to carry if that state recognizes Louisiana's license:

"A current and valid concealed handgun permit issued by another state to an individual having attained the age of twenty-one years shall be deemed to be valid for the out-of-state permit holder to carry a concealed weapon within this state if a current and valid concealed handgun permit issued by Louisiana is valid in those states."

Anyone contemplating reciprocal carry should check with the official list maintained by the Louisiana State Police at the point in time the reciprocal carry is to occur. Reference Louisiana's reciprocity agreements here: [http://gunla.ws/la2]

D. Duty to Inform Officers

A permittee armed with a handgun must notify a LEO who approaches the permittee in an official manner or with an identified official purpose that he has a weapon on his person, submit to a pat down, and allow the officer to temporarily disarm him. Whenever a LEO is made aware that an individual is carrying a concealed handgun and the LEO has reasonable grounds to believe that the individual is under the influence of either alcohol or a controlled dangerous substance, the LEO may take temporary take possession of the handgun and request submission of the individual to a department certified chemical test for determination of the chemical status of the individual. Whenever an officer is made aware that an individual is behaving in a criminally negligent manner, or is negligent in the carrying of a concealed handgun, the LEO may seize the handgun, until adjudication by a judge. [http://gunla.ws/t7lm]

E. NFA Items

Louisiana permits ownership of all NFA items, provided they are legally obtained pursuant to federal law. Hunting with suppressors is legal.

F. Carrying Firearms in Vehicles

Louisiana permits anyone who is legally allowed to possess a firearm to transport or store such firearm in a locked, privately-owned motor vehicle in any parking lot, parking garage, or other designated parking area. [http://gunla.ws/la3]

G.   Self-defense Laws

Louisiana has both Castle Doctrine and SYG laws. There is no duty to retreat from any place You have a legal right to be. You may use force, including deadly force, in defense of yourself or others if You reasonably believe it is necessary to prevent imminent death, SBI, the commission of a forcible felony, or to stop the unlawful & forcible entry into Your dwelling, place of business, or occupied motor vehicle. Deadly force may also be used if reasonably necessary to stop an intruder from using unlawful force against an occupant of a dwelling, business, or occupied motor vehicle in the course of a robbery.
[http://gunla.ws/la4]

H.   Criminal Provisions

Under Louisiana law, a license to carry a handgun is not valid in any of the following places or circumstances:

- On school property, a school sponsored event, or in a firearm-free zone (including within 1,000 feet of school property, any school campus, or school bus)
- While on the premises of an alcoholic beverage outlet, or any portion of an establishment selling alcoholic beverages for consumption on the premises, unless You are the owner or an employee. (There remains a conflicting statute in place that permits carry into a place that serves alcohol if it has a Class A-Restaurant permit)
- While under the influence of alcohol or a controlled dangerous substance (under the influence of alcohol is considered a blood alcohol level of .05)
- Any place banned by federal law
- A law enforcement office, station or building

- A detention facility, prison or jail
- A courthouse or courtroom
- Any polling place
- Any meeting place of a governing authority
- The state capitol building
- Any areas within an airport which carrying is prohibited by federal law (unless in a carrying case and properly prepared to be checked as luggage)
- A place of worship (church, synagogue, mosque, etc.)
- A parade or demonstration
- Any portion of an establishment selling alcoholic beverages for consumption on the premises

For a list of places where carrying a firearm is prohibited, see: [http://gunla.ws/la5]

I.   Do "No Gun Signs" Have the Force of Law?

Yes. If a property or establishment has a "No Guns" sign or the person in lawful possession communicates to you that guns are not allowed, You are prohibited from carrying on the property or into the establishment. Failure to obey such signs or verbal warnings constitutes trespass. Furthermore, no individual to whom a concealed handgun permit is issued may carry such concealed handgun into the private residence of another without first receiving the consent of that person. [http://gunla.ws/fxbn]

J.   Carry in Restaurants That Serve Alcohol

Louisiana law generally prohibits a person from intentionally carrying a firearm, openly or concealed, while on the premises of an alcoholic beverage outlet, which includes any commercial establishment in which alcoholic beverages are sold in individual servings for consumption on the premises, whether or not such sales are a primary or incidental purpose of the business of the establishment. However, this prohibition does not apply to the owner, lessee, or employee of such an outlet, to law enforcement officers, or to a person possessing a firearm in accordance with a concealed handgun permit on the premises of an alcoholic beverage outlet which has been issued a Class A-Restaurant permit. [http://gunla.ws/r570]

K.   Open Carry

Open carry is legal in Louisiana without a permit. Places listed in the "Criminal Provisions" above apply to those who open carry. The state preempts all firearm laws in the state and local authorities cannot have laws/ordinances prohibiting open carry unless such law of a local government was in place before July 15, 1985.

 **MAINE GUN LAWS**

Introduction

Maine is located along the Atlantic Coast of the U.S. and bordered by water on two sides, the south and east. New Hampshire borders Maine to the west, and Quebec and New Brunswick, Canada both border to the north. Maine has a population of about 1,300,000 and is the only state to border only one other state.

A.   State Constitution

Regarding the right to bear arms, the Maine Constitution states:

"Every citizen has a right to keep and bear arms and this right shall never be questioned." [http://gunla.ws/me1]

B.   Scope of Preemption

The controlling language of the Maine preemption statute is set forth as follows:

"The State intends to occupy and preempt the entire field of legislation concerning the regulation of firearms, components, ammunition and supplies. Except as provided in subsection 3, any existing or future order, ordinance, rule or regulation in this field of any political subdivision of the State is void." Local governments may restrict the discharge of firearms. [http://gunla.ws/me2]

C.   Reciprocal Carry

By statute, Maine will recognize another state's license to carry if that state recognizes Maine's license:

"A handgun carried by a person to whom a valid permit to carry a concealed firearm has been issued by another state if a permit to carry a concealed firearm issued from that state has been granted reciprocity. The Chief of the State Police may enter into reciprocity agreements with any other states that meet the requirements of this paragraph. Reciprocity may be granted to a permit to carry a concealed firearm issued from another state if: (1) The other state that issued the permit to carry a concealed firearm has substantially equivalent or stricter requirements for the issuance of a permit to carry a concealed firearm; and (2) The other state that issued the permit to carry a concealed firearm observes the same rules of reciprocity regarding a person issued a permit to carry a concealed firearm under this chapter" [http://gunla.ws/me3]

Since there is no national carry license, as with the other states, some states are reciprocal with Maine and some are not. Anyone contemplating reciprocal carry should check with the official list maintained by the Maine State Police at the point in time the reciprocal carry is to occur. Reference Maine's reciprocity agreements online. [http://gunla.ws/wcv6]

D.   NFA Items

Maine permits ownership of all NFA items, provided they are legally obtained pursuant to federal law. Hunting with suppressors is legal. CLEOs are required to sign an application for the transfer of any item regulated under the NFA within 15 days if the applicant is not prohibited by law from receiving it. [http://gunla.ws/qppw]

E.   Duty to Inform Officers

Maine does not require individuals to inform a LEO of a permit or license to carry unless they are carrying without a permit. If an individual carrying without a permit is stopped by a LEO, they have a duty to inform the Officer that they are carrying a firearm. Every permit holder, including a nonresident who holds a permit issued by the nonresident's state of residence, must have the holder's permit in the holder's immediate possession at all times when carrying a concealed handgun and must display the same on demand of any LEO. Those carrying under permitless carry must inform immediately. Those with a permit/license that Maine honors must present their permit/license to carry and proper identification when asked. [http://gunla.ws/jw1a] & [http://gunla.ws/rjmp]

F.   Carrying Firearms in Vehicles

Maine permits anyone who is legally allowed to possess firearms to carry them in a motor vehicle, concealed or openly. Long guns must be unloaded. If You are 21 years of age, 18 to 20 if in the military or veteran, and can legally possess a firearm, You are permitted to carry a loaded, concealed handgun on your person anywhere it is legal to carry in Maine without any type of permit/license. This includes automobiles. [http://gunla.ws/me4]

G.   Self-defense Laws

Maine has a Castle Doctrine but no SYG law. There is no duty to retreat when in Your home or place of business. You may use force, including deadly force, in defense of yourself or others

254

if You reasonably believe it is necessary to prevent imminent death, SBI, the commission of a forcible felony, arson, or to stop the unlawful entry into a dwelling or residence if You reasonably believe the intruder intends to inflict bodily injury against an occupant of the dwelling. However, if You do not reasonably believe that the intruder intends arson or bodily harm, You may use deadly force only if You first demand the intruder to terminate the criminal trespass and the trespasser fails to immediately comply with the demand. [http://gunla.ws/me5] & [http://gunla.ws/me6]

H.   Constitutional Carry

As of 10/15/15, Maine permits anyone who is at least 21 (or 18 if they are active duty military or an honorably discharged veteran) and not prohibited from owning a firearm to legally carry a handgun without a permit, openly or concealed. [http://gunla.ws/me7]

I.   Criminal Provisions

Under Maine law, a license to carry a handgun is not valid in any of the following places or circumstances:

- In any establishment licensed for consumption of liquor, if the establishment has posted a "no gun sign."
- On public school property and a person may not discharge a firearm within 500 feet of school property
- Discharging within 100 yards of a residential dwelling, absent permission by the owner or adult occupant
- Any place where federal law prohibits the carrying
- Possession while under the influence of intoxicating liquor or drugs, or both
- While in a courthouse
- State Parks

- Acadia National Park
- State Capitol area
- Wildlife Sanctuaries
- Labor disputes and strikes
- Baxter State Park
- Allagash Wilderness Waterway

For a list of places where carrying a firearm is prohibited, see: [http://gunla.ws/me8]

J.   Do "No Gun Signs" Have the Force of Law?

Yes. If a property or establishment has a "No Guns" sign or the person in lawful possession communicates to you that guns are not allowed, You are prohibited from carrying on the property or into the establishment. Failure to obey such signs or verbal warnings constitutes trespass. [http://gunla.ws/47ee]

K.   Carry in Restaurants The Serve Alcohol

Yes, if not posted. You are prohibited from carrying a concealed firearm into an establishment that is licensed for on-premises consumption of liquor and has a sign posted to prohibit or restrict the possession of firearms. Failure to comply may result in a 5-year suspension of Your eligibility to apply for a permit to carry a concealed handgun in Maine. [http://gunla.ws/y7i9]

L.   Open Carry

Open carry is legal in Maine. Places listed in the "Criminal Provisions" above apply to those who open carry. Open carry is prohibited in State Parks and in the Allagash Wilderness Waterway. The state preempts all firearm laws in the state and local authorities cannot have laws/ordinances against open carry.

256

Remember that if you enter any property and the owner/responsible person asks you to leave, you must leave. Failure to leave can result in trespass charges. The minimum age for open carry is 18.

 **MARYLAND GUN LAWS**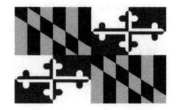

Introduction

Maryland is surrounded by Virginia, West Virginia, and the District of Columbia to the south and west and by Pennsylvania to the north and Delaware to the east. Maryland is a small state, comparable in size to Hawaii, the next smallest state. However, Maryland has the 19th largest population in the United States with over 6,000,000 residents. Open carry is legal in Maryland with a valid license to carry. The Firearm Safety Act 2013 was enacted to ban 45 different semi-automatic handguns and rifles from sale and ownership within the state. [http://gunla.ws/afns]

A.   State Constitution

Maryland has no "right to bear arms" granted in its constitution. [http://gunla.ws/md1]

B.   Scope of Preemption

The controlling language of the Maryland preemption statute is set forth as follows:

"Except as otherwise provided in this section, the State preempts the right of a county, municipal corporation, or special taxing district to regulate the purchase, sale, taxation, transfer, manufacture, repair, ownership, possession, and transportation of: (1) a handgun, rifle, or shotgun; and (2) ammunition for and components of a handgun, rifle, or shotgun." [http://gunla.ws/md2]

C. Reciprocal Carry

Maryland does not have a statutory reciprocity provision and does not recognize permits issued in any other state.

D. Assault Weapons Ban

It is illegal to possess an assault weapon, unless it was possessed before October 1, 2013 or the individual received a certificate of possession from the Maryland State Police prior to October 1, 2013. Assault weapons may not be sold or transferred to any person other than a licensed gun dealer or any individual who is going to relinquish it to the police.

Under Maryland's Firearms Safety Act, certain models of firearms are banned as assault pistols and assault long guns. It is illegal to possess an assault weapon or a copycat weapon with two or more specified features (folding stock, grenade/flare launcher, or flash suppressor) unless owned before October 1, 2013, or received through inheritance from a lawful possessor and not otherwise forbidden to possess. [http://gunla.ws/kl5i]

E. Universal Background Checks

Maryland requires that all sales and transfers of handguns or assault weapons, even between private parties, go through a FFL who must conduct a background check. Background checks are not required for private sales of long guns. [http://gunla.ws/gpgi]

F. Permit to Purchase Handguns

As of 10/1/13, Maryland requires a permit in order to

purchase handguns. You must pass a background check and complete a 4-hour safety course in order to obtain a permit to purchase handguns. Active duty or retired law enforcement officers or military members are exempt from this law and may purchase handguns without obtaining this permit. [http://gunla.ws/m1im]

G.   NFA Items

Maryland permits ownership of automatic firearms, SBSs, and SBRs, provided they are legally obtained pursuant to federal law. The law is still silent in regards to DDs and AOWs. MGs must be registered with the Secretary of State Police within 24 hours of acquisition, and must be re-registered annually. Hunting with suppressors is legal.

H.   High-Capacity Magazine Ban

Maryland bans the intrastate manufacture, sale, and transfer of magazines capable of holding more than 10 rounds. Note that possession of high-capacity magazines is legal, and Maryland residents can possess high-capacity magazines they lawfully owned before 10/1/13. Maryland residents can also purchase or import high-capacity magazines from out of state. These may not, however, be transferred to a subsequent owner unless done so outside the state of Maryland.

I.   Waiting Period

Maryland imposes a seven (7) day waiting period before purchasing any firearm other than a rifle or shotgun. [http://gunla.ws/wsge]

J.   Carrying Firearms in Vehicles

It is illegal to carry any loaded firearm in any vehicle in Maryland, regardless of whether You have a permit. Maryland generally bans the carrying of firearms without a permit. Someone without a permit may only transport a handgun if it is unloaded and secured in an enclosed case or holster, and may only transport the handgun to or from: the place of purchase or repair, Your home or business, a shooting range, shooting event, or hunting activity. [http://gunla.ws/md4]

K.   Self-defense Laws

Maryland does not have a Castle Doctrine or SYG law, however Maryland courts have consistently recognized a right of self-defense similar to a castle doctrine law. Because there is no statute to explain when the use of deadly force is appropriate, there is uncertainty over the details of when deadly force may be used, and Maryland only allows the use of deadly force in narrow circumstances. There is no duty to retreat when in Your home. You may use force, including deadly force, in defense of yourself or others if You reasonably believe it is necessary to prevent imminent death or SBI. [http://gunla.ws/db8q]

L.   Duty to Inform Officer

No. A person to whom a permit is issued or renewed shall carry the permit in the person's possession whenever the person carries, wears, or transports a handgun. You must present Your permit on demand. [http://gunla.ws/j7zk]

M.   Criminal Provisions

A Maryland-issued license to carry a handgun is not valid

in any of the following places or circumstances:

- On any kind of public school property
- At demonstrations in a public place or in a vehicle that is within 1,000 feet of a demonstration in a public place
- State parks
- State/national forests
- In legislative buildings
- In/on State public buildings and grounds
- State Highway Rest Areas

For a list of places where carrying a firearm is prohibited, see: [http://gunla.ws/md5]

N.   Carry in Restaurants That Serve Alcohol

Yes. Maryland has no laws prohibiting the carrying of firearms in restaurants that serve alcohol. You can carry in a restaurant that serves alcohol. Places like Fridays or Chili's unless they have a "No Gun Sign," then You are prohibited from carrying into the establishment. This does not include a bar or the bar area of a restaurant. You can carry your firearm into a restaurant that serves alcohol, but you are prohibited from consuming alcohol while carrying a firearm.

O.   Open Carry

There is no statute in Maryland law that prohibits a Maryland license holder from carrying a handgun openly. Places listed in the "Criminal Provisions" above apply to those who open carry. The minimum age for open carry is 18.

Pending Court case:

Note that on 2/4/16 a federal court cast doubt on the constitutionality of Maryland's ban on assault weapons and high-capacity magazines, suggesting that these items may be protected by the Second Amendment, and that the government has a high burden to prove that these laws are constitutional. However, the 4th Circuit Court of Appeals recently overturned the 2016 federal court decision. Unless and until the U.S. Supreme Court rules otherwise, Maryland's Firearms Safety Act remains in force.

MASSACHUSETTS
GUN LAWS

Introduction

Massachusetts is officially known as the Commonwealth of Massachusetts and is located in the New England area of the United States. Rhode Island and Connecticut border it to the south, with Vermont and New Hampshire bordering on the north. New York borders on the west, and the Atlantic Ocean borders on the east. Massachusetts has a rich history; Plymouth Colony was formed on its lands. It was also home to the Salem Witch Trials. Open carry is legal in Massachusetts with a valid license to carry, but is frowned upon by local authorities.

A.   State Constitution

Regarding the right to bear arms, the Massachusetts Constitution states:

> "The people have a right to keep and to bear arms for the common defense. And as, in time of peace, armies are dangerous to liberty, they ought not to be maintained without the consent of the legislature; and the military power shall always be held in an exact subordination to the civil authority, and be governed by it."
> [http://gunla.ws/ma1]

B.   Scope of Preemption

Massachusetts does not have a preemption clause.

C.   Reciprocal Carry

Massachusetts does not recognize another state's license to carry. A permit is required in order to purchase a firearm, and You must pass a background check to obtain this permit. A nonresident may apply for a temporary license:

> "A Class A or Class B temporary license to carry firearms or feeding devices or ammunition therefor, within the commonwealth, may be issued by the colonel of state police, or persons authorized by him, to a nonresident or any person not falling within the jurisdiction of a local licensing authority or to an alien that resides outside the commonwealth for purposes of firearms competition and subject to such terms and conditions as said colonel may deem proper" [http://gunla.ws/ma2]

Class A and Class B licenses are defined as:

> "A Class A license shall entitle a holder thereof to purchase, rent, lease, borrow, possess and carry: (i) firearms, including large capacity firearms, and feeding devices and ammunition therefor, for all lawful purposes... and (ii) rifles and shotguns, including large capacity weapons, and feeding devices and ammunition therefor"; And
> "A Class B license shall entitle a holder thereof to purchase, rent, lease, borrow, possess and carry: (i) non-large capacity firearms and feeding devices and ammunition therefor" [http://gunla.ws/ma3]

D. High-Capacity Magazine Ban

Massachusetts bans the sale, transfer, and possession of high-capacity magazines unless they were legally owned on or before 9/13/94, and You have a class A or class B license. High-capacity magazines are defined as those capable of holding more than ten (10) rounds or more than five (5) shotgun shells. Internal tube/helical magazines for .22 firearms are not considered high-capacity magazines, even if capable of holding more than 10 rounds.

E. NFA Items

The only NFA items allowed in Massachusetts are SBR, SBS, MGs, AOWs and DDs., provided they are legally obtained pursuant to federal law and comply with MA's assault weapons ban. SBRs, SBSs and AOWs must have proper approval from the ATF(E). A state license is needed to own a MG, and some localities prohibit DDs. Suppressors are permitted only for LEOs or licensed manufacturers. [http://gunla.ws/3ryl]

F. Assault Weapons Ban

Massachusetts bans the sale, transfer, and possession of assault weapons, unless they were legally possessed before 7/13/94.

The definitions for "Assault Weapon", "Large Capacity Feeding Device" (magazine), and "Large Capacity Weapon" can be found at the following hyperlink: [http://gunla.ws/ma4]

"Large Capacity Weapons" are more available than "Assault Weapons" and may still be manufactured, sold, and owned, but they require a Class A license to obtain, and there are additional regulations governing how You may transport them.

G.   Universal Background checks

Massachusetts requires background checks be conducted on all sales of firearms, even between private parties. [http://gunla.ws/c0i0]

H.   Carrying Firearms in Vehicles

Massachusetts generally prohibits carrying firearms in vehicles without a permit. Handguns may not be carried in vehicles without a permit. Long guns may only be carried without a permit if they are unloaded and secured in a locked container. Large Capacity Weapons may only be carried if they are unloaded and contained within the locked trunk of the vehicle or in a locked case or other secure container. [http://gunla.ws/ma5]

I.   Self-defense Laws

Massachusetts has a Castle Doctrine but no SYG law. There is no duty to retreat when in Your home or place of business. You may use force, including deadly force, in defense of yourself or others if You reasonably believe it is necessary to prevent imminent death, SBI, or against an unlawful intruder into Your dwelling if You reasonably believe the intruder is about to inflict death or SBI to a lawful occupant of the dwelling. [http://gunla.ws/ma6]

J.   Duty to Inform Officer

No. You must have your license to carry with You at all times when You carry a concealed firearm in Massachusetts. Upon demand from a LEO, You must display your license. Failure to do so may result in forfeiture of Your firearm. [http://gunla.ws/lg44]

K. Criminal Provisions

Under Massachusetts law, a license to carry a handgun is not valid in any of the following places or circumstances:

- Class B licensee cannot carry a concealed and loaded firearm in a public place, or possess a firearm as defined by the Class A license statute [http://gunla.ws/ja48]
- While under the influence of intoxicating liquor, marijuana, narcotic drugs, depressants, stimulant substances, or the vapors of glue [http://gunla.ws/ma7]
- One may not discharge a firearm within 500 feet of a dwelling or other building in use, except with the consent of the owner or legal occupant
- While carrying a concealed weapon, one cannot occupy, or attempt to enter or occupy, a secure area of an airport or the cabin of an airplane
- On 3/21/16 the Supreme Court unanimously struck down MA's ban on stun guns as a violation of the Second Amendment. Stun guns are now legal in MA.

For a list of places where carrying a firearm is prohibited, see: [http://gunla.ws/ma8]

L. Do "No Gun Signs" Have the Force of Law?

No. "No Firearm" signs in Massachusetts do not have the force of law unless they are posted on property that is specifically mentioned in State law as being off limits to those with a permit/license to carry. However, as a possessor with a real property interest, a retailer, has the right to limit, and qualify the right to enter the property, subject to not carrying a handgun. It would be improper to enter, and the licensee would be subject to ejection for possession of a handgun threat. Failure to leave once requested would subject the licensee to arrest for criminal trespass.

M.   Carry in Restaurants That Serve Alcohol

Yes. Massachusetts has no laws prohibiting the carrying of firearms in restaurants that serve alcohol. You can carry in a restaurant that serves alcohol. Places like Fridays or Chili's unless they have a "No Gun Sign," then it is suggested that You not carry into the establishment. This does not include a bar or the bar area of a restaurant. You can carry Your firearm into a restaurant that serves alcohol, but You are prohibited from consuming alcohol while carrying a firearm.

N.   Open Carry

You are allowed to carry handguns openly. An individual with a Class A unrestricted license to carry firearms (LTC-A) does not have to conceal a handgun in public. In 2013, the Massachusetts Supreme Judicial Court ruled that the holder of a LTC-A license is not responsible for alarm caused by licensed carry of a handgun, and that a permit cannot be revoked for suitability purposes under these circumstances. If police demand to see the permit, it must be produced. Failure to produce a LTC upon demand by a LEO is probable cause for arrest. Open carry of long guns is prohibited, except while hunting.

 **MICHIGAN GUN LAWS**

Introduction

Michigan is found in the Great Lakes Region of the U.S., and is bordered to the north by four of the five Great Lakes. Indiana and Ohio border Michigan to the south, with water separating Michigan from Canada on the east side and Wisconsin to the west. Michigan has a large tourist economy, and is known for its involvement in the car industry. Open carry of a handgun is legal in Michigan even without a valid license to carry.

A.   State Constitution

Regarding the right to bear arms, the Michigan Constitution states:

"Every person has a right to keep and bear arms for the defense of himself and the state." [http://gunla.ws/mi1]

B.   Scope of Preemption

The controlling language of the Michigan preemption statute is set forth as follows:

"A local unit of government shall not impose special taxation on, enact or enforce any ordinance or regulation pertaining to, or regulate in any other manner the ownership, registration, purchase, sale, transfer, transportation, or possession of pistols or other firearms, ammunition for pistols or other firearms, or components of pistols or other firearms, except as otherwise provided by federal law or a law of this state." [http://gunla.ws/mi2]

C.   Reciprocal Carry

By statute, Michigan will recognize another state's license to carry if that state has a licensing scheme, which is consistent with Michigan's:

"An individual who is not a resident of this state is not required to obtain a license under this section if all of the following conditions apply: (a) The individual is licensed in his or her state of residence to purchase, carry, or transport a pistol. (b) The individual is in possession of the license described in subdivision (a). (c) The individual is the owner of the pistol he or she possesses, carries, or transports. (d) The individual possesses the pistol for a lawful purpose … (e) The individual is in this state for a period of 180 days or less and does not intend to establish residency in this state." [http://gunla.ws/mi3]

D.   Duty to Inform Officer

Yes. When stopped or approached by a LEO, Michigan requires all individuals possessing a firearm to inform the LEO of that fact immediately. This is true for passengers in a vehicle as well. When carrying a concealed firearm, you must have your license/permit with you at all times. [http://gunla.ws/3t3j]

E.   NFA Items

Michigan permits ownership of all NFA items, provided they are legally obtained pursuant to federal law, but imposes additional state regulations. SBR and SBS with an overall length under 26" are considered pistols in MI, and are subject to the same rules as pistols, including a requirement that they be registered with the state police. Hunting with suppressors is legal.

F.   Carrying Firearms in Vehicles

Michigan generally prohibits carrying firearms in vehicles without a permit. Someone without a permit may only carry a firearm in their vehicle if it is unloaded and secured in a locked container in an area of the car that is not readily accessible (such as the trunk). [http://gunla.ws/mi4]

G.   Self-defense Laws

Michigan has both Castle Doctrine and SYG laws. There is no duty to retreat from any place You have a legal right to be. You may use force, including deadly force, in defense of yourself or others if You reasonably believe it is necessary to prevent imminent death, SBI, rape, or to stop the unlawful & forcible entry into a dwelling or business, or to stop an aggressor from removing another person from a dwelling, business or occupied motor vehicle against their will. [http://gunla.ws/mi5]

H.   Criminal Provisions

Under Michigan law, a license to carry a handgun is not valid in any of the following places or circumstances:

- A nonresident carrying a concealed weapon pursuant to another state's license must present the license upon demand of a police officer
- A school or school property (A parent or legal guardian may carry a concealed weapon while in his or her

vehicle while on school property, if the vehicle is on school grounds for the purpose of picking up or dropping off his or her child from school.)

- A public or private child care center, day care center, or child-placing agency
- Any place where the owner of the property verbally states that guns are not allowed on the property
- A sports arena, stadium, or other large entertainment facility (with a seating capacity of 2,500 or more)
- A bar or tavern licensed where liquor is sold and consumed on the premises
- On the property of a church, synagogue, mosque, temple, or other place of worship (unless the presiding official permit carrying on that property)
- A hospital
- In a dormitory or classroom of a community college, college, or university.
- A permit is required in order to purchase a handgun, and You must pass a background check to obtain this permit

For a list of places where carrying a firearm is prohibited, see: [http://gunla.ws/mi6]

I.   Do "No Gun Signs" Have the Force of Law?

No. "No Firearm" signs in Michigan do not have the force of law unless they are posted on property that is specifically mentioned in State Law as being off limits to those with a permit/license to carry. However, as a possessor with a real property interest, a retailer, has the right to limit, and qualify the right to enter the property, subject to not carrying a handgun. It would be improper to enter, and the licensee would be subject to ejection for possession of a handgun threat. Failure to leave once requested would subject the licensee to arrest for criminal trespass.

J.   Carry in Restaurants That Serve Alcohol

Yes. Michigan has no laws prohibiting the carrying of firearms in restaurants that serve alcohol. You can carry in a restaurant that serves alcohol. Places like Fridays or Chili's unless they have a "No Guns" sign, then it is suggested that You not carry into the establishment. This does not include the bar or bar area of a restaurant. You can carry Your firearm into a restaurant that serves alcohol, but You are prohibited from consuming alcohol while carrying a firearm. [http://gunla.ws/7zuy]

K.   Open Carry

Open carry is legal with restrictions. You must have a valid permit/license to carry a loaded handgun in a vehicle in Michigan. For residents of Michigan without a CPL, You must carry a firearm registered to You. For non-residents, if You do not have a permit/license from Your state of residence, concealed and/or open carry is prohibited. Those who open carry without a valid permit/license to carry cannot carry on the property of businesses that sell alcohol and this includes grocery stores that sell alcohol. [http://gunla.ws/5b8p]

MINNESOTA GUN LAWS

Introduction

Minnesota is nicknamed the Land of 10,000 Lakes and is found in the Midwest of the United States. As the second northernmost state (second only to Alaska), Minnesota is bordered to the north by Canada, North and South Dakota to the west, Iowa to the south, and Wisconsin to the east. Minnesota makes up almost 2.25% of the entire area of the United States. Open carry is legal in Minnesota with a valid license to carry.

A.   State Constitution

The Minnesota Constitution does not have a provision for the right to bear arms. [http://gunla.ws/mn1]

B.   Scope of Preemption

The controlling language of the Minnesota preemption statute is set forth as follows:

> "The legislature preempts all authority of a home rule charter or statutory city including a city of the first class, county, town, municipal corporation, or other governmental subdivision, or any of their instrumentalities, to regulate firearms, ammunition, or their respective components to the complete exclusion of any order, ordinance or regulation by them except that:

(a) a governmental subdivision may regulate the discharge of firearms; and

(b) a governmental subdivision may adopt regulations identical to state law.

Local regulation inconsistent with this section is void." [http://gunla.ws/mn2]

C.   Reciprocal Carry

Minnesota will recognize another state's license to carry, at the discretion of the Commissioner of Public Safety. [http://gunla.ws/mnrc]

D.   Duty to Inform Officer

Minnesota does not require individuals to inform a LEO of a permit or license to carry by state law, but some municipalities and localities do have such a requirement. The holder of a permit to carry must have a permit card and a driver's license, state identification card, or other government-issued photo identification in immediate possession at all times when carrying a pistol and must display the permit card and identification document upon lawful demand by a LEO. [http://gunla.ws/cmlw]

E.   NFA Items

Minnesota permits ownership of all NFA items, provided they are legally obtained pursuant to federal law, but imposes additional state regulations. MGs and SBRs are only legal if they count as curio & relics, and You must register them with the state within 10 days of acquisition. Some destructive devices are prohibited in most cases. Hunting with suppressors is legal. Persons

18 and older may purchase assault weapons with a permit to purchase (or permit to carry for persons 21 and older). [http://gunla.ws/tjxp] & [http://gunla.ws/dqzu]

F.   Carrying Firearms in Vehicles

Minnesota allows the transportation of firearms in a motor vehicle if the gun is unloaded and either: 1) in a gun case made to contain the firearm, and the case fully encloses the firearm by being zipped, snapped, buckled, tied or otherwise fastened, without any portion of the gun exposed; or 2) in the closed trunk. [http://gunla.ws/mn3]

G.   Self-defense Laws

Minnesota has a Castle Doctrine but no SYG law. There is no duty to retreat when in Your home or place of business. You may use force, including deadly force, in defense of yourself or others if You reasonably believe it is necessary to prevent imminent death, SBI, or the commission of a forcible felony within Your dwelling. [http://gunla.ws/mn4]

H.   Criminal Provisions

Under Minnesota law, a license to carry a handgun is not valid in any of the following places or circumstances:

- Possession or storage of a firearm while knowingly on school property, including:
  - A public or private elementary, middle, or secondary school (whether leased or owned by the school)
  - A child care center while children are present and participating in the child care program

- A school bus when that bus is being used by a school to transport one or more students to and from school-related activities (which includes curricular and extracurricular activities)

- It be a felony to recklessly discharge a firearm from a motor vehicle [http://gunla.ws/uu8n]
- Private property if no gun sign is posted or requested to leave by owner, except employees may keep a firearm in their car on the parking lot of their employer
- Churches if they have a ban on firearms in the building and parking lot
- Authorities are prohibited from confiscating firearms during states of emergency
- Any correctional facility or state hospital
- In a public place while under the influence of alcohol, a controlled substance, or a combination thereof
- Minnesota residents may now purchase firearms in any state so long as the purchase is permitted by federal law and the law of that state

For a list of places where carrying a firearm is prohibited, see: [http://gunla.ws/mn5]

Under Minnesota law, a license to carry a handgun is valid in the following exceptions:

- That portion of a building or facility under the temporary, exclusive control of a public or private school, a school district, or an association of such entities where conspicuous signs are prominently posted at each entrance that give actual notice to persons of the school-related use
- The above does not apply to:

- Active licensed peace officers;
- Military personnel or students participating in military training, who are on-duty, performing official duties;
- Persons authorized to carry a pistol under section 624.714 while in a motor vehicle or outside of a motor vehicle to directly place a firearm in, or retrieve it from, the trunk or rear area of the vehicle;
- Persons who keep or store in a motor vehicle pistols in accordance with section 624.714 or 624.715 or other firearms in accordance with section 97B.045;
- Firearm safety or marksmanship courses or activities conducted on school property;
- Possession of dangerous weapons, BB guns, or replica firearms by a ceremonial color guard;
- A gun or knife show held on school property;
- Possession of dangerous weapons, BB guns, or replica firearms with written permission of the principal or other person having general control and supervision of the school or the director of a child care center; or
- Persons who are on unimproved property owned or leased by a child care center, school, or school district unless the person knows that a student is currently present on the land for a school-related activity [http://gunla.ws/60966]

I.   Waiting Period

Minnesota imposes a seven (7) day waiting period before purchasing a handgun or assault weapon. This waiting period is waived for people who possess a valid Minnesota carry license. [http://gunla.ws/5zvn]

J.   Do "No Gun Signs" Have the Force of Law?

No. "No Firearm" signs in Minnesota do not have the force of law unless they are posted on property that is specifically mentioned in State law as being off limits to those with a permit/license to carry. However, as a possessor with a real property interest, a retailer, has the right to limit, and qualify the right to enter the property, subject to not carrying a handgun. It would be improper to enter, and the licensee would be subject to ejection for possession of a handgun thereat. Failure to leave once requested would subject the licensee to criminal charges. [http://gunla.ws/gevj]

K.   Carry in Restaurants That Serve Alcohol

Yes. Minnesota has no laws prohibiting the carrying of firearms in restaurants that serve alcohol. You can carry in a restaurant that serves alcohol. Places like Fridays or Chili's unless they have a "No Gun Sign," then it is suggested that You not carry into the establishment. This does not include a bar or the bar area of a restaurant. You can carry your firearm into a restaurant that serves alcohol, but you are prohibited from consuming alcohol while carrying a firearm.

L.   Open Carry (Without a Valid Permit/License)

Open carry is legal in Minnesota but you must have a valid permit/license to carry openly. Places as listed in the "Criminal Provisions" above apply to those who open carry. The state preempts all firearm laws in the state and local authorities cannot have laws/ordinances against open carry. Remember that if you enter any property and the owner/responsible person asks You to leave, You must leave. Failure to leave can result in trespass charges.

Whoever carries a BB gun, rifle, or shotgun on or about their person in a public place is guilty of a gross misdemeanor, unless they have a license/permit. A person under the age of 21 who carries a semiautomatic military-style assault weapon on or about their person in public is guilty of a felony. [http://gunla.ws/fude]

MISSISSIPPI GUN LAWS

Introduction

Mississippi is located in the Southern United States. Alabama borders Mississippi to the east, with Tennessee bordering on the north. Louisiana borders to the south, and the Gulf of Mexico to the west. Mississippi is made up heavily of trees and forests. Open carry is legal in Mississippi even without a valid license to carry.

A. State Constitution

Regarding the right to bear arms, the Mississippi Constitution states:

> "The right of every citizen to keep and bear arms in defense of his home, person, or property, or in aid of the civil power when thereto legally summoned, shall not be called in question, but the legislature may regulate or forbid carrying concealed weapons." [http://gunla.ws/ms1]

B. Scope of Preemption

The controlling language of the Mississippi preemption statute is set forth as follows:

> "[s]ubject to the provisions of Section 45-9-53, no county or municipality may adopt any ordinance that restricts the

282

possession, carrying, transportation, sale, transfer or ownership of firearms or ammunition or their components."

Counties and Municipalities may adopt some regulations governing the discharge of firearms, or the carrying of firearms in local parks and government buildings. [http://gunla.ws/ms2]

C.   Reciprocal Carry

By statute, Mississippi will recognize another state's license to carry if that state recognizes Mississippi's license:

"Mississippi recognizes valid, unrevoked and unexpired license to carry stun guns, concealed pistols, or revolvers issued in other states. Also, the Department of Public Safety is authorized to enter into reciprocal agreements with other states if those states require a written agreement for reciprocity. Mississippi has written reciprocity agreements with the following states: Alabama, Alaska, Arizona, Arkansas, Colorado, Connecticut, Florida, Georgia, Idaho, Indiana, Iowa, Kansas, Kentucky, Louisiana, Maine, Michigan, Minnesota, Missouri, Montana, Nebraska, Nevada, New Hampshire, New Mexico, North Carolina, North Dakota, Ohio, Oklahoma, Oregon, Pennsylvania, Rhode Island, South Carolina, South Dakota, Tennessee, Texas, Utah, Virginia, Washington, West Virginia, Wisconsin, Wyoming."

.

Mississippi Law § 97-37-1 (2) states:

"It shall not be a violation of this section for any person over the age of eighteen (18) to carry a firearm or deadly weapon concealed in whole or in part within the confines of his own home or his place of business, or any real property

283

associated with his home or business or within any motor vehicle.

If You will be traveling on the Natchez Trace Federal Parkway, please contact them directly at (662)842-1572 for their rules & regulation on transporting Your firearm."

Anyone contemplating reciprocal carry should check with the current official list maintained by the Mississippi Department of Public Safety at the point in time the reciprocal carry is to occur. [http://gunla.ws/ms3]

D.   NFA Items

Mississippi permits ownership of all NFA items, provided they are legally obtained pursuant to federal law. Hunting with suppressors is legal.

E.   Carrying Firearms in Vehicles

Mississippi permits anyone who may legally possess a firearm to carry it in a motor vehicle without a permit, openly or concealed. [http://gunla.ws/ms4]

F.   Self-defense Laws

Mississippi has both Castle Doctrine and SYG laws. There is no duty to retreat from any place You have a legal right to be. You may use force, including deadly force, in defense of yourself or others if You reasonably believe it is necessary to prevent imminent death, SBI, the commission of a forcible felony, or to stop the commission of any felony against You, upon or in any dwelling, in any occupied vehicle, in any place of business. [http://gunla.ws/ms5]

G. Constitutional Carry

As of 4/15/16, Mississippi permits anyone who is at least 21 years old and not prohibited from owning firearms to carry a handgun without a permit, openly or concealed. [http://gunla.ws/ms6]

H. Criminal Provisions

Mississippi citizens are eligible for an enhanced permit, which requires different criteria to be met to obtain the license. These permit holders can carry firearms in specialized locations. [http://gunla.ws/qs3v] Under Mississippi law, a license to carry a handgun is not valid in any of the following places or circumstances, whether it is issued by Mississippi, or a person is carrying pursuant to a reciprocity agreement between his or her state of license and Mississippi:

- Possessing or carrying a firearm of any kind on educational property
- Exhibiting a firearm in a rude, angry, or threatening manner in the presence of three or more persons, which is not in necessary self-defense
- A police, sheriff or highway patrol station
- A detention facility, prison or jail
- A courthouse or courtroom
- A polling place
- Any meeting place of the governing body of any governmental entity
- A school, including:
  - Elementary or secondary school facilities
  - A junior college, community college, college or university facility

- A school, college or professional athletic event not related to firearms
- An establishment dispensing alcoholic beverages for consumption on the premises
- Inside the passenger terminal of any airport (unless it is encased for shipment, and checking as baggage)
- A church or other place of worship
- Where carrying is prohibited by federal law
- Any place where notice is posted prohibiting firearms [http://gunla.ws/msfp]

For a list of places where carrying firearms is prohibited, see: [http://gunla.ws/ms7]

I.   Duty to Inform Officer

No. The licensee must carry the license, together with valid identification, at all times in which the licensee is carrying a stun gun, concealed pistol or revolver and must display both the license and proper identification upon demand by a LEO. [http://gunla.ws/1rw8]

J.   Do "No Gun Signs" Have the Force of Law?

Yes, for both non-enhanced permit holders and enhanced permit holders. If a property or establishment has a "No Guns" sign or the person in lawful possession communicates to you that guns are not allowed, You are prohibited from carrying on the property or into the establishment. Failure to obey such signs or verbal warnings constitutes trespass. [http://gunla.ws/vvcf]

K.   Carry in Restaurants That Serve Alcohol

Yes. Mississippi has no laws prohibiting the carrying of

firearms in restaurants that serve alcohol. You can carry in a restaurant that serves alcohol. Places like Fridays or Chili's unless they have a "No Gun Sign," then You are prohibited from carrying a firearm into the establishment. This does not include a bar or the bar area of a restaurant – You are prohibited from carrying into these areas. You can carry Your firearm into a restaurant that serves alcohol, but you are prohibited from consuming alcohol while carrying a firearm.

L.   Open Carry

You can open carry in Mississippi without any type of permit/license. Places as listed in the "Criminal Provisions" above would apply to those who open carry. Remember that if You enter any property and the owner/responsible person asks You to leave, You must leave. Failure to leave can result in trespass charges. The minimum age for open carry is 18. [http://gunla.ws/mtfz]

MISSOURI GUN LAWS

Introduction

Missouri is bordered by eight states including: Arkansas, Iowa, Illinois, Kansas, Kentucky, Nebraska, Oklahoma, and Tennessee. It is located in the Midwest and has the 18th largest population of the United States. Open carry is legal in Missouri with a valid license to carry.

A.   State Constitution

Regarding the right to bear arms, the Missouri Constitution states:

> "That the right of every citizen to keep and bear arms in defense of his home, person and property, or when lawfully summoned in aid of the civil power, shall not be questioned; but this shall not justify the wearing of concealed weapons." [http://gunla.ws/mo1]

B.   Scope of Preemption

The controlling language of the Missouri preemption statute is set forth as follows:

> "The general assembly hereby occupies and preempts the entire field of legislation touching in any way firearms, components, ammunition and supplies to the complete exclusion of any order, ordinance or regulation by any

political subdivision of this state. Any existing or future orders, ordinances or regulations in this field are hereby and shall be null and void." [http://gunla.ws/mo2]

C.   Reciprocal Carry

At present, Missouri's concealed carry law recognizes all out-of-state licenses. Mo. Rev. Stat. §§ 571.010 to 571.510. Nevertheless, not all states recognize Missouri's license. You can apply for a Missouri carry license at age 19. [http://gunla.ws/mo3]

D.   Constitutional Carry

Missouri law does not plainly state that you do not need a permit to carry. The definition of "Unlawful use of a weapon" was changed to only apply when a person carries a weapon into a place that is off limits according to Missouri law. Anyone who is at least 19 years old may legally possess a firearm without a permit, openly or concealed. This is not limited to Missouri residents. Anyone who can legally possess a firearm may carry it openly or concealed, except where firearms are restricted under section 571.107. [http://gunla.ws/0vyk]

E.   NFA Items

Missouri permits ownership of all NFA items except for destructive devices, provided they are legally obtained pursuant to federal law. Hunting with suppressors is legal.

F.   Carrying Firearms in Vehicles

Missouri permits anyone who is legally allowed to possess a firearm to carry it without a permit as long as it is not readily accessible, or unloaded (provided the ammunition is not readily accessible). [http://gunla.ws/mo4]

G. Self-defense Laws

Missouri has a Castle Doctrine but no SYG law. There is no duty to retreat when in Your home or motor vehicle. You may use force, including deadly force, in defense of yourself or others if You reasonably believe it is necessary to prevent imminent death, SBI, the commission of a forcible felony, or to stop the unlawful & forcible entry into Your dwelling, place of business, or occupied motor vehicle. [http://gunla.ws/hcpu]

H. Criminal Provisions

In accordance with Mo. Rev. Stat. § 571.107, a person may not carry a concealed weapon (including firearm) in any of the following places, some of which may involve consent:

- Any police, sheriff or Highway Patrol office or station, without consent
- Within 25 feet of any polling place or station on Election Day
- Any adult or juvenile jail or institution
- Any courthouse or facilities related to courts
- Any meeting of a government body
- Any bar, tavern, or the like, without consent
- Airports except as allowed by law, such as commercial transportation in checked baggage
- Schools
- Child care facilities, without consent
- Riverboat gambling facility
- Any gated area of an amusement park
- Public Buses
- Any church or place of worship, without consent

- Any sports arena or stadium (with seating for more than 5,000)
- Any hospital accessible by the public
- Private or public property where posted. Note that cities and localities do not have the authority to ban open carry.
- Specially trained school employees and teacher with carry permits can carry on their school's campus

However, possession of a firearm in a vehicle on the premises of any of these locations is permitted so long as the firearm is not removed from the vehicle or brandished while in the vehicle on the premises. As a general rule, carrying a concealed firearm in these locations is not a criminal act. However, You may be denied access to these places or removed for doing so. If a police officer is summoned, there is increasingly more sanction for violation.

It is unlawful for any person to discharge a firearm while intoxicated, except in self-defense. [http://gunla.ws/mocwl]

For a list of places where carrying firearms is prohibited, see: [http://gunla.ws/mo6]

I.   Duty to Inform Officer

No. Any person issued a CCP or a concealed carry endorsement issued prior to August 28, 2013, must carry the CCP or endorsement at all times the person is carrying a concealed firearm and must display the CCP and a state or federal government-issued photo identification or the endorsement or permit upon request of any LEO. [http://gunla.ws/h13m]

J.   Do "No Gun Signs" Have the Force of Law?

Yes/No, but such signs have no penalty unless You refuse to leave or repeat the offense in a set time period. Carrying into an establishment that is not prohibited in the "Criminal Provisions" but has a "no gun" sign is not a criminal act, but may subject the individual to denial to the premises or removal from the premises. If such person refuses to leave the premises and a LEO is summoned, such person may be issued a citation for up to $100 for the first offense. If a second citation is issued for a similar violation occurring within a six-month period, such person shall be fined up to $200 or his or her CCP shall be suspended for one year. If a third citation is issued within one year of the first citation, such person shall be fined up to $500 and have their CCP revoked and will not be eligible for a CCP for three years. [http://gunla.ws/qxas]

K.   Carry in Restaurants That Serve Alcohol

Yes, subject to the "No Gun Signs" provision above. Missouri has no laws prohibiting the carrying of firearms in restaurants that serve alcohol. You can carry in a restaurant that serves alcohol. Places like Fridays or Chili's unless they have a "No Gun Sign." This does not include a bar or the bar area of a restaurant – You are prohibited from carrying into these areas. You can carry your firearm into a restaurant that serves alcohol, but you are prohibited from consuming alcohol while carrying a firearm. [http://gunla.ws/t1ja]

L.   Open Carry

Open Carry is legal with a valid permit/license. Places as listed in the "Criminal Provisions" above would apply to those who open carry. Remember that if you enter any property and the owner/responsible person asks you to leave, you must leave. Failure to leave can result in trespass charges. As of October 11, 2014, a valid CCW overrides local laws against open carry, state wide. [http://gunla.ws/z2zh] & [http://gunla.ws/dphq]

MONTANA
GUN
LAWS

Montana is the fourth-largest state and is surrounded by Canada to the north, North and South Dakota to the east, Wyoming to the south, and Idaho to the southwest. Although it is a large state, the population is small and spread out, with Montana being only the seventh least-populous state in the United States. Open carry is legal in Montana even without a license to carry.

A.   State Constitution

Regarding the right to bear arms, the Montana Constitution states:

> "The right of any person to keep or bear arms in defense of his own home, person, and property, or in aid of the civil power when thereto legally summoned, shall not be called in question, but nothing herein contained shall be held to permit the carrying of concealed weapons."
> [http://gunla.ws/mt1]

B.   Scope of Preemption

The controlling language of the Montana preemption statute is set forth as follows:

> "(1) Except as provided in subsection (2), a county, city, town, consolidated local government, or other local government unit may not prohibit, register, tax, license, or regulate the purchase, sale or other transfer (including delay

in purchase, sale, or other transfer), ownership, possession, transportation, use, or unconcealed carrying of any weapon, including a rifle, shotgun, handgun, or concealed handgun.

(2) (a) For public safety purposes, a city or town may regulate the discharge of rifles, shotguns, and handguns. A county, city, town, consolidated local government, or other local government unit has power to prevent and suppress the carrying of concealed or unconcealed weapons to a public assembly, publicly owned building, park under its jurisdiction, or school, and the possession of firearms by convicted felons, adjudicated mental incompetents, illegal aliens, and minors." [http://gunla.ws/mt2]

The plain language of this statutory provision leaves preemption an open question. However, each county sheriff can provide information on where concealed weapons are prohibited in their counties. Specifically, be sure to check local regulations, which may restrict carrying concealed weapons at public meetings, and in public parks and buildings. While this is a "friendly" carry state, specific county lists should be gathered to comply with all laws.

C.   Reciprocal Carry

By statute, Montana will recognize another state's license to carry if that state recognizes Montana's license:

"A concealed weapon permit from another state is valid in this state if: (a) the person issued the permit has the permit in the person's immediate possession; (b) the person bearing the permit is also in possession of an official photo identification of the person, whether on the permit or on other identification; and (c) the state that issued the permit requires a criminal records background check of permit applicants prior to issuance of a permit."

Since there is no national carry license, as with the other states, some states are reciprocal with Montana and some are not. Anyone contemplating reciprocal carry should check with the official list maintained by the Montana AG at the point in time the reciprocal carry is to occur. States add *and* delete states with reciprocity agreements over time. Link to Montana AG list of permits it recognizes: [http://gunla.ws/mtcw]

D.   NFA Items

Montana permits ownership of all NFA items, provided they are legally obtained pursuant to federal law. Hunting with suppressors is legal.

E.   Carrying Firearms in Vehicles

Montana permits anyone who is legally allowed to possess firearms to carry them in a motor vehicle without a permit, openly or concealed. The only exception is that a permit is needed to carry a handgun that is "wholly or partially covered by clothing or wearing apparel". Therefore a permit would be needed to carry a concealed handgun on Your person, but not in the glove box. [http://gunla.ws/mt3]

F.   Self-defense Laws

Montana has both Castle Doctrine and SYG laws. There is no duty to retreat from any place You have a legal right to be. You may use force, including deadly force, in defense of yourself or others if You reasonably believe it is necessary to prevent imminent death, SBI, the commission of a forcible felony, or to stop the

unlawful & forcible entry into an occupied structure if You reasonably believe deadly force is necessary to prevent from assaulting an occupant of the structure or committing a forcible felony in the structure.
[http://gunla.ws/mt4] & [http://gunla.ws/mt5]

G.   Criminal Provisions

Under Montana law, a license to carry a handgun is not valid in any of the following places or circumstances, whether it is issued by Montana, or a person is carrying pursuant to a reciprocity agreement:

- In school buildings
- Buildings owned or leased by the federal, state or local government
- Financial institutions
- In local areas, some public meetings, and in public parks and buildings [http://gunla.ws/mtcw]

For a list of places where carrying a firearm is prohibited, see: [http://gunla.ws/mt6]

H.   Duty to Inform Officer

No. Non-residents must always have their permit/license and photo identification with them whenever they carry a concealed weapon and present them to a LEO upon request. [http://gunla.ws/0tog]

I.   Do "No Gun Signs" Have the Force of Law?

No. "No Firearm" signs in Montana do not have the force of law unless they are posted on property that is specifically mentioned in State law as being off limits to those with a permit/license to carry. However, as a possessor with a real property interest, a retailer, has the right to limit, and qualify the right to enter the property, subject to not carrying a handgun. It would be improper to enter, and the licensee would be subject to ejection for possession of a handgun thereat. Failure to leave once requested would subject the licensee to criminal charges.

J.   Carry in Restaurants That Serve Alcohol

In Montana you cannot carry concealed, but you are permitted to carry openly in a restaurant that serves alcohol. Places like Fridays or Chili's unless they have a "No Gun Sign," then it is suggested that You not carry into the establishment. This does not include a bar or the bar area of a restaurant – You are prohibited from carrying into these areas. You can carry your firearm into a restaurant that serves alcohol, but you are prohibited from consuming alcohol while carrying a firearm. [http://gunla.ws/su39]

K.   Open Carry (Without a Valid Permit/License)

Open Carry is legal in Montana. Places listed in the "Criminal Provisions" above may apply to those who open carry. The state preempts all firearm laws in the state and local authorities cannot have laws/ordinances against open carry. Federal law prohibits possession by a person under 18.

NEBRASKA GUN LAWS

Introduction

Nebraska is bordered by South Dakota to the north. It also shares borders with Iowa, Missouri, Kansas, Colorado and Wyoming. The state of Nebraska is divided into two (2) time zones, and its largest city is Omaha. Open carry is legal in Nebraska with a valid license to carry, and You can have a handgun in Your vehicle without a permit so long as it is clearly visible.

A.   State Constitution

Regarding the right to bear arms, the Nebraska Constitution states:

> "All persons are by nature free and independent, and have certain inherent and inalienable rights; among these are … the right to keep and bear arms for security or defense of self, family, home, and others, and for lawful common defense, hunting, recreational use, and all other lawful purposes, and such rights shall not be denied or infringed by the state or any subdivision thereof. To secure these rights, and the protection of property, governments are instituted among people, deriving their just powers from the consent of the governed." [http://gunla.ws/ne1]

B.   Scope of Preemption

The controlling language of the Nebraska preemption statute is set forth as follows:

> "The Legislature hereby finds and declares that the state has a valid interest in the regulation of the purchase, lease, rental, and transfer of handguns and that requiring a certificate prior to the purchase, lease, rental, or transfer of a handgun serves a valid public purpose."
> And
> "Any city or village ordinance existing on September 6, 1991, shall not be preempted by sections 69-2401 to 69-2425." [http://gunla.ws/ne2]

Nebraska has some level of preemption, but local governments may regulate the discharge of firearms, and some local governments may place some regulations on handguns as long as they are consistent with the state concealed carry laws. The city of Omaha requires people without a Nebraska carry permit to register their handguns with the city. [http://gunla.ws/ne3]

C.   Reciprocal Carry

By statute, Nebraska will recognize another state's license to carry if that state recognizes Nebraska's license:

> "A valid license or permit to carry a concealed handgun issued by any other state or the District of Columbia shall be recognized as valid in this state under the Concealed Handgun Permit Act if (1) the holder of the license or permit is not a resident of Nebraska and (2) the Attorney General has determined that the standards for issuance of such license or permit by such state or the District of

Columbia are equal to or greater than the standards imposed by the act."

Since there is no national carry license, as with the other states, some states are reciprocal with Nebraska and some are not. Anyone contemplating reciprocal carry should check with the official list maintained by the Nebraska AG at the point in time the reciprocal carry is to occur. All states add *and* delete states with which they have reciprocity agreements over time. [http://gunla.ws/ne4]

D. Duty to Inform Officer

Yes. Whenever a permitholder who is carrying a concealed handgun is in contact with a LEO or emergency services personnel, the permitholder must immediately inform the LEO or emergency services personnel that the permitholder is carrying a concealed handgun. A permitholder must carry his or her CCP and his or her Nebraska driver's license or government issued ID any time he or she carries a concealed handgun and must display both when asked to do so by a LEO or emergency services personnel. During contact with a permitholder, a LEO or emergency services personnel may secure the handgun if they determine it is necessary for their safety. [http://gunla.ws/6eau]

E. NFA Items

Nebraska permits ownership of all NFA items, provided they are legally obtained pursuant to federal law. Hunting with suppressors is legal.

F. Carrying Firearms in Vehicles

Nebraska permits anyone who is legally allowed to possess

a firearm to carry it openly in a vehicle without a permit. Long guns and handguns may be carried openly (however it is illegal to carry a loaded shotgun in a vehicle), however a loaded handgun must be visible from outside the vehicle. [http://gunla.ws/ne5]

G.   Self-defense Laws

Nebraska has a modified form of Castle Doctrine but no SYG law. There is no duty to retreat when in Your dwelling or place of business. You may use force, including deadly force, in defense of yourself or others if You reasonably believe it is necessary to prevent imminent death, SBI, kidnapping, or rape. [http://gunla.ws/ne6]

H.   Criminal Provisions

Under Nebraska law, a license to carry a handgun is not valid in any of the following places or circumstances, whether it is issued by Nebraska, or a person is carrying pursuant to reciprocity between his or her state of license and Nebraska:

- Police, sheriff, or Nebraska State Patrol station or office
- Detention facility, prison, or jail
- Courtroom or building which contains a courtroom
- Polling place during an election
- Meeting of the Legislature or a committee of the Legislature
- Financial institution
- Professional or semiprofessional athletic event
- A school building, grounds, vehicle, or school sponsored activity or athletic event, including:
  - A public school
  - A private school
  - A denominational school

- A parochial elementary, vocational, or secondary school
- A private post-secondary career school
- A community college
- A public or private college, junior college, or university
- Place of worship
- Hospital, emergency room, or trauma center
- Political rally or fundraiser
- An establishment having a license issued under the Nebraska Liquor Control Act that derives over one-half of its total income from the sale of alcoholic liquor
- Private property where there is a prohibition against carrying concealed firearms
- Any employer may prohibit employees from carrying concealed handguns in vehicles owned by the employer
- While consuming alcohol or while the permit holder has remaining in his or her blood, urine, or breath any previously consumed alcohol or any controlled substance
- A permit is required in order to purchase a handgun, and You must pass a background check to obtain this permit.
- Into or onto any other place or premises where handguns are prohibited by state law or by the establishment itself

For a list of places where carrying firearms is prohibited, see: [http://gunla.ws/ne7]

I.   Do "No Gun Signs" Have the Force of Law?

Yes. "No Guns" signs have the force of law in Nebraska. A permit holder who carries a firearm into an establishment that has a "no guns" sign conspicuously posted is guilty of a Class III misdemeanor for the first violation and a Class I misdemeanor for any subsequent violation. [http://gunla.ws/42dh]

J.   Carry in Restaurants That Serve Alcohol

Yes, subject to the "No Gun Signs" provision above. Nebraska only prohibits carrying in establishments that derive more than one-half of their total income from the sale of alcohol. This does not include the bar or bar area of a restaurant – You are prohibited from carrying into these areas. You can carry your firearm into a restaurant that serves alcohol, but you are prohibited from consuming alcohol while carrying a firearm. [http://gunla.ws/vvnw]

K.   Open Carry (Without a Valid Permit/License)

Open carry is legal in Nebraska, but state preemption allows local governments to regulate the open carrying of firearms. Nebraska preemption only covers the carrying of "concealed firearms." Places listed in the "Criminal Provisions" above apply to those who open carry. The Minimum age for open carry is 18. For open carry in a vehicle, the firearm must be clearly visible. [http://gunla.ws/upfg]

L.   Background Checks

Background checks are not required for purchases of long guns. A person acquiring a handgun must have either a handgun certificate or a CCP and has therefore been subjected to a background check. [http://gunla.ws/lhxi]

NEVADA GUN LAWS

Introduction

Nevada is largely composed of desert, and over two-thirds of the population of the state lives in the Las Vegas Metropolitan Area. California borders to the west, Arizona to the southeast, Utah to the east, and Oregon and Idaho to the north. Open carry is legal in Nevada with a valid license to carry, and one may possess a handgun in their vehicle without a permit so long as it is visible.

A.   State Constitution

Regarding the right to bear arms, the Nevada Constitution states:

"Every citizen has the right to keep and bear arms for security and defense, for lawful hunting and recreational use and for other lawful purposes." [http://gunla.ws/nv1]

B.   Scope of Preemption

The controlling language of the Nevada preemption statute is set forth as follows:

"Except as otherwise provided by specific statute, the Legislature reserves for itself such rights and powers as are necessary to regulate the transfer, sale, purchase, possession, ownership, transportation, registration and licensing of firearms and ammunition in Nevada, and no county may infringe upon those rights and powers, except that a town board may proscribe by ordinance or regulation the unsafe discharge of firearms." [http://gunla.ws/nv2]

C.   Reciprocal Carry

By statute, Nevada will recognize another state's license to carry if that state recognizes Nevada's license:

"A person who possesses a permit to carry a concealed firearm that was issued by a state included in the list prepared pursuant to NRS 202.3689 may carry a concealed firearm in this State in accordance with the requirements set forth in NRS 202.3653 to 202.369, inclusive."
[http://gunla.ws/nv3]

Anyone contemplating reciprocal carry should check with the official list maintained by the Nevada Law Enforcement Agency at the time the reciprocal carry is to occur. Nevada's reciprocity agreements can be viewed online. [http://gunla.ws/nv4]

D.   Duty to Inform Officers

Nevada does not require individuals to inform a LEO of a permit or license to carry but if an Officer asks about a weapon, by law, an answer must be supplied. Each permittee must carry their permit and proper identification whenever they are in actual possession of a concealed firearm. Both the permit and proper identification must be presented if requested by a LEO. [http://gunla.ws/ox3c]

E.   NFA Items

Nevada permits ownership of all NFA items, provided they are legally obtained pursuant to federal law. Hunting with suppressors is legal.

F.   Carrying Firearms in Vehicles

Nevada permits anyone who is legally allowed to possess firearms to carry them in a vehicle without a permit, openly or concealed. Long guns must be unloaded when transporting in an automobile unless You are paraplegic or have had a leg amputated. [http://gunla.ws/nv5]

F.   Self-defense Laws

Nevada has both Castle Doctrine and SYG laws. There is no duty to retreat from any place You have a legal right to be. You may use force, including deadly force, in defense of yourself or others if You reasonably believe it is necessary to prevent imminent death, SBI, the commission of a forcible felony, or to stop the unlawful & forcible entry into a dwelling with intent to harm an occupant. [http://gunla.ws/nv6]

H.   Criminal Provisions

Under Nevada law, a license to carry a handgun is not valid in any of the following places or circumstances, whether it is issued by Nevada, or a person is carrying pursuant to a reciprocity between his or her state of license and Nevada:

- While under the influence of alcohol (a blood-alcohol concentration of .10 or more) [http://gunla.ws/nv7]
- While on the property of the Nevada Higher Education or a private or public school grounds or school vehicle
- Any public building who has posted that carry is prohibited
- Any public building located on the property of a public

306

airport

- A public building that has a metal detector at each public entrance, or where a sign is posted at each public entrance
- While hunting from an aircraft, helicopter or motor driven vehicle, including snowmobiles. A paraplegic hunter may shoot from any stopped motor vehicle which is not parked on the traveled portion of a public highway
- Discharge a firearm from, upon, or across any federal or state highway/county road
- Discharge in any public place where any person might be endangered

For a list of places where carrying firearms is prohibited, see: [http://gunla.ws/nv8]

I.   Do "No Gun Signs" Have the Force of Law?

No. "No Firearm" signs in Nevada do not have the force of law unless they are posted on property that is specifically mentioned in State Law as being off limits to those with a permit/license to carry. However, as a possessor with a real property interest, a retailer, has the right to limit, and qualify the right to enter the property, subject to not carrying a handgun. It would be improper to enter, and the licensee would be subject to ejection for possession of a handgun threat. Failure to leave once requested would subject the licensee to criminal charges.

J.   Carry in Restaurants the Serve Alcohol

Yes. Nevada has no laws prohibiting the carrying of firearms in restaurants that serve alcohol. You can carry in a restaurant that serves alcohol. Places like Fridays or Chili's unless they have a "No Gun Sign," then it is suggested that You not carry into the establishment. This does not include a bar or the bar area of a restaurant – You are prohibited from carrying into these areas. You can carry Your firearm into a restaurant that serves alcohol, but You are prohibited from carrying while intoxicated (having a blood alcohol level of .10 or greater). [http://gunla.ws/t28z]

K.   Open Carry

Open carry is legal in Nevada. Places listed in the "Criminal Provisions" above may not be off limits to those who open carry. The state preempts all firearm laws in the state and local authorities cannot have laws/ordinances against open carry. Remember that if You enter any property and the owner/responsible person asks You to leave, You must leave. Failure to leave can result in trespass charges. The minimum age to open carry is 18. [http://gunla.ws/1y2y]

 # NEW HAMPSHIRE GUN LAWS

Introduction

New Hampshire is located in the Northeast, surrounded by Maine to the east, Canada to the north, Vermont to the west, and Massachusetts to the south. New Hampshire is the home of the first primary during Presidential election years. Open carry is legal in New Hampshire even without a valid license to carry, but a license is needed to carry in a vehicle.

A.   State Constitution

Regarding the right to bear arms, the New Hampshire Constitution states:

> "All persons have the right to keep and bear arms in defense of themselves, their families, their property and the state." [http://gunla.ws/nh1]

B.   Scope of Preemption

The controlling language of the New Hampshire preemption statute is set forth as follows:

> "To the extent consistent with federal law, the state of New Hampshire shall have authority and jurisdiction over the sale, purchase, ownership, use, possession, transportation, licensing, permitting, taxation, or other matter pertaining to

firearms, firearms components, ammunition, firearms supplies, or knives in the state. Except as otherwise specifically provided by statute, no ordinance or regulation of a political subdivision may regulate the sale, purchase, ownership, use, possession, transportation, licensing, permitting, taxation, or other matter pertaining to firearms, firearms components, ammunition, or firearms supplies in the state." [http://gunla.ws/nh2]

C.   Reciprocal Carry

By statute, New Hampshire will recognize another state's license to carry if that state recognizes New Hampshire's license:

"No nonresident holding a current and valid license to carry a loaded pistol or revolver in the state in which he resides or who is a peace officer in the state in which he resides, shall be required to obtain a license to carry a loaded pistol or revolver within this state if: I. Such nonresident carries upon his person the license held from the state in which he resides; and II. The state in which such person is a resident provides a reciprocal privilege for residents of this state."

Anyone contemplating reciprocal carry should check with the official list maintained by the New Hampshire State Police at the point in time the reciprocal carry is to occur. For, hopefully, the most up-to-date list see this following link: [http://gunla.ws/nhfp]

D.   Constitutional Carry

New Hampshire permits anyone who is over the age of 18 and may legally possess a firearm to carry a handgun concealed or openly without a permit. [http://gunla.ws/r6up]

E. NFA Items

New Hampshire permits ownership of all NFA items, provided they are legally obtained pursuant to federal law.

F. Carrying Firearms in Vehicles

New Hampshire generally prohibits carrying loaded firearms in vehicles. Loaded long guns may not be carried in vehicles, and handguns may only be carried without a permit if they are unloaded and secured in a locked container that is not readily accessible. [http://gunla.ws/nh3]

G. Self-defense Laws

New Hampshire has a Castle Doctrine but no SYG law. There is no duty to retreat when in Your dwelling or place of business. You may use force, including deadly force, in defense of yourself or others if You reasonably believe it is necessary to prevent imminent death, SBI, kidnapping, or rape. [http://gunla.ws/nh4]

H. Criminal Provisions

Under New Hampshire law, a license to carry a handgun is not valid in any of the following places or circumstances, whether it is issued by New Hampshire or a person is carrying pursuant to reciprocity between his or her state of license and New Hampshire:

- In a courtroom, or area used by the court
- Discharge of a firearm within 15 feet of the traveled portion of or across any state highway [http://gunla.ws/nh5]
- On posted property

- Discharge on the land of another within 300 feet of a permanently occupied building without the permission of the owner [http://gunla.ws/nh6]

For a list of places where carrying firearms is prohibited, see: [http://gunla.ws/nh7]

I. Duty to Inform Officer

No. There is no duty to inform a LEO immediately on contact that you possess a firearm. You are required to have Your permit/license and proper identification with You at all times when You carry a concealed firearm and must present both if the LEO demands. [http://gunla.ws/8ks0]

J. Do "No Gun Signs" Have the Force of Law?

No. "No Firearm" signs in New Hampshire do not have the force of law unless they are posted on property that is specifically mentioned in State law as being off limits to those with a permit/license to carry. However, as a possessor with a real property interest, a retailer, has the right to limit, and qualify the right to enter the property, subject to not carrying a handgun. It would be improper to enter, and the licensee would be subject to ejection for possession of a handgun thereat. Failure to leave once requested would subject the licensee to criminal charges.

K. Carry In Restaurants That Serve Alcohol

Yes. New Hampshire has no laws prohibiting the carrying of firearms in restaurants that serve alcohol. You can carry in a restaurant that serves alcohol. Places like Fridays or Chili's unless they have a "No Gun Sign," then it is suggested that You not carry

312

into the establishment. This does not include a bar or the bar area of a restaurant – You are prohibited from carrying into these areas. You can carry your firearm into a restaurant that serves alcohol, but You are prohibited from carrying while You consume alcohol.

L.   Open Carry (Without a Valid Permit/License)

Open carry is legal. New Hampshire has permitless carry. Anyone who can legally possess a firearm can carry open or concealed without any type of permit/license. The state preempts all firearm laws in the state and local authorities cannot have laws/ordinances against open carry. Remember that if You enter any property and the owner/responsible person asks You to leave, You must do so. Failure to leave can result in trespass charges. The minimum age to open carry is 18.

 **NEW
JERSEY
GUN
LAWS**

Introduction

New Jersey is the most densely populated state in all of the United States. Recently New Jersey has been the center of many firearm related issues. Please reference the New Jersey Department of Law and Public Safety to make sure You have the most current information. [http://gunla.ws/v6fa] It is bordered by New York on the north and east, Pennsylvania to the west, Delaware to the southwest, and the Atlantic Ocean to the south.

A.   State Constitution

New Jersey does not have a "right to bear arms" constitutional provision. [http://gunla.ws/nj1]

B.   Scope of Preemption

The controlling language of the New Jersey preemption statute is set forth as follows:

"The governing body of every municipality may make, amend, repeal and enforce ordinances to: ...Regulate and prohibit the sale and use of guns, pistols, firearms, and fireworks of all descriptions." [http://gunla.ws/nj2]

C.   Reciprocal Carry

New Jersey does not recognize any other state's CCW license.

D.   Assault Weapons Ban

It is illegal to possess an assault weapon, unless it was possessed before May 1, 1990 and registered with the state. Assault weapons may not be sold or transferred to any person other than a licensed gun dealer or any individual who is going to relinquish it to the police. [http://gunla.ws/nj3]

E.   NFA Items

The only NFA items legal in New Jersey are MGs and AOWs, and they are subject to additional state regulation. Possession of a MG requires a state license, which is granted on a "may-issue" basis by a county superior court judge. MG licenses are rarely granted. [http://gunla.ws/mjr7] & [http://gunla.ws/cayv]

F.   Carrying Firearms in Vehicles

New Jersey generally prohibits carry firearms in vehicles without a permit. People without permits may only carry a firearm if it is unloaded and either secured in a locked container or locked in the trunk. It is illegal to carry a loaded long gun in a vehicle. Furthermore, without a permit, firearms may only be carried to or from: the place of purchase or repair, Your home or business, a shooting range, or hunting activities. [http://gunla.ws/nj4]

G. Self-defense Laws

New Jersey has a Castle Doctrine but no SYG law. There is no duty to retreat when in Your dwelling. You may use force, including deadly force, in defense of yourself or others if You reasonably believe it is necessary to prevent imminent death, SBI, the commission of a forcible felony, or to prevent an unlawful intruder in a dwelling from inflicting unlawful force against an occupant of the dwelling. [http://gunla.ws/nj5]

H. High-Capacity Magazine Ban

New Jersey bans the intrastate manufacture, sale, transportation, and possession of magazines with the capacity to hold more than 15 rounds of ammunition. In addition, possession and transportation of hollow point ammunition is generally prohibited except on or to one's private property, a shooting range, or a gun club registered with the New Jersey state police.

I. Waiting Period

New Jersey imposes a seven (7) day waiting period before purchasing a firearm.

J. Criminal Provisions

To obtain a firearm in New Jersey an individual must first obtain a Firearms Purchaser Identification Card (FPID), which requires passing a background check. It is *required* for any person to purchase a gun. There is a separate FPID for the purchase of a handgun than for the purchase a rifle or shotgun. A handgun FPID is valid for the purchase of one handgun and lasts for ninety (90) days from issue, and a long gun FPID allows the purchase of an unlimited number of shotguns or rifles. Only one handgun can be

316

purchased within a 30-day period. A New Jersey-specific license to carry a handgun, if You are somehow able to obtain one via a showing of a "compelling need", is not valid in any of the following places or circumstances:

- On school, college, or university grounds
- On or in a casino
- Motor vehicles can be impounded if the driver unlawfully has a gun inside the vehicle
- State Parks
- Firearm owners cannot purchase more than one handgun in any thirty (30) day period
- Theft or loss of any firearm must be reported to the police within thirty-six (36) hours of the discovery of the theft or loss

For a list of places where carrying firearms is prohibited, see: [http://gunla.ws/nj6]

K.   Background Checks

A person acquiring a handgun must have a permit to purchase a handgun. A person acquiring a long gun must have a Firearms Purchaser Identification Card. Private sale of a long gun does not require a background check. [http://gunla.ws/803e]

L.   Duty to Inform Officer

No. There is no duty to inform a LEO immediately on contact that you possess a firearm. You are required to have Your permit/license and proper identification with You at all times when You carry a concealed firearm and must present both if the LEO demands.

M. Carry in Restaurants That Serve Alcohol

Yes. New Jersey has no laws prohibiting the carrying of firearms in restaurants that serve alcohol. You can carry in a restaurant that serves alcohol. Places like Fridays or Chili's unless they have a "No Gun Sign," then it is suggested that You not carry into the establishment. This does not include a bar or the bar area of a restaurant – You are prohibited from carrying into these areas. You can carry Your firearm into a restaurant that serves alcohol, but You are prohibited from carrying while you consume alcohol.

N. Open Carry

Open carry is illegal in New Jersey. There is no law against open carry, but You must have a "License to Carry Firearm Concealed" to carry a firearm in New Jersey. The license gives You the ability to carry only a concealed firearm and not to open carry a firearm. Thus, You have to have a license to carry any firearm in New Jersey and that license is only for carrying a firearm concealed.

NEW MEXICO GUN LAWS

Introduction

New Mexico is bordered by Arizona to the west, Colorado to the north, and Texas to the east, with corners touching Utah and Oklahoma. New Mexico has a rich history, and houses the second-highest percentage of Native Americans in the United States. Open carry is legal in New Mexico even without a license to carry.

A.   State Constitution

Regarding the right to bear arms, the New Mexico Constitution states:

> "No law shall abridge the right of the citizen to keep and bear arms for security and defense, for lawful hunting and recreational use and for other lawful purposes, but nothing herein shall be held to permit the carrying of concealed weapons." [http://gunla.ws/nm1]

B.   Scope of Preemption

The controlling language of the New Mexico preemption statute is set forth as follows:

> "No municipality or county shall regulate, in any way, an incident of the right to keep and bear arms."

And also:

"A concealed handgun license shall not be valid on tribal land, unless authorized by the governing body of an Indian nation, tribe or pueblo."

It is important to remember that although New Mexico has strong preemption laws, these do not apply to Indian reservations, which comprise a significant portion of New Mexico. [http://gunla.ws/nm2]

C.   Reciprocal Carry

By statute, New Mexico will recognize another state's license to carry if that state recognizes New Mexico's license:

"The department shall promulgate rules necessary to implement the provisions of the Concealed Handgun Carry Act. The rules shall include: E. provision of discretionary state authority for the transfer, recognition or reciprocity of a concealed handgun license issued by another state if the issuing authority for the other state: (1) includes provisions at least as stringent as or substantially similar to the Concealed Handgun Carry Act; (2) issues a license or permit with an expiration date printed on the license or permit; (3) is available to verify the license or permit status for law enforcement purposes within three business days of a request for verification; (4) has disqualification, suspension and revocation requirements for a concealed handgun license or permit; and (5) requires that an applicant for a concealed handgun license or permit: (a) submit to a national criminal history record check; (b) not be prohibited from possessing firearms pursuant to federal or state law; and (c) satisfactorily complete a firearms safety program that covers deadly force issues, weapons care and maintenance, safe handling and storage of firearms and marksmanship."

Since there is no national carry license, as with the other states, some states are reciprocal with New Mexico and some are not. Anyone contemplating reciprocal carry should check with the official list maintained by the New Mexico Department of Public Safety at the point in time the reciprocal carry is to occur. [http://gunla.ws/nm3]

D.   NFA Items

New Mexico permits ownership of all NFA items, provided they are legally obtained pursuant to federal law. Hunting with suppressors is legal.

E.   Carrying Firearms in Vehicles

New Mexico law allows a person who is not otherwise prohibited to have a concealed, loaded firearm in his/her vehicle (including motorcycles and bicycles). If You are not licensed to carry concealed in New Mexico or in a state that New Mexico recognized, You may not have the weapon concealed on Your person when you exit Your vehicle or motorcycle. [http://gunla.ws/7caj]

F.   Self-defense Laws

New Mexico has a Castle Doctrine but no SYG law. There is no duty to retreat when in Your dwelling. You may use force, including deadly force, in defense of yourself or others if You reasonably believe it is necessary to prevent imminent death, SBI, unlawful action against You or Your family, or the commission of a forcible felony. [http://gunla.ws/nm5]

G. Criminal Provisions

Under New Mexico law, a license to carry a handgun is not valid in any of the following places or circumstances:

- Into or on premises where to do so would be in violation of state or federal law
- On premises of elementary school, middle school or high school
- On the premises of a preschool
- In a courthouse or court facility
- On Tribal land
- On public buses
- Airport security zones or any Federal property
- On private property if the owner posted signs or verbally communicates that firearms are prohibited
- While consuming alcohol or while impaired by the use of alcohol or other substances
- Handling it in a negligent manner
- Discharge within 150 yards of an inhabited dwelling or building without the permission of the owner or lessee

Additionally:

- The current law allows You to carry only one (1) concealed firearm. You can carry one (1) concealed and 50 openly - but not two (2) concealed.
- Firearms and ammunition may be stored in a locked vehicle while on a college/university campus, and may be carried while driving in a vehicle on campus, but may not be carried on foot while on campus. Exceptions exist for university-sponsored shooting events and ROTC programs. [http://gunla.ws/y19c]

For a list of places where carrying firearms is prohibited, see: [http://gunla.ws/nm6]

H.   Duty to Inform Officer

No. You must have your License/Permit with You at all times when You carry a concealed firearm in New Mexico. Upon demand from a LEO, You must display Your license. [http://gunla.ws/1cms]

I.   Do "No Gun Signs" Have the Force of Law?

Yes. Licensees may not carry a concealed handgun on or about their person on private property that has signs posted prohibiting the carrying of concealed weapons or when verbally told so by a person lawfully in possession of the property. Failure to obey such signs or verbal warnings constitutes trespass. [http://gunla.ws/ht2t]

J.   Carry in Restaurants That Serve Alcohol

Yes, but only if you have a License/Permit and only into a restaurant licensed to sell only beer and wine that derives no less than 60% of its annual gross receipts from the sale of food for consumption on the premises, unless the restaurant has a sign posted that prohibits the carrying of firearms, or You are verbally instructed by the owner or manager that carrying of a firearm is not permitted in the restaurant. [http://gunla.ws/bpz7]

K.   Open Carry

Open carry is legal and common in New Mexico. Places as listed in the "Criminal Provisions" above apply to those who open carry. New Mexico Code states that only a person with a valid

Concealed Firearms License can carry into any establishment that dispenses alcohol. So open carry would be prohibited into any place that sells any alcohol for consumption off the premises without a valid license. This would include any store that sells alcohol, such as Walmart. The minimum age for open carry is 19. [http://gunla.ws/50rb]

 **NEW YORK GUN LAWS**

Introduction

New York is bordered by Connecticut, Massachusetts, and Vermont to the east, New Jersey and Pennsylvania to the south, and Canada to the north and west, and has a maritime border with Rhode Island. New York City is the most populous city in all of the United States and has recently experienced many changes in their gun law. If You have further questions, reference the Governor's website: [http://gunla.ws/byc8]

A.   State Constitution

New York does not have a constitutional provision for the right to bear arms. [http://gunla.ws/ny1]

However, New York's Civil Rights Code states:

"A well-regulated militia being necessary to the security of a free state, the right of the people to keep and bear arms cannot be infringed." [http://gunla.ws/ny2]

B.   Scope of Preemption

New York does not have a preemption statute; however, the resident licensing statute states:

"Any license issued pursuant to this section shall be valid notwithstanding the provisions of any local law or ordinance. ... A license to carry or possess a pistol or revolver, not otherwise limited as to place or time of possession, shall be effective throughout the state, except that the same shall not be valid within the city of New York unless a special permit granting validity is issued by the police commissioner of that city." [http://gunla.ws/ny3]

Some cases have held that some local ordinances are impermissible due to state preemption. Therefore, one must check with local ordinances regarding carrying of a firearm within any city or municipality, *especially within New York City*. It is highly recommended one consult with a New York licensed attorney as recent cases may change the law and scope of preemption. New York City has much stricter gun laws than the rest of the state, and generally does not recognize carry permits, even those issued by New York State.

C.   Reciprocal Carry

By statute, New York will not recognize another state's license to carry, however one may transport a firearm in the state pursuant to:

"Sections 265.01, 265.02, 265.03, 265.04, 265.05, 265.10, 265.11, 265.12, 265.13, 265.15 and 270.05 shall not apply to: ... 13. Possession of pistols and revolvers by a person who is a nonresident of this state while attending or traveling to or from, an organized competitive pistol match or league competition under auspices of, or approved by, the National Rifle Association and in which he is a competitor, within forty-eight hours of such event or by a person who is a non-resident of the state while attending or traveling to or from an organized match sanctioned by the International Handgun Metallic Silhouette Association and in which he is a competitor, within forty-eight hours of such event, provided that he has not been previously convicted of a felony or a crime which, if committed in New York, would constitute a felony, and further provided that the pistols or revolvers are transported unloaded in a locked opaque container together with a copy of the match program, match schedule or match registration card. Such documentation shall constitute *prima facie* evidence of exemption, providing that such person also has in his possession a pistol license or firearms registration card issued in accordance with the laws of his place of residence."

D.   NFA Items

Ownership of MGs, suppressors, SBRs, and SBSs are prohibited to the average citizen. DDs are permitted except for rockets with greater than 3 ounces of propellant, which are prohibited. AOWs are legal to own but are still required to be on a pistol permit. AOWs disguised as non-firearms are illegal. [http://gunla.ws/hv8w]

E.   License is Required to own Pistols

New York requires a pistol permit in order to purchase, possess, or transport a handgun. This permit is different from a permit to carry a pistol. Even after You receive a pistol permit, You must make a separate application for each pistol You wish to buy or sell. In order to purchase a handgun, the holder of a pistol permit must apply for an amendment to their permit to include the new gun, and can make the purchase only after this application is granted. Once purchased, each handgun must be registered and a description of it (by make, model, caliber, and serial number) must be added to the pistol permit. Applying for a pistol permit can take 4-6 months and requires a background check, and for the applicant to list several character references. The pistol permit must be renewed every 5 years.

F.   Universal Background Checks

Background checks are mandatory for all firearm sales, and every firearm sale (except between family members) must go through an FFL. Documentation of the check must be provided to the New York State Police and You must keep a record of the transaction. [http://gunla.ws/slwt]

G.   Regulation of Ammunition Sales

Currently all sales of ammunition must go through a registered ammunition dealer, who is to record and report each sale. Internet purchases of ammunition must be sent to an ammunition dealer for pickup, all sales of ammunition must be conducted face to face. This law also mandated that ammunition dealers will be required to conduct background checks on the sale of ammunition, however on 7/10/15 the government suspended implementation of this background check law because the technology to create the ammo background check system is not yet operational. As of 10/3/17 this ammo background check provision is not currently in effect, but it will likely be implemented in the future once the background check system is ready.

H.   High-Capacity Magazine Ban

New York bans the manufacture, sale, transportation, and possession of magazines with the capacity to hold more than 10 rounds of ammunition. This ban does not grandfather in previously

328

legal magazines, and people were required to dispose of any magazine holding more than 10 rounds by 2/15/13. The only exceptions are for internal tubular/helical magazines chambered in .22, which are allowed to contain more than 10 rounds and antique high-quality magazines, if registered to an associated antique assault weapon. [http://gunla.ws/iq83]

I.   Assault Weapons Ban

New York maintains an assault weapons ban. The manufacture and sale of assault weapons is prohibited. Possession of assault weapons is prohibited unless they were legally owned by 1/15/13 and registered with the state by 1/15/14. New York does not allow the registration of new assault weapons, and the registration of existing assault weapons must be renewed every 5 years. The definition of assault weapons can be found here: [http://gunla.ws/ny4]

J.   Carrying Firearms in Vehicles

New York generally prohibits the carrying of firearms in vehicles by people without a carry permit. Long guns may be carried only if they are unloaded and secured in a locked container that is not readily accessible. Handguns may only be carried by people with carry permits. [http://gunla.ws/ny5]

K.   Self-defense Laws

New York has a Castle Doctrine but no SYG law. There is no duty to retreat when in Your dwelling. You may use force, including deadly force, in defense of yourself or others if You reasonably believe it is necessary to prevent imminent use of deadly force by the aggressor, kidnapping, forcible rape, robbery, arson, or burglary of an occupied building. [http://gunla.ws/ny6]

L.   Criminal Provisions

Under New York law, a license to carry a handgun is not valid in any of the following places or circumstances:

- In a building or on the grounds of an educational institution, including:
  - Any school
  - A college or university
  - On a school bus
- Court houses
- Any place that Federal Law prohibits the carry
- If transporting a firearm through New York (that is NY is not Your destination *and* You are traveling to a state where possession is permitted) do keep the firearm locked away, unloaded and not easily accessible by driver or passenger
- Note: there are even stricter rules when/if the Mayor has declared a state of emergency in New York City
- Gun owners are required to report theft of any of their guns within 24 hours of discovering that theft
- Requires that guns be safely stored such that they are inaccessible to any household member who has been convicted of a felony or domestic violence crime, been involuntarily committed, or is currently under an order of protection
- Police are authorized to seize guns from someone who has been certified by a medical professional to be too mentally unstable to safely possess rifles or shotguns

For a list of places where carrying firearms is prohibited, see: [http://gunla.ws/ny7]

M. Duty to Inform LEO Immediately on Contact?

No. While carrying a pistol or revolver, every licensee must have on his or her person a license to carry the same. Every person licensed to possess a pistol or revolver on particular premises shall have the license for the same on such premises. Upon demand, the license must be exhibited for inspection to any LEO. [http://gunla.ws/zy1d]

N. Carry in Restaurants That Serve Alcohol

Yes. New York has no laws prohibiting the carrying of firearms in restaurants that serve alcohol, so long as You possess the appropriate Permit/License. Places like Fridays or Chili's unless they have a "No Gun Sign," then it is suggested that You not carry into the establishment. This does not include a bar or the bar area of a restaurant – You are prohibited from carrying into these areas. You can carry Your firearm into a restaurant that serves alcohol, but You are prohibited from carrying while You consume alcohol or are under the influence of alcohol.

O. Open Carry

The law in New York is extremely vague on open carry. Open carry in public is not legal in most instances. While no law specifically bans open carry, a license to carry is issued to carry concealed as per N.Y. Penal Law § 400. [http://gunla.ws/yygx] Therefore, pistol permit holders must carry concealed. Open carry is permitted while hunting and on one's own property. Open carry of unloaded long guns is not explicitly prohibited by any law, but is generally not practiced. [http://gunla.ws/wcu6]

NORTH CAROLINA GUN LAWS

Introduction

North Carolina is bordered to the north by Virginia, to the west by Tennessee, to the southwest by Georgia, and to the south by South Carolina. Being bordered on the east by the Atlantic Ocean, there is a wide range of elevation in the state from the coast to the mountains. Open carry is generally legal in North Carolina even without a license to carry, but some localities restrict it.

A.   State Constitution

Regarding the right to bear arms, the North Carolina Constitution states:

> "A well regulated militia being necessary to the security of a free State, the right of the people to keep and bear arms shall not be infringed; and, as standing armies in time of peace are dangerous to liberty, they shall not be maintained, and the military shall be kept under strict subordination to, and governed by, the civil power. Nothing herein shall justify the practice of carrying concealed weapons, or prevent the General Assembly from enacting penal statutes against that practice." [http://gunla.ws/nc1]

B.   Scope of Preemption

The controlling language of the North Carolina preemption statute is set forth as follows:

"It is declared by the General Assembly that the regulation of firearms is properly an issue of general, statewide concern, and that the entire field of regulation of firearms is preempted from regulation by local governments except as provided by this section." [http://gunla.ws/nc2]

C.   Reciprocal Carry

By statute, North Carolina will recognize another state's license to carry.

§ 14-415.24. Reciprocity; out-of-state handgun permits.

(a) A valid concealed handgun permit or license issued by another state is valid in North Carolina.

(b) Repealed by Session Laws 2011-268, s. 22(a), effective December 1, 2011.

(c) Every 12 months after the effective date of this subsection, the Department of Justice shall make written inquiry of the concealed handgun permitting authorities in each other state as to: (i) whether a North Carolina resident may carry a concealed handgun in their state based upon having a valid North Carolina concealed handgun permit and (ii) whether a North Carolina resident may apply for a concealed handgun permit in that state based upon having a valid North Carolina concealed handgun permit. The Department of Justice shall attempt to secure from each state permission for North Carolina residents who hold a valid North Carolina concealed handgun permit to carry a concealed handgun in that state, either on the basis of the North Carolina permit or on the basis that the North Carolina permit is sufficient to permit the issuance of a similar license or permit by the other state. (2003-199, s. 1; 2011-268, s. 22(a).) [http://gunla.ws/14415]

Anyone contemplating reciprocal carry should check with the official list maintained by the North Carolina AG at the point in time the reciprocal carry is to occur. States add *and* delete states with reciprocity agreements over time. North Carolina's reciprocity agreement can be viewed online. [http://gunla.ws/rw5b]

D.   Duty to Inform Officers

Yes. North Carolina requires holders of permit or license to carry who are approached or addressed by a LEO to inform the Officer that they possess a firearm and provide the Officer with their permit and identification. [http://gunla.ws/m90a]

E.   NFA Items

North Carolina permits ownership of all NFA items, provided they are legally obtained pursuant to federal law. It is legal to use suppressors for hunting. CLEOs are required to sign an application for the transfer of any item regulated under the NFA within 15 days if the applicant is not prohibited by law from receiving it. [http://gunla.ws/e494]

F.   Carrying Firearms in Vehicles

North Carolina permits anyone who is legally allowed to possess a firearm to carry it openly in a motor vehicle without a

334

permit, as long as it is readily visible from outside. Concealed carry requires a permit. A handgun is concealed in a vehicle if a person approaching cannot readily see it and if it is readily accessible. A handgun under the front seat or in an unlocked glove box or console is illegal. A handgun openly displayed or in a locked glove box, locked console, or in the trunk is lawful. [http://gunla.ws/nc3]

G.   Self-defense Laws

North Carolina has both Castle Doctrine and SYG laws. There is no duty to retreat from any place You have a legal right to be. You may use force, including deadly force, in defense of yourself or others if You reasonably believe it is necessary to prevent imminent death, SBI, or to stop the unlawful & forcible entry into Your dwelling, place of business, or occupied motor vehicle. [http://gunla.ws/nc4]

H.   Criminal Provisions

Under North Carolina law, it shall be unlawful for any person willfully and intentionally to carry concealed about his person any pistol or gun except in the following circumstances:

(1) The person is on the person's own premises

(2) The deadly weapon is a handgun, the person has a concealed handgun permit issued in accordance with Article 54B of this Chapter or considered valid under G.S. 14-415.24, and the person is carrying the concealed handgun in accordance with the scope of the concealed handgun permit as set out in G.S. 14-415.11I. [http://gunla.ws/nc3]

Under North Carolina law, a license to carry a handgun is

not valid in any of the following places or circumstances, whether it is issued by North Carolina, or a person is carrying pursuant to a reciprocity agreement between his or her state of license and North Carolina:

- While participating in, affiliated with, or present as a spectator at:
    - A picket line
    - A demonstration at a private health care facility or public place owned by the State (or political subdivisions)
- On educational property or to a curricular or extracurricular activity sponsored by a school, unless kept in a closed container in a locked automobile in the parking lot of a public institution of higher learning
- In any place where a 'no guns' sign is posted
- Hunting on Sunday, with any firearm
- Note: weapons on certain State property and in courthouses, as stated above, is unlawful. This rule, however, does not apply to any of the following: A person with a permit issued in accordance with Article 54B of this Chapter or considered valid under G.S. 14-415.24 who has a firearm in a closed compartment or container within the person's locked vehicle or in a locked container securely affixed to the person's vehicle. A person may unlock the vehicle to enter or exit the vehicle provided the firearm remains in the closed compartment at all times and the vehicle is locked immediately following the entrance or exit.
- In a law enforcement or correctional facility
- A permit is required in order to purchase a handgun, and You must pass a background check to obtain this permit

For a list of places where carrying firearms is prohibited, see: [http://gunla.ws/nc5]

I.   Do "No Gun Signs" Have the Force of Law?

Yes. A permit does not authorize a person to carry a concealed handgun on any private premises where notice that carrying a concealed handgun is prohibited by the posting of a conspicuous notice or statement by the person in legal possession or control of the premises. Failure to obey such signs or verbal warnings constitutes trespass.
[http://gunla.ws/4beh]

J.   Carry in Restaurants That Serve Alcohol

Yes, so long as You possess a Permit/License. You can carry a concealed firearm into bars and restaurants that serve alcohol unless a "No Guns Sign" is posted or the owner or manager informs You that guns are prohibited. You are prohibited from carrying while You consume alcohol or are under the influence of alcohol. [http://gunla.ws/37ea]

K.   Open Carry

Open carry is legal, but local governments have some limited authority to restrict firearms in some locations. Whether these local ordinances violate the State's firearm preemption laws has not yet been tested in North Carolina courts. Places as listed in the "Criminal Provisions" above apply to those who open carry. The minimum age for open carry is 18.

L.   Background Checks

A person acquiring a handgun must have either a permit to

purchase a handgun or a concealed handgun permit. A background check is required to obtain either of these permits. A background check is not required for the sale of long guns. [http://gunla.ws/hf99]

NORTH DAKOTA GUN LAWS

Introduction

North Dakota is bordered to the north by Canada, the south by South Dakota, the west by Montana, and the east by Minnesota. It is the third least-populous state in the United States, and agriculture is its largest economic industry. Open carry is legal in North Dakota with a valid license to carry, but You can carry an unloaded handgun without a license during daylight hours, or at any time on Your property.

A.   State Constitution

Regarding the right to bear arms, the North Dakota Constitution states:

> "All individuals are by nature equally free and independent and have certain inalienable rights, among which are those of …to keep and bear arms for the defense of their person, family, property, and the state, and for lawful hunting, recreational, and other lawful purposes, which shall not be infringed." [http://gunla.ws/nd1]

B.   Scope of Preemption

The controlling language of North Dakota's preemption statute is set forth as follows:

"A political subdivision, including home rule cities or counties, may not enact any ordinance relating to the purchase, sale, ownership, transfer of ownership, registration, or licensure of fire arms and ammunition which is more restrictive than state law. All such existing ordinances are void." [http://gunla.ws/nd2]

C.   Reciprocal Carry

By statute, North Dakota will recognize another state's license to carry if that state recognizes North Dakota's license:

"A person who has a valid license issued by another state to carry a concealed firearm or dangerous weapon in that state and whose state grants to residents of this state the right to carry a concealed firearm or dangerous weapon without requiring a separate license to carry a concealed firearm or dangerous weapon issued by that state may carry, subject to the provisions of this state's law, a concealed firearm or dangerous weapon in this state, and the other state's license is valid in this state."

Non-residents must have a valid concealed weapons license from their home state, which is determined by their driver's license and the state must have reciprocity with North Dakota. Anyone contemplating reciprocal carry should check with the official list maintained by the North Dakota State Police at the point in time the reciprocal carry is to occur. States add *and* delete states with reciprocity agreements over time. [http://gunla.ws/nftr]

D.   Constitutional Carry

North Dakota residents who are over the age of 18 and legally permitted to possess a firearm may carry a handgun openly or concealed without a permit. North Dakota's Permitless Carry Law only applies to North Dakota residents who have possessed a valid North Dakota driver's license or non-driver identification card for a minimum of 1 year. [http://gunla.ws/vxd6]

E.   NFA Items

North Dakota permits ownership of all NFA items, provided they are legally obtained pursuant to federal law. It is legal to use suppressors for hunting. CLEOs are required to sign an application for the transfer of any item regulated under the NFA within 30 days if the applicant is not prohibited by law from receiving it. NFA-compliant automatic firearms must be registered with the county sheriff and the state Bureau of Criminal Investigation. [http://gunla.ws/naxz]

F.   Carrying Firearms in Vehicles

North Dakota permits anyone who may legally possess a firearm to carry it in a vehicle without a permit, openly or concealed, so long as the firearm is unloaded. A carry permit is generally required to carry a loaded firearm in a vehicle. [http://gunla.ws/nd3]

G.   Self-defense Laws

North Dakota has a Castle Doctrine but no SYG law. There is no duty to retreat when in Your dwelling. You may use force, including deadly force, in defense of yourself or others if You reasonably believe it is necessary to prevent imminent death, SBI, the commission of a forcible felony, or if necessary to protect Your dwelling, place of business, or occupied motor home from arson, burglary, robbery, or other forcible felonies. [http://gunla.ws/nd4]

H.   Criminal Provisions

Under North Dakota law, a license to carry a handgun is not valid in any of the following places or circumstances, whether it is issued by North Dakota, or a person is carrying pursuant to a reciprocity agreement between his or her state of license and North Dakota:

- In a government building
- A gaming (gambling) establishment
- At a public gathering, which includes:
  - Athletic or sporting events
  - Schools or school functions, except college students or employees with a valid license may keep a firearm in a locked vehicle on campus
  - Churches or church functions, except with permission
  - Political rallies or functions
- Publicly owned and operated buildings
- MGs must be registered with the North Dakota Bureau of Criminal Investigation and the county sheriff

For a list of places where carrying firearms is prohibited, see: [http://gunla.ws/nd5]

I.   Duty to Inform Officer

If You are a North Dakota Resident carrying under permitless carry, You must immediately inform the LEO that You are carrying a firearm. If You have a permit/license issued by North Dakota or a state they honor, You do not need to inform the LEO unless they ask. Every individual while carrying a concealed firearm or dangerous weapon, for which a license to carry concealed is required, must have on one's person the license issued

342

by North Dakota or another state and must provide it to any LEO for an inspection upon demand by the LEO. [http://gunla.ws/asbn]

J.   Do "No Gun Signs" Have the Force of Law?

No. "No Firearm" signs in North Dakota do not have the force of law unless they are posted on property that is specifically mentioned in State Law as being off limits to those with a permit/license to carry. However, as a possessor with a real property interest, a retailer, has the right to limit, and qualify the right to enter the property, subject to not carrying a handgun. It would be improper to enter, and the licensee would be subject to ejection for possession of a handgun thereat. Failure to leave once requested would subject the licensee to criminal charges.

K.   Carry in Restaurants That Serve Alcohol

Yes. North Dakota has no laws prohibiting the carrying of firearms in restaurants that serve alcohol. Places like Fridays or Chili's unless they have a "No Gun Sign," then it is suggested that You not carry into the establishment. This does not include a bar or the bar area of a restaurant – You are prohibited from carrying into these areas. You can carry Your firearm into a restaurant that serves alcohol, but You are prohibited from carrying while You consume alcohol or are under the influence of alcohol. [http://gunla.ws/i5w2]

L.   Open Carry

Open carry is legal, but non-residents must have a valid permit/license to carry a concealed handgun that North Dakota issues or honors in order to open carry. North Dakota residents who have been a resident of North Dakota for at least one year can carry without a permit. Open carry of long guns is generally permitted.

Non-permit holders may carry one hour before sunrise until one hour after sunset, provided the firearm is unloaded and in plain sight. The minimum age for open carry is 18. [http://gunla.ws/ar25]

 # OHIO GUN LAWS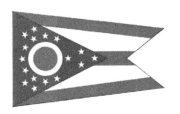

Introduction

Ohio is bordered to the north by Michigan and Lake Erie, which separates Ohio from Canada. To the south, Ohio is bordered by West Virginia and Kentucky, to the west by Indiana, and to the east by Pennsylvania. Ohio has the tenth-largest highway network, and is in a prime location for commercial travel.

A.   State Constitution

Regarding the right to bear arms, the Ohio Constitution states:

> "The people have the right to bear arms for their defense and security; but standing armies, in time of peace, are dangerous to liberty, and shall not be kept up; and the military shall be in strict subordination to the civil power." [http://gunla.ws/oh1]

B.   Scope of Preemption

The controlling language of Ohio's preemption statute is set forth as follows:

> "Municipalities shall have authority to exercise all powers of local self-government and to adopt and enforce within their limits such local police, sanitary and other similar regulations, as are not in conflict with general laws."

[http://gunla.ws/oh2]

Whereas:

(A) The individual right to keep and bear arms, being a fundamental individual right that predates the U.S. Constitution and Ohio Constitution, and being a constitutionally protected right in every part of Ohio, the general assembly finds the need to provide uniform laws throughout the state regulating the ownership, possession, purchase, other acquisition, transport, storage, carrying, sale, or other transfer of firearms, their components, and their ammunition. Except as specifically provided by the U.S. Constitution, Ohio Constitution, state law, or federal law, a person, without further license, permission, restriction, delay, or process, may own, possess, purchase, sell, transfer, transport, store, or keep any firearm, part of a firearm, its components, and its ammunition.

(B) In addition to any other relief provided, the court shall award costs and reasonable attorney fees to any person, group, or entity that prevails in a challenge to an ordinance, rule, or regulation as being in conflict with this section.

(C) As used in this section: (1) The possession, transporting, or carrying of firearms, their components, or their ammunition include, but are not limited to, the possession, transporting, or carrying, openly or concealed on a person's person or concealed ready at hand, of firearms, their components, or their ammunition. (2) "Firearm" has the same meaning as in § 2923.11 of the Revised Code.

(D) This section does not apply to either of the following: (1) A zoning ordinance that regulates or prohibits the

346

commercial sale of firearms, firearm components, or ammunition for firearms in areas zoned for residential or agricultural uses; (2) A zoning ordinance that specifies the hours of operation or the geographic areas where the commercial sale of firearms, firearm components, or ammunition for firearms may occur, provided that the zoning ordinance is consistent with zoning ordinances for other retail establishments in the same geographic area and does not result in a *de facto* prohibition of the commercial sale of firearms, firearm components, or ammunition for firearms in areas zoned for commercial, retail, or industrial uses. [http://gunla.ws/ohccw]

C.   Reciprocal Carry

By statute, Ohio will recognize another state's license to carry if that state recognizes Ohio's license:

"The attorney general shall negotiate and enter into a reciprocity agreement with any other license-issuing state under which a license to carry a concealed handgun that is issued by the other state is recognized in this state if the attorney general determines that both of the following apply: (a) The eligibility requirements imposed by that license-issuing state for that license are substantially comparable to the eligibility requirements for a license to carry a concealed handgun issued under § 2923.125 of the Revised Code; (b) That license-issuing state recognizes a license to carry a concealed handgun issued under § 2923.125 of the Revised Code."

Residents of other states who hold a valid carry permit from another state and are visiting Ohio will have their permit recognized during their temporary stay in Ohio, even if their permit is from a state that does not have a reciprocity agreement with Ohio.

Anyone contemplating reciprocal carry should check with the official list maintained by the Ohio AG at the point in time the reciprocal carry is to occur. For information about transporting a firearm within Your vehicle, please follow this link. [http://gunla.ws/oh3]

D.   Duty to Inform Officers

Yes. A holder of a permit to carry who is in a motor vehicle that is stopped by LEO has a duty to inform any Officer who approached the vehicle that they possess a permit to carry and a concealed weapon. Additionally, Ohio law requires that you remain in the vehicle while stopped (unless asked to exit) and keep Your hands in plain sight for the duration of the stop. [http://gunla.ws/5efa]

E.   NFA Items

Ohio permits ownership of all NFA items, provided they are legally obtained pursuant to federal law. It is legal to use suppressors for hunting. CLEOs are required to sign an application for the transfer of any item regulated under the NFA within 45 days if the applicant is not prohibited by law from receiving it. [http://gunla.ws/tfkl] & [http://gunla.ws/fw8g]

F.   Carrying Firearms in Vehicles

Ohio generally prohibits carrying loaded firearms in vehicles without a permit. Someone without a permit may carry a firearm in a vehicle only if it is unloaded and: carried in a sealed box or case, or in a compartment that can be reached only by leaving the vehicle, or in plain sight and secured in a rack or holder

348

made for the purpose. [http://gunla.ws/oh4]

G.   Self-defense Laws

Ohio has a Castle Doctrine but no SYG law. There is no duty to retreat when in Your dwelling or vehicle. You may use force, including deadly force, in defense of yourself or others if You reasonably believe it is necessary to prevent imminent death, SBI, or to stop the unlawful & forcible entry into Your dwelling or occupied motor vehicle. Note that Ohio is the only state where the burden of proof is on You to prove that You acted in self-defense, except in cases of unlawful entry into Your dwelling or occupied motor vehicle. This means that You may be charged with homicide after using deadly force against an aggressor, and You must then prove that Your use of force was legally justified. [http://gunla.ws/oh5]

H.   Criminal Provisions

Under Ohio law, any license to carry a handgun does not permit concealed carry in any of the following places or circumstances:

- A police station, sheriff's office, or state highway patrol station
- Discharge near or across a roadway or near a building
- Into a premises controlled by the Bureau of Criminal Identification and Investigation
- A state correctional institution, jail, workhouse, or other detention facility
- An airport passenger terminal
- Discharge in, at, or on a school safety zone
- Discharge within 100 yards of a cemetery
- A courthouse, or building where a courtroom is located

- A public or private college, university, or other higher education institution, though possession is permitted in the parking areas thereto so long as the handgun remains secured in his vehicle
- Any church, synagogue, mosque, or other place of worship (unless the establishment permits carry)
- A child day care facility
- An aircraft
- Any government building or facility
- Any place which federal law prohibits
- Any place where a "no guns" sign is clearly posted
- While under the influence of alcohol or drugs
- Residents of Ohio may now purchase shotguns, rifles, and ammunition in any other state from licensed firearms dealers, in accordance with federal law and the laws of that state
- People with a valid carry permit are exempt from background checks when buying guns

For a list of places where carrying firearms is prohibited, see: [http://gunla.ws/oh6]

I.   Do "No Gun Signs" Have the Force of Law?

Yes. If a property or establishment has a "No Guns" sign or the person in lawful possession communicates to You that guns are not allowed, You are prohibited from carrying on the property or into the establishment. Failure to obey such signs or verbal warnings constitutes trespass.
[http://gunla.ws/o4l8]

J.   Carry in Restaurants That Serve Alcohol

Yes, so long as you possess a valid concealed handgun

license. Places like Fridays or Chili's unless they have a "No Gun Sign," then it is suggested that You not carry into the establishment. This does not include a bar or the bar area of a restaurant – You are prohibited from carrying into these areas. You can carry Your firearm into a restaurant that serves alcohol, but you are prohibited from carrying while you consume alcohol or are under the influence of alcohol. [http://gunla.ws/8bn1]

K.   Open Carry

Open carry is legal, but you must have a valid permit/license to carry a handgun in a vehicle unless it is unloaded and: carried in a sealed box or case, or in a compartment that can be reached only by leaving the vehicle, or in plain sight and secured in a rack or holder made for the purpose. Places as listed in the "Criminal Provisions" above apply to those who open carry. The minimum age to open carry is 18. [http://gunla.ws/8wi5]

 # OKLAHOMA
GUN LAWS

Introduction

Oklahoma is bordered to the north by Kansas, with corners touching Missouri, Colorado, and New Mexico. To the south and west is Texas, and to the east is Arkansas. Oklahoma's major industries include oil, natural gas, and agriculture. Open carry is legal in Oklahoma with a valid license to carry.

A.   State Constitution

Regarding the right to bear arms, the Oklahoma Constitution states:

> "The right of a citizen to keep and bear arms in defense of his home, person, or property, or in aid of the civil power, when thereunto legally summoned, shall never be prohibited; but nothing herein contained shall prevent the Legislature from regulating the carrying of weapons." [http://gunla.ws/ok1]

B.   Scope of Preemption

The controlling language of Oklahoma's preemption statute is set forth as follows:

> "The State Legislature hereby occupies and preempts the entire field of legislation in this state touching in any way

352

firearms, components, ammunition, and supplies to the complete exclusion of any order, ordinance, or regulation by any municipality or other political subdivision of this state. Any existing or future orders, ordinances, or regulations in this field, except as provided for in paragraph 2 of this subsection and subsection C of this section, are null and void." [http://gunla.ws/ok2]

C.   Reciprocal Carry

By statute, Oklahoma will recognize another state's license to carry:

"The State of Oklahoma hereby recognizes any valid concealed carry weapons permit or license issued by another state."

Additionally, Oklahoma will allow those from Permit-less carry states (Alaska, Arizona, Vermont and Wyoming):

"Starting November 1, 2012, the state of Oklahoma will allow You to carry a concealed handgun without a license only if You are allowed to do so in Your own state." [http://gunla.ws/ok3]

D.   Duty to Inform Officers

Yes. Oklahoma does not require individuals to inform a LEO of a permit or license to carry unless they are actually in possession of a firearm, in which case they must inform any LEO they come in contact with of that fact. You must possess your permit/license and Oklahoma State photo identification any time you carry a pistol. [http://gunla.ws/8wi5]

E. NFA Items

Oklahoma permits ownership of all NFA items, provided they are legally obtained pursuant to federal law. It is legal to use suppressors for hunting. CLEOs are required to sign an application for the transfer of any item regulated under the NFA within 15 days if the applicant is not prohibited by law from receiving it. [http://gunla.ws/ori7]

F. Carrying Firearms in Vehicles

Oklahoma permits anyone who may legally possess a firearm to carry it unloaded without a permit. Long guns may be carried openly or concealed behind a seat or within the interior of the vehicle, and handguns may be carried openly or within a firearms case, gun rack, or in the trunk. [http://gunla.ws/ok4]

G. Self-defense Laws

Oklahoma has both Castle Doctrine and SYG laws. There is no duty to retreat from any place You have a legal right to be. You may use force, including deadly force, in defense of yourself or others if You reasonably believe it is necessary to prevent imminent death, SBI, the commission of a forcible felony, or to stop the unlawful & forcible entry into a dwelling, place of business, or occupied motor vehicle. [http://gunla.ws/ok5]

H. Criminal Provisions

Under Oklahoma law, a license to carry a handgun is not valid in any of the following places or circumstances, whether it is issued by Oklahoma, or a person is carrying pursuant to a reciprocity agreement between his or her state of license and Oklahoma:

354

- Carrying with the intent to unlawfully injure another person
- Pointing a gun, whether loaded or unloaded, at another person, except in self-defense
- Any building or office space used (owned or leased) by a city, town, county, state, or federal government authority
- At a meeting place of any city, town, county, state or federal officials, school board members, legislative members, or elected or appointed officials
- A prison, jail, detention facility
- An elementary, secondary school, college, university or Technology Center
- Any sports arena during a professional sporting event
- Any place where pari-mutuel wagering is authorized by law (i.e. gambling, horse racing, etc.)
- On school property (either public or private), school bus, or other vehicle used by any school for transportation of students
- While under the influence of beer, intoxicating liquors, hallucinogenic drugs, unprescribed drugs, or prescribed drugs which affect mental, emotional, or physical processes
- Oklahoma has a max size for the caliber of firearm You can carry. The max caliber You can carry legally is .45.
- People convicted of a misdemeanor drug offense may now apply for a license to carry, provided their sentence was completed at least 10 years ago

Note: Beginning November 1, 2017, individuals with a valid carry permit will be allowed to bring a firearm on public buses.

For a list of places where carrying firearms is prohibited, see: [http://gunla.ws/ok6]

I. Do "No Gun Signs" Have the Force of Law?

No. "No Firearm" signs in Oklahoma do not have the force of law unless they are posted on property that is specifically mentioned in State law as being off limits to those with a permit/license to carry. However, as a possessor with a real property interest, a retailer, has the right to limit, and qualify the right to enter the property, subject to not carrying a handgun. It would be improper to enter, and the licensee would be subject to ejection for possession of a handgun thereat. Failure to leave once requested would subject the licensee to criminal charges. [http://gunla.ws/4na9]

J. Carry in Restaurants That Serve Alcohol

Yes, if you possess a valid concealed handgun license. Places like Fridays or Chili's unless they have a "No Gun Sign," then it is suggested that You not carry into the establishment. This does not include a bar or the bar area of a restaurant – You are prohibited from carrying into these areas. You can carry Your firearm into a restaurant that serves alcohol, but You are prohibited from carrying while You consume alcohol or are under the influence of alcohol. [http://gunla.ws/4na9]

K. Open Carry

Open carry is legal in Oklahoma only for those who have a valid permit/license to carry a firearm or those from the permitless carry states of AK, AZ, VT and WY. Places listed in the "Criminal Provisions" above apply to those who open carry. The minimum age to open carry is 21.

OREGON
GUN
LAWS

Introduction

Oregon is located in the Northwest and is bordered to the north by Washington State, with California and Nevada to the south, Idaho to the east, and the Pacific Ocean to the west. Oregon is home to dense forests and deserts alike. Open carry is generally legal in Oregon with a valid license to carry, although some localities prohibit it.

A.   State Constitution

Regarding the right to bear arms, the Oregon Constitution states:

> "The people shall have the right to bear arms for the defense of themselves, and the State, but the Military shall be kept in strict subordination to the civil power"
> [http://gunla.ws/or1]

B.   Scope of Preemption

The controlling language of Oregon's preemption statute is set forth as follows:

> "Except as expressly authorized by state statute, the authority to regulate in any matter whatsoever the sale, acquisition, transfer, ownership, possession, storage,

transportation or use of firearms or any element relating to firearms and components thereof, including ammunition, is vested solely in the Legislative Assembly."
[http://gunla.ws/or2]

C.   Reciprocal Carry

Oregon does not recognize another state's license to carry a concealed weapon.

D.   NFA Items

Oregon permits ownership of all NFA items, provided they are legally obtained pursuant to federal law. It is legal to use suppressors for hunting.

E.   Carrying Firearms in Vehicles

Oregon permits anyone who may legally possess a firearm to carry it openly in a motor vehicle without a permit, provided it is visible from outside the vehicle. People without carry permits may not carry a loaded handgun that is concealed and readily accessible. People without carry permits may carry concealed handguns if they are not readily accessible, such as being locked in the trunk. [http://gunla.ws/or3]

F.   Self-defense Laws

Oregon has a Castle Doctrine, and while they do not explicitly have a SYG law, the Oregon Supreme Court has ruled that there is no duty to retreat from any place You have a legal right to be, which is essentially the same thing as a SYG law. You may use force, including deadly force, in defense of yourself or others if You reasonably believe it is necessary to prevent imminent death, SBI, or the commission of a forcible felony. [http://gunla.ws/or4]

G. Universal Background Checks

Background checks are mandatory for all firearm sales, and transfers between private parties must go through a licensed dealer. [http://gunla.ws/kks4]

H. Criminal Provisions

Cities may have ordinances that are more restrictive or broad than the State laws. Under Oregon law:

"When a sheriff issues a concealed handgun license under this section, the sheriff shall provide the licensee with a list of those places where carrying concealed handguns is prohibited or restricted by state or federal law."

Ultimately, a person carrying a handgun must comply with § 166.370(2)(B)(3)(d). Under Oregon law, it is unlawful, specifically, to:

- Possess a firearm on school property unless it is possessed by someone who is allowed to possess it and the firearm is unloaded and locked in a motor vehicle
- Possess a firearm in a public building or court facility [http://gunla.ws/tjhn]
- Hunt in a cemetery
- Discharge a weapon on or across highway, ocean shore recreation area or public utility facilities
- Discharge a weapon or throw objects at trains
- Discharge a weapon across airport operational services [http://gunla.ws/orfw]

For a list of places where carrying firearms is prohibited, see: [http://gunla.ws/or5]

I. Duty to Inform Officers

No. You are not required to inform a LEO that you possess a handgun immediately on contact. However, You are required to possess Your license/permit and photo identification any time You carry a handgun. You must present Your license/permit and photo identification to a LEO upon request. [http://gunla.ws/gyee]

J. Do "No Gun Signs" Have the Force of Law?

No. "No Firearm" signs in Oregon do not have the force of law unless they are posted on property that is specifically mentioned in State Law as being off limits to those with a permit/license to carry. However, as a possessor with a real property interest, a retailer, has the right to limit, and qualify the right to enter the property, subject to not carrying a handgun. It would be improper to enter, and the licensee would be subject to ejection for possession of a handgun threat. Failure to leave once requested would subject the licensee to criminal charges.

K. Carry in Restaurants That Serve Alcohol

Yes, if you possess a valid concealed handgun license. Places like Fridays or Chili's unless they have a "No Gun Sign," then it is suggested that You not carry into the establishment. This does not include a bar or the bar area of a restaurant – You are prohibited from carrying into these areas. You can carry Your firearm into a restaurant that serves alcohol, but you are prohibited from carrying while you consume alcohol or are under the influence of alcohol.

L.   Open Carry (Without a Valid Permit/License)

Open carry is legal, but the State has given local governments the right to adopt laws/ordinances on carrying loaded firearms by those without a permit/license to carry. Some cities and towns have adopted such laws/ordinances. Places as listed in the "Criminal Provisions" above apply to those who open carry. All public buildings are off limits to those who open carry without a permit/license. The minimum age to open carry is 18.

PENNSYLVANIA GUN LAWS

Introduction

The Commonwealth of Pennsylvania is located in the Mid-Atlantic region of the United States. The centrally located state borders Delaware and Maryland to the south, West Virginia to the southwest, Ohio to the west, New York to the north, and New Jersey to the east. Open carry is legal in Pennsylvania with a valid license to carry, except in Philadelphia.

A.   State Constitution

Regarding the right to bear arms, the Pennsylvania Constitution states:

> "The right of the citizens to bear arms in defense of themselves and the State shall not be questioned."
> [http://gunla.ws/pa1]

B.   Scope of Preemption

The controlling language of Pennsylvania's preemption statute is set forth as follows:

> "No county, municipality or township may in any manner regulate the lawful ownership, possession, transfer or transportation of firearms, ammunition or ammunition components when carried or transported for purposes not prohibited by the laws of this Commonwealth."

[http://gunla.ws/pa2]

Cities and municipalities may regulate the unsafe discharge of firearms.

C. Reciprocal Carry

By statute, Pennsylvania will recognize another state's license to carry if that state recognizes Pennsylvania's license:

> "The Attorney General shall have the power and duty to enter into reciprocity agreements with other states providing for the mutual recognition of a license to carry a firearm issued by the Commonwealth and a license or permit to carry a firearm issued by the other state." [http://gunla.ws/pa3]

Anyone contemplating reciprocal carry should check with the official list maintained by the Pennsylvania AG at the point in time the reciprocal carry is to occur. Pennsylvania's reciprocity agreement can be viewed here: [http://gunla.ws/pa4]

D. NFA Items

Pennsylvania permits ownership of all NFA items, provided they are legally obtained pursuant to federal law. It is legal to use suppressors for hunting.

E. Carrying Firearms in Vehicles

Pennsylvania generally prohibits carrying firearms in vehicles without a permit. Carrying a loaded long gun is illegal. People without permits may only carry firearms in their vehicle if they are unloaded, and they are transporting it to or from: the place of purchase or repair, a shooting range, or hunting activities. [http://gunla.ws/pa5]

F.   Self-defense Laws

Pennsylvania has a Castle Doctrine but no SYG law. There is no duty to retreat when in Your dwelling. You may use force, including deadly force, in defense of yourself or others if You reasonably believe it is necessary to prevent imminent death, SBI, the commission of a forcible felony, or if necessary to protect Your dwelling, place of business, or occupied motor home from arson, burglary, robbery, or other forcible felonies. [http://gunla.ws/pa6]

G.   Universal Background Checks

Pennsylvania requires that every sale of a handgun go through an FFL to conduct a background check.

H.   Criminal Provisions

Under Pennsylvania law, a license to carry a handgun is not valid in any of the following places or circumstances, whether it is issued by Pennsylvania, or a person is carrying pursuant to a reciprocity agreement between his or her state of license and Pennsylvania:

- When carrying a firearm concealed on one's person or in a vehicle pursuant to a license to carry, upon lawful demand of a law enforcement officer, one must produce the license for inspection
- Some cities have passed ordinances that restricts carrying of firearms within City Parks be sure to check the ordinances of the City which You plan to be in ahead of time, although carry in State Parks by licensees is

permitted
- Mental hospitals
- Casinos
- Court houses
- On school property

For a list of places where carrying firearms is prohibited, see: [http://gunla.ws/pa7]

I.   Duty to Inform Officers

No. When carrying a firearm concealed on or about one's person or in a vehicle, an individual licensed to carry must produce their license/permit to carry a firearm for inspection upon the request from a LEO. [http://gunla.ws/w9rh]

J.   Do "No Gun Signs" Have the Force of Law?

No. "No Firearm" signs in Pennsylvania do not have the force of law unless they are posted on property that is specifically mentioned in State law as being off limits to those with a permit/license to carry. However, as a possessor with a real property interest, a retailer, has the right to limit, and qualify the right to enter the property, subject to not carrying a handgun. It would be improper to enter, and the licensee would be subject to ejection for possession of a handgun thereat. Failure to leave once requested would subject the licensee to criminal charges.

K.   Carry in Restaurants That Serve Alcohol

Yes, if you possess a valid concealed handgun license. Places like Fridays or Chili's unless they have a "No Gun Sign," then it is suggested that You not carry into the establishment. This does not include a bar or the bar area of a restaurant – You are prohibited from carrying into these areas. You can carry Your firearm into a restaurant that serves alcohol, but You are prohibited from carrying while You consume alcohol or are under the influence of alcohol.

L.   Open Carry (Without a Valid Permit/License)

Open carry is legal, except a valid permit/license is needed to carry a loaded handgun openly or concealed in a vehicle and for openly carrying in the city of Philadelphia. Places as listed in the "Criminal Provisions" above apply to those who open carry. Philadelphia has laws/ordinances concerning open carry and only those with a valid permit/license to carry can open carry in Philadelphia. [http://gunla.ws/u50p] The minimum age to open carry is 18.

 # RHODE ISLAND GUN LAWS

Rhode Island's full name is State of Rhode Island and Providence Plantations, and is the least extensive of the United States. It is bordered by Massachusetts to the north and east, Connecticut to the west, with the Atlantic Ocean to the South. Open carry is legal in Rhode Island with a valid license to carry only if the license was issued by the state Attorney General.

A.   State Constitution

Regarding the right to bear arms, the Rhode Island Constitution states:

"The right of the people to keep and bear arms shall not be infringed." [http://gunla.ws/ri1]

B.   Scope of Preemption

The controlling language of Rhode Island's preemption statute is set forth as follows:

"The control of firearms, ammunition, or their component parts regarding their ownership, possession, transportation, carrying, transfer, sale, purchase, purchase delay, licensing, registration, and taxation shall rest solely with the state, except as otherwise provided in this chapter."
[http://gunla.ws/ri2]

C.   Reciprocal Carry

Rhode Island does not recognize another state's license to carry a concealed weapon.

D.   Duty to Inform Officers

Yes. Rhode Island does not require individuals to inform a LEO of a permit or license to carry, however an Officer may arrest anyone in possession of a firearm if the Officer believes that person is carrying or using that firearm illegally. Anyone so arrested must then prove that their possession or use of a firearm was legal, such as by producing a permit to carry. For this reason it is highly recommended that anyone in possession of a firearm always have their license/permit with them and notify LEO of their permit to carry immediately. [http://gunla.ws/ttuh]

E.   NFA Items

Rhode Island bans all NFA Items. [http://gunla.ws/ze3y]

F.   Carrying Firearms in Vehicles

Rhode Island generally prohibits carrying firearms in vehicles without a permit. Carrying loaded long guns is illegal. Someone without a permit may carry a handgun provided that it is disassembled, unloaded and carried openly or secured in a separate container, and You are carrying it to or from: the place of purchase or repair, a shooting range, or when moving from one home to another. [http://gunla.ws/ri3]

G.   Waiting Period

Rhode Island imposes a seven (7) day waiting period before

purchasing a firearm.

H.   Universal Background Checks

Background checks are mandatory for all firearm sales, and transfers between private parties, except between family members, must go through a licensed dealer. Holders of a valid Rhode Island license to carry are exempt from this requirement.

I.   Self-defense Laws

Rhode Island has a Castle Doctrine but no SYG law. There is no duty to retreat when in Your dwelling. You may use force, including deadly force, in defense of yourself or others if You reasonably believe it is necessary to prevent imminent death, SBI, or to stop the unlawful & forcible entry into a dwelling, place of business, or occupied motor vehicle. [http://gunla.ws/ri4]

J.   Criminal Provisions

Under Rhode Island law, a license to carry a handgun is not valid in any of the following places or circumstances:

- Parks
- Hospitals
- Places of worship
- Sports arenas
- Gambling facilities
- Polling places
- Public and private school grounds
- Discharge of a firearm on another's property without their permission [http://gunla.ws/mqet]
- Discharge of a firearm across a public road, street, square, or lane

- While intoxicated or under the influence of intoxicating liquor or narcotic drugs [http://gunla.ws/ri5]

For a list of places where carrying firearms is prohibited, see: [http://gunla.ws/ws41]

K. Carry in Restaurants That Serve Alcohol

Yes, if you possess a valid concealed handgun license. Places like Fridays or Chili's unless they have a "No Gun Sign," then it is suggested that You not carry into the establishment. This does not include a bar or the bar area of a restaurant – You are prohibited from carrying into these areas. You can carry Your firearm into a restaurant that serves alcohol, but you are prohibited from carrying while you consume alcohol or are under the influence of alcohol.

L. Open Carry

Open carry of handguns is permitted for only those with a carry permit issued by the AG of Rhode Island. Open carry is not permitted for those whose handgun permits were issued by local authorities. Long gun open carry with or without a permit is not prohibited by law. Places as listed in the "Criminal Provisions" above apply to those who open carry. [http://gunla.ws/ebkt]

 # SOUTH CAROLINA GUN LAWS

Introduction

South Carolina is bordered to the north by North Carolina, to the west and south by Georgia, and to the east by the Atlantic Ocean. It was the founding state of the Confederacy as it was the first to secede from the Union during the Civil War.

A.   State Constitution

Regarding the right to bear arms, the South Carolina Constitution states:

> "A well regulated militia being necessary to the security of a free State, the right of the people to keep and bear arms shall not be infringed. As, in times of peace, armies are dangerous to liberty, they shall not be maintained without the consent of the General Assembly. The military power of the State shall always be held in subordination to the civil authority and be governed by it. No soldier shall in time of peace be quartered in any house without the consent of the owner nor in time of war but in the manner prescribed by law." [http://gunla.ws/sc1]

B.   Scope of Preemption

The controlling language of South Carolina's preemption statute is set forth as follows:

"No governing body of any county, municipality, or other political subdivision in the State may enact or promulgate any regulation or ordinance that regulates or attempts to regulate: (1) the transfer, ownership, possession, carrying, or transportation of firearms, ammunition, components of firearms, or any combination of these things."
[http://gunla.ws/sc2]

C.   Reciprocal Carry

By statute, South Carolina will recognize another state's license to carry if that state recognizes South Carolina's license:

"Valid out-of-state permits to carry concealable weapons held by a resident of a reciprocal state must be honored by this State, provided, that the reciprocal state requires an applicant to successfully pass a criminal background check and a course in firearm training and safety. A resident of a reciprocal state carrying a concealable weapon in South Carolina is subject to and must abide by the laws of South Carolina regarding concealable weapons."
[http://gunla.ws/sc2]

Anyone contemplating reciprocal carry should check with the official list maintained by the South Carolina State Law Enforcement Division (SLED) at the point in time the reciprocal carry is to occur. South Carolina's reciprocity agreement can be viewed here: [http://gunla.ws/mwcy]

D.   Duty to Inform Officers

South Carolina requires holders of a permit or license to carry to notify and present their permit to any Officer that identifies themselves as a LEO or asks for identification or a driver's license. [http://gunla.ws/x5vp]

E.   NFA Items

South Carolina permits ownership of all NFA items, provided they are legally obtained pursuant to federal law. It is legal to use suppressors for hunting. [http://gunla.ws/396w]

F.   Carrying Firearms in Vehicles

South Carolina generally prohibits carrying handguns in vehicles without a permit. The exceptions are that You may transport a handgun to and from a place where You may legally possess a handgun, to or from a hunting trip, or in a vehicle if the handgun is secured in a closed glove compartment, closed console, closed trunk or closed container secured by an integral fastener and transported in the "luggage compartment" of the vehicle. [http://gunla.ws/sc3]

G.   Self-defense Laws

South Carolina has both Castle Doctrine and SYG laws. There is no duty to retreat from any place You have a legal right to be. You may use force, including deadly force, in defense of yourself or others if You reasonably believe it is necessary to prevent imminent death, SBI, the commission of a forcible felony, or to stop the unlawful & forcible entry into a dwelling, place of business, or occupied motor vehicle. People are immune from civil liability from lawsuits arising from their lawful use of force in self-defense. [http://gunla.ws/sc4]

H.   Criminal Provisions

Under South Carolina law, a license to carry a handgun is not valid in any of the following places or circumstances, whether it is issued by South Carolina, or a person is carrying pursuant to a reciprocity agreement between his or her state of license and South Carolina:

- Upon request by an owner or occupant of a business to not carry on their property
- A private or public school, college, university, technical college, or other post-secondary institution
- On a bus
- Any publicly owned building without express permission
- Any other law enforcement office or facility
- A detention facility, prison, or jail
- Any place with a posted 'no guns' sign [http://gunla.ws/vchb]
- A courthouse or courtroom
- Any polling place on an election day
- An office or meeting place of a governing body of any county, public school district, municipality, or special purpose district
- A daycare or preschool facility
- A school or college athletic event (which is not related to firearms)
- A church or other religious sanctuary
- Any place prohibited by federal law
- A hospital, medical clinic, doctor's office, or any other facility where medical services are performed
- Into the residence of another person without express permission to carry
- Discharge while under the influence of alcohol

For a list of places where carrying firearms is prohibited, see: [http://gunla.ws/sc5]

I.   Do "No Gun Signs" Have the Force of Law?

Yes. If a property or establishment has a "No Guns" sign or the person in lawful possession communicates to You that guns are not allowed, You are prohibited from carrying on the property or into the establishment. Failure to obey such signs or verbal warnings constitutes trespass. [http://gunla.ws/2bsc]

J.   Carry in Restaurants That Serve Alcohol

Yes, if you possess a valid concealed handgun license/permit. Places like Fridays or Chili's unless they have a "No Gun Sign," then You are prohibited from carrying into the establishment. This does not include a bar or the bar area of a restaurant – You are prohibited from carrying into these areas.

You are not prohibited from carrying a firearm while consuming alcohol, but You are prohibited from discharging a firearm while intoxicated. [http://gunla.ws/jmhx]

K.   Open Carry

Open carry of a handgun is illegal in South Carolina. Even those with a valid permit/license to carry a concealed firearm are prohibited from carrying openly. Open carry of long guns is permitted while hunting.

SOUTH DAKOTA GUN LAWS

South Dakota is bordered to the north by North Dakota, to the west by Montana and Wyoming, to the south by Nebraska, and to the east by Iowa and Minnesota. The Missouri River bifurcates the state into two districts, known as East River and West River to South Dakota inhabitants. Open carry is legal in South Dakota with a valid license to carry.

A.   State Constitution

Regarding the right to bear arms, the South Dakota Constitution states:

> "The right of the citizens to bear arms in defense of themselves and the state shall not be denied."
> [http://gunla.ws/sd1]

B.   Scope of Preemption

The controlling language of South Dakota's preemption statute is set forth as follows:

> "No county, [township, or municipality] may pass any ordinance that restricts possession, transportation, sale, transfer, ownership, manufacture, or repair of firearms or ammunition or their components. Any ordinances

prohibited by this section are null and void."
[http://gunla.ws/sd2]

C.   Reciprocal Carry

By statute, South Dakota will recognize another state's license to carry if that state recognizes South Dakota's license:

"Any valid permit to carry a concealed pistol, issued to a nonresident of South Dakota, is valid in South Dakota according to the terms of its issuance in the state of its issue, but only to the extent that the terms of issuance comply with any appropriate South Dakota statute or promulgated rule. However, if the holder of such a nonresident permit to carry a concealed pistol becomes, at any time, a legal resident of South Dakota, the provisions of this section no longer apply." [http://gunla.ws/sd3]

And,

"The attorney general shall compare South Dakota permit issuance statutes with the permit issuance statutes in states with which reciprocity is sought or requested in order to determine whether the laws of the other state meet or exceed the requirements of this chapter for the issuance of a permit. The secretary of state may enter into reciprocity agreements with other states after the attorney general has notified the secretary of state that the other states' laws meet or exceed the provisions of this chapter."
[http://gunla.ws/sd4]

Since there is no national carry license, as with the other states, some states are reciprocal with South Dakota and some are not. Anyone contemplating reciprocal carry should check with the official list. South Dakota's reciprocity agreements can be viewed here: [http://gunla.ws/7w8p]

South Dakota issues both regular and enhanced carry permits, as well as "gold" carry permits. Information about these permits and the differences between them can be viewed here: [http://gunla.ws/sd5]

D.   NFA Items

South Dakota permits ownership of all NFA items, provided they are legally obtained pursuant to federal law. It is legal to use suppressors for hunting.

E.   Carrying Firearms in Vehicles

South Dakota generally prohibits carrying concealed handguns in vehicles without a permit, unless the handgun is unloaded and is carried for any lawful use within a trunk or other closed compartment of a vehicle or in a closed container that cannot be concealed on the person. [http://gunla.ws/sd6]

F.   Self-defense Laws

South Dakota has both Castle Doctrine and SYG laws. There is no duty to retreat from anywhere You have a legal right to be. You may use force, including deadly force, in defense of yourself or others if You reasonably believe it is necessary to prevent imminent death, SBI, the commission of a forcible felony, or to stop the unlawful & forcible entry into a dwelling, place of business, or occupied motor vehicle. [http://gunla.ws/sd7]

G.   Criminal Provisions

Under South Dakota law, a license to carry a handgun is not

valid in any of the following places or circumstances:

- It is a crime to discharge a firearm from a motor vehicle
- Any school premises, school vehicle, or building used for school functions, if not for supervised gun training sessions
- Any courthouse
- The state capitol
- In a bar
- While operating or riding a snowmobile (unless the firearm is unloaded and within a carrying case)

For a list of places where carrying firearms is prohibited, see: [http://gunla.ws/sd8]

H.   Duty to Inform LEO Immediately on Contact?

No. You must possess a valid South Dakota permit to carry any time you carry a concealed pistol. You are not required to inform a LEO that you are carrying a firearm immediately on contact, but if a LEO requests, you must display Your license/permit. [http://gunla.ws/seu5]

I.   Do "No Gun Signs" Have the Force of Law?

No. "No Firearm" signs in South Dakota do not have the force of law unless they are posted on property that is specifically mentioned in state law as being off limits to those with a permit/license to carry. However, as a possessor with a real property interest, a retailer, has the right to limit, and qualify the right to enter the property, subject to not carrying a handgun. It would be improper to enter, and the licensee would be subject to ejection for possession of a handgun threat. Failure to leave once requested would subject the licensee to criminal charges.

J. Carry in Restaurants That Serve Alcohol

Yes, if you possess a valid concealed handgun license/permit. Places like Fridays or Chili's unless they have a "No Gun Sign," then it is suggested that You not carrying into the establishment. This does not include a bar or the bar area of a restaurant – You are prohibited from carrying into these areas. You can carry Your firearm into a restaurant that serves alcohol, but you are prohibited from carrying while you consume alcohol or are under the influence of alcohol. [http://gunla.ws/zjvk]

K. Open Carry

Open carry is legal in South Dakota. Places as listed in the "Criminal Provisions" above apply to those who open carry. For open carry in a vehicle, the firearm must be clearly visible. The minimum age for open carry is 18.

TENNESSEE GUN LAWS

Introduction

Tennessee is surrounded by many states including Kentucky, Missouri, Arkansas, Mississippi, Alabama, Georgia, North Carolina, and Virginia. While Nashville is the state capital, Memphis is the most populated city in Tennessee. Open carry is legal in Tennessee with a valid license to carry.

A.   State Constitution

Regarding the right to bear arms, the Tennessee Constitution states:

"That the citizens of this State have a right to keep and to bear arms for their common defense; but the Legislature shall have power, by law, to regulate the wearing of arms with a view to prevent crime." [http://gunla.ws/tn1]

B.   Scope of Preemption

The controlling language of Tennessee's preemption statute is set forth as follows:

"(a) Except as provided in § 39-17-1311(d), which allows counties and municipalities to prohibit the possession of handguns while within or on a public park, natural area, historic park, nature trail, campground, forest, greenway, waterway or other similar public place that is owned or operated by a county, a municipality or instrumentality thereof, no city, county, or urban-county government shall occupy any part of the field of regulation of the transfer, ownership, possession or transportation of firearms, ammunition or components of firearms or combinations thereof; provided, that the provisions of this section shall be prospectively only and shall not affect the validity of any ordinance or resolution lawfully enacted before April 8, 1986." Tenn. Code Ann. § 39-17-1314. [http://gunla.ws/tn2]

C.   Reciprocal Carry

By statute, Tennessee will recognize another state's license to carry if that state recognizes Tennessee's license:

"(1) A facially valid handgun permit, firearms permit, weapons permit or license issued by another state shall be valid in this state according to its terms and shall be treated as if it is a handgun permit issued by this state; provided, however, the provisions of this subsection (r) shall not be construed to authorize the holder of any out-of-state permit or license to carry, in this state, any firearm or weapon other than a handgun. (2) For a person to lawfully carry a handgun in this state based upon a permit or license issued in another state, the person must be in possession of the permit or license at all times the person carries a handgun in this state."

Note: Tennessee is willing to recognize the handgun carry permits or equivalents of any state that issues them, not just the ones with which it has entered into reciprocity agreements.

Anyone contemplating reciprocal carry should check with the official list maintained by the Tennessee Commissioner of Safety at the point in time the reciprocal carry is to occur. States add *and* delete states with reciprocity agreements over time. Tennessee's reciprocity agreement can be viewed here: [http://gunla.ws/tn3]

D. NFA Items

Tennessee permits ownership of all NFA items, provided they are legally obtained pursuant to federal law. It is legal to use suppressors for hunting. CLEOs are required to sign an application for the transfer of any item regulated under the NFA within 15 days if the applicant is not prohibited by law from receiving it. [http://gunla.ws/n17s]

E. Carrying Firearms in Vehicles

Tennessee permits anyone who may legally possess a firearm to carry a firearm in a motor vehicle without a permit. [http://gunla.ws/tn4]

F. Self-defense Laws

Tennessee has both Castle Doctrine and SYG laws. There is no duty to retreat from any place You have a legal right to be. You may use force, including deadly force, in defense of yourself or others if You reasonably believe it is necessary to prevent imminent death, SBI, or to stop the unlawful & forcible entry into a dwelling, place of business, or occupied motor vehicle. [http://gunla.ws/tn5]

G.   Criminal Provisions

Under Tennessee law, a license to carry a handgun does not carry in any of the following places or circumstances, even when the license was issued by Tennessee, or a person is carrying pursuant to a reciprocity agreement between his or her state of license and Tennessee:

- While inside any room in which judicial proceedings are in progress
- In a public or private school building, bus, campus, grounds, recreational area, athletic field, or any other property owned or used by a board of education, school, college, or university board of trustees, regents or directors for the administration of the educational institution, or any other facility where school sponsored athletic events are conducted
- While under the influence of alcohol or any controlled substance
- Where any individual, corporation, business entity, or local, state or federal government entity owned, operated or managed property has posted notice prohibiting the carrying of a concealed firearm
- In airports, military institutions, and other areas prohibited by federal law
- It is legal to store a loaded firearm in Your car even without a permit to carry
- Permit holders may store firearms and ammunition in their vehicles parked at work so long as they are locked up out of sight and secured within the vehicle
- Full time employees of public universities may carry on property owned, operated, or used by their university, provided they have a valid carry permit
- Public universities are prohibited from taking any

adverse action against an employee or student who lawfully transports or stores firearms or ammunition in their parked motor vehicle
- The governing entity of all private K-12 schools and private universities may develop a policy on handguns that either permits or prohibits people with valid carry permits from carrying on school property.

For a list of places where carrying firearms is prohibited, see: [http://gunla.ws/tn6]

H.   Duty to Inform Officers

No. You must have a valid license/permit to carry in Your possession any time you carry a concealed pistol. You are not required to inform a LEO that You are carrying a firearm immediately on contact, but if a LEO requests, You must display Your license/permit. [http://gunla.ws/n17s]

I.   Do "No Gun Signs" Have the Force of Law?

Yes. "No Guns" signs have the force of law. If a property or establishment has a "No Guns" sign or the person in lawful possession communicates to You that guns are not allowed, You are prohibited from carrying on the property or into the establishment. Carrying a firearm onto a property or into a building that has such a sign posted is a Class B misdemeanor. [http://gunla.ws/d2y8]

J.   Carry in Restaurants That Serve Alcohol

Yes, if you possess a valid concealed handgun license/permit. You are allowed to carry into any establishment that serves alcohol, including bars, unless there is a "No Guns Sign," then you are prohibited from carrying into the establishment. You are prohibited from carrying while You consume alcohol or are under the influence of alcohol.

K.　Open Carry

Open Carry of loaded handguns is only legal for those with a valid permit/license to carry a concealed firearm. Places as listed in the "Criminal Provisions" above apply to those who open carry. Long guns may only be carried unloaded unless You are hunting in an approved area. [http://gunla.ws/z42z]

Note: As of July 1, 2017, persons who can legally possess/purchase a firearm and are protected by a protection order may carry a handgun without a license for 60 days from the date the protection order was issued.

 **TEXAS GUN LAWS**

Introduction

Texas is bordered to the south by Mexico and the Gulf of Mexico, to the north by Oklahoma, to the west by New Mexico, and to the east by Arkansas and Louisiana. Texas is both the second most populous and the second most extensive of the U.S. Open carry is legal in Texas with a valid license to carry.

A.   State Constitution

Regarding the right to bear arms, the Texas Constitution states:

> "Every citizen shall have the right to keep and bear arms in the lawful defense of himself or the State; but the Legislature shall have power, by law, to regulate the wearing of arms, with a view to prevent crime."
> [http://gunla.ws/tx1]

B.   Scope of Preemption

The controlling language of Texas' preemption statute is set forth as follows:

> "(a) ...a municipality may not adopt regulations relating to:
> (1) the transfer, private ownership, keeping, transportation,

licensing, or registration of firearms, ammunition, or firearm supplies." [http://gunla.ws/tx2]

C.   Reciprocal Carry

By statute, Texas will recognize another state's license to carry if that state recognizes Texas' license:

"The governor shall negotiate an agreement with any other state that provides for the issuance of a license to carry a concealed handgun under which a license issued by the other state is recognized in this state or shall issue a proclamation that a license issued by the other state is recognized in this state if the AG of the State of Texas determines that a background check of each applicant for a license issued by that state is initiated by state or local authorities or an agent of the state or local authorities before the license is issued."
[http://gunla.ws/tx3]

Since there is no national carry license, as with the other states, some states are reciprocal with Texas and some are not. Anyone contemplating reciprocal carry should check with the official list maintained by the Texas AG at the point in time the reciprocal carry is to occur. [http://gunla.ws/94ds]

D.   Duty to Inform Officers

Yes. If a license holder is carrying a handgun on or about the license holder's person when a LEO demands that the license holder display identification, the license holder must display both their license to carry and driver's license. [http://gunla.ws/f0v2]

E. NFA Items

Texas permits ownership of all NFA items, provided they are legally obtained pursuant to federal law. It is legal to use suppressors for hunting.
[http://gunla.ws/2xmx] & [http://gunla.ws/k108]

F. Carrying Firearms in Vehicles

Texas permits anyone who is legally allowed to possess firearms to carry them in vehicles without a permit. People without permits must keep handguns concealed and out of sight when in vehicle. [http://gunla.ws/tx4]

G. Open Carry

Open carry is legal in Texas, but You must have a license to carry issued by Texas or a permit/license that Texas honors. If open carrying, the firearm must either be in a shoulder holster or a belt holster. LEOs have the authority to ask if You have a permit/license to carry when open carrying. If asked, You must display Your license/permit.

Open carry is not allowed on the campuses of any four-year public college/university/Jr. or community colleges. Beginning August 1, 2017 public four-year universities and public two-year colleges must allow concealed carry in campus buildings. Universities are allowed to designate certain sensitive areas as "gun free zones." [http://gunla.ws/pueq]

H. Self-defense Laws

Texas has both Castle Doctrine and SYG laws. There is no duty to retreat from any place You have a legal right to be. You may use force, including deadly force, in defense of yourself or others if You reasonably believe it is necessary to prevent imminent death, SBI, the commission of a forcible felony, or to stop the unlawful & forcible entry into a dwelling, place of business, or occupied motor vehicle. [http://gunla.ws/tx5]

I.   Criminal Provisions

In Texas it is unlawful to possess a firearm in the following prohibited places:

- A license holder may carry concealed, but not openly, on the premises of an institute of higher education.
  - No private or public institution of higher education may enact any regulation prohibiting or restricting the storage or transportation of a firearm or ammunition in a locked, privately owned vehicle including a student enrolled at the institution [http://gunla.ws/sqen]
  - The president of institutions of higher education must develop reasonable rules and regulations governing the carrying of handguns by license holders on campus, and these rules must not have the effect of general prohibiting license holders from carrying on campus
  - An institute of higher education may develop rules and regulations governing the storage of handguns in dormitories and residential facilities owned or operated by that institution and located on its campus
- On the premises of a polling place on the day of an election or while early voting is in progress
- On the premises of any government court or offices utilized by the court, unless pursuant to written

regulations or written authorization of the court
- On the premises of a racetrack
- In or into a secured area of an airport. Note that You cannot be arrested solely for possessing a handgun You're licensed to carry in the secure part of an airport, unless You fail to leave immediately upon being asked to by a police officer
- In or at any penal institution
- Hotels unless the hotel has notified the guest upon reservation confirmation [http://gunla.ws/psen]
- A hospital
- An amusement park
- A church, synagogue, or other established place of religious worship
  - Beginning 9/1/17 an exemption exists for volunteers providing security at places of worship who have a LTC and are approved by the congregation leaders. [http://gunla.ws/2ooh]
- Within 1,000 feet of premises the location of which is designated by the Texas Department of Criminal Justice as a place of execution under Article 43.19, Code of Criminal Procedure, on a day that a sentence of death is set to be imposed on the designated premises and the person received notice [http://gunla.ws/4601]
- State agencies or political subdivisions are prohibited from posting signs prohibiting license holders from carrying on their premises, except for the locations listed above where carrying weapons is already prohibited
- Carrying on the grounds or in the building of any K-12 school is prohibited. [http://gunla.ws/serp]
  - Beginning September 1, 2017 employees of school districts, open-enrollment charter schools and private elementary schools who possess valid LTCs

are permitted to transport and store firearms in their locked cars and trucks. [http://gunla.ws/2toh]

For a list of places where carrying firearms is prohibited, see: [http://gunla.ws/tx6]

J.   Do "No Gun Signs" Have the Force of Law?

Yes. If a property or establishment has a "No Guns" sign or the person in lawful possession communicates to You that guns are not allowed, You are prohibited from carrying on the property or into the establishment. Failure to obey such signs or verbal warnings constitutes trespass. [http://gunla.ws/51jo]

K.   Carry in Restaurants That Serve Alcohol

Yes, if you possess a valid concealed handgun license/permit and the establishment derives less than 51% of its income from the sale of alcohol for onsite consumption. If there is a "No Gun Sign," You are prohibited from carrying into the establishment. You are prohibited from carrying while You consume alcohol or are under the influence of alcohol. [http://gunla.ws/sc8g]

UTAH GUN LAWS

Introduction

Utah is located in the Western United States. Most of its 2,940,000 people live along the Wasatch Front, which is centered in Salt Lake City, and much of the state is nearly uninhabited. Utah is bordered by Arizona to the south, Colorado to the east, Wyoming on the northeast, Idaho to the north and Nevada to the west, as well as a corner of New Mexico. Open carry is legal in Utah with a valid license to carry, and is legal even without a license so long as at least two actions are required to fire the gun, such as racking the slide and pulling the trigger.

A.   State Constitution

Regarding the right to bear arms, the Utah Constitution states:

"The individual right of the people to keep and bear arms for security and defense of self, family, others, property, or the state, as well as for other lawful purposes shall not be infringed; but nothing herein shall prevent the Legislature from defining the lawful use of arms." [http://gunla.ws/ut1]

B.   Scope of Preemption

The controlling language of Utah's preemption statute is set forth as follows:

"(2) ... All authority to regulate firearms shall be reserved to the state except where the Legislature specifically delegates responsibility to local authorities or state entities. Unless specifically authorized by the Legislature by statute, a local authority or state entity may not enact or enforce any ordinance, regulation, or rule pertaining to firearms." [http://gunla.ws/ut2]

C.   Reciprocal Carry

By statute, Utah will recognize another state's license to carry.

"The provisions of Subsections 76-10-504 (1) and (2), and Section 76-10-505 do not apply to any person to whom a permit to carry a concealed firearm has been issued: ... (b) by another state or county." [http://gunla.ws/ut3]

Utah's reciprocity agreements can be viewed here: [http://gunla.ws/ut4]

D.   NFA Items

Utah permits ownership of all NFA items, provided they are legally obtained pursuant to federal law. It is legal to use suppressors for hunting. CLEOs are required to sign an application for the transfer of any item regulated under the NFA within 15 days if the applicant is not prohibited by law from receiving it. [http://gunla.ws/ig84]

E.   Carrying Firearms in Vehicles

Utah generally prohibits carrying concealed firearms in vehicles without a permit. It is illegal to possess a loaded long gun

394

in a vehicle. You may only carry a handgun without a permit if: (1) You are legally in possession of the vehicle; (2) have the consent of the owner; (3) are over 18 years old; and (4) the firearm is unloaded; securely encased (not including glove box or console box) and is not readily accessible for immediate use. [http://gunla.ws/ut5]

F.   Self-defense Laws

Utah has both Castle Doctrine and SYG laws. There is no duty to retreat from anywhere You have a legal right to be. You may use force, including deadly force, in defense of yourself or others if You reasonably believe it is necessary to prevent imminent death, SBI, the commission of a forcible felony, or to stop the unlawful & forcible entry into Your dwelling, if You reasonably believe the intruder intended to harm an occupant of the dwelling or commit a felony inside it. [http://gunla.ws/ut6]

G.   Criminal Provisions

Under Utah law, a license to carry a handgun is not valid in any of the following places or circumstances, whether it is issued by Utah, or a person is carrying pursuant to a reciprocity agreement between his or her state of license and Utah:

- Any secured area in which firearms are prohibited and notice is posted. Including:
  - A school or educational facility that has prohibited carrying pursuant to § 53B-3-103
  - Correctional facility, as defined by § 76-8-311.3
  - Law enforcement facility
  - Mental health facility, as defined by § 62A-15-602
  - A courtroom or courthouse which has prohibited carrying pursuant to § 78A-2-203

■ Any airport secure area

For a list of places where carrying firearms is prohibited, see: [http://gunla.ws/ut7]

H. Duty to Inform Officers

No. Although there is no legal requirement to disclose to a LEO that You are carrying a firearm, it is recommended to do so. If a LEO sees a gun on Your person during their contact with You, and You have not identified Yourself as a permit holder in legal possession of a firearm, the officer may assume You are carrying illegally and may take defensive action. [http://gunla.ws/5xu4]

I. Do "No Gun Signs" Have the Force of Law?

It depends. "No Guns" signs have the force of law if they are posted at a house of worship or private residence. Firearms are also prohibited where the owner or responsible person has verbally communicated that firearms are not permitted. Failure to leave or disarm constitutes trespass. [http://gunla.ws/kcxm]

J. Carry in Restaurants That Serve Alcohol

Yes. If You possess a license/permit, You are allowed to carry into all establishments that serve alcohol. You are allowed to consume alcohol while You carry, but it is illegal to carry while intoxicated (blood alcohol level over .08%) [http://gunla.ws/06w8]

K. Open Carry

Open carry of a loaded firearm is legal for those with a valid permit/license. Open carry of a firearm without a permit is allowed as long as the gun is at least two actions from being fired, i.e., no bullet in the chamber. Places as listed in the "Criminal Provisions" above apply to those who open carry.

VERMONT GUN LAWS

Introduction

Vermont is located in the Northeast, surrounded by New York, New Hampshire, Massachusetts, and Canada. It is the only state in the New England area that does not touch the Atlantic Ocean. It is the second least populous of the fifty (50) states. Vermont was the first state to enact constitutional carry laws, which are sometimes referred to as Vermont style carry.

A.   State Constitution

Regarding the right to bear arms, the Vermont Constitution states:

> "That the people have a right to bear arms for the defense of themselves and the State – and as standing armies in time of peace are dangerous to liberty, they ought not to be kept up; and that the military should be kept under strict subordination to and governed by the civil power."
> [http://gunla.ws/vt1]

B.   Scope of Preemption

The controlling language of Vermont's preemption statute is set forth as follows:

> "Except as otherwise provided by law, no town, city or incorporated village, by ordinance, resolution or other

enactment, shall directly regulate hunting, fishing and trapping or the possession, ownership, transportation, transfer, sale, purchase, carrying, licensing or registration of traps, firearms, ammunition or components of firearms or ammunition. This section shall not limit the powers conferred upon a town, city or incorporated village under section 2291(8) of this title. The provisions of this section shall supersede any inconsistent provisions of a municipal charter." [http://gunla.ws/vt2]

C.   Reciprocal Carry

Vermont does not require a permit to carry a concealed or open weapon within the state.

D.   NFA Items

Vermont permits ownership of all NFA items, provided they are legally obtained pursuant to federal law.

E.   Carrying Firearms in Vehicles

Vermont permits any who may legally possess firearms to carry them in vehicles, but long guns must be kept unloaded. [http://gunla.ws/vt3]

F.   Self-defense Laws

Vermont does not have a Castle Doctrine or SYG law, but courts have consistently ruled that there is no duty to retreat when attacked in Your dwelling. You may use force, including deadly force, in defense of yourself or others if You reasonably believe it is necessary to prevent imminent death, SBI, or the commission of a forcible felony.

G.   Criminal Provisions

Under Vermont law, one cannot carry a handgun in any of the following places or circumstances:

- A person who carries a dangerous or deadly weapon, openly or concealed, with the intent or avowed purpose of injuring a fellow man, or who carries a dangerous or deadly weapon within any state institution or upon the grounds or lands owned or leased for the use of such institution, without the approval of the warden or superintendent of the institution, shall be imprisoned not more than two (2) years or fined not more than $200.00, or both.
- Intentionally point or aim a firearm towards another, except in self-defense
- Within a courthouse
- On a school bus or in a school building or on school property, unless the board of school directors authorizes the use of firearms for instructional purposes
- On the grounds of a state institution, unless the Warden gives permission (e.g., prisons, mental hospital, state colleges, etc.)
- On the grounds of a residential treatment program

For a list of places where carrying firearms is prohibited, see: [http://gunla.ws/vt4]

Vermont Statutes can be accessed at: [http://gunla.ws/vt5]

H.   Duty to Inform Officers

No. Vermont allows anyone who can legally possess a

firearm to carry it concealed without a permit of any kind.

I. Do "No Gun Signs" Have the Force of Law?

Yes. If a property or establishment has a "No Guns" sign or the person in lawful possession communicates to You that guns are not allowed, You are prohibited from carrying on the property or into the establishment. Failure to obey such signs or verbal warnings constitutes Unlawful Trespass and is punishable by up to three years in prison or a fine of up to $500. [http://gunla.ws/53ns]

J. Carry in Restaurants That Serve Alcohol

Yes. You are allowed to carry into any establishment that serves alcohol, including bars. If there is a "No Guns" sign, You are prohibited from carrying into the establishment. [http://gunla.ws/7wpq]

K. Open Carry

Open carry is legal in Vermont. Places as listed in the "Criminal Provisions" above apply to those who open carry. The minimum age for open carry is lower in Vermont, but federal law states that you must be 18 to possess a handgun.

 # VIRGINIA
GUN
LAWS

Introduction

Virginia is bordered to the north by Maryland and the District of Columbia, to the northwest by West Virginia, to the west by Kentucky, and to the south by Tennessee and North Carolina. It is officially named the Commonwealth of Virginia and is situated on the Atlantic Coast. Open carry is generally legal in Virginia even without a valid license to carry, although some localities ban or restrict this.

A.   State Constitution

Regarding the right to bear arms, the Virginia Constitution states:

> "That a well regulated militia, composed of the body of the people, trained to arms, is the proper, natural, and safe defense of a free state, therefore, the right of the people to keep and bear arms shall not be infringed; that standing armies, in time of peace, should be avoided as dangerous to liberty; and that in all cases the military should be under strict subordination to, and governed by, the civil power." [http://gunla.ws/du3a]

B.   Scope of Preemption

The controlling language of Virginia's preemption statute is set forth as follows:

402

"No locality shall adopt or enforce any ordinance, resolution or motion, as permitted by § 15.2-1425, and no agent of such locality shall take any administrative action, governing the purchase, possession, transfer, ownership, carrying, storage or transporting of firearms, ammunition, or components or combination thereof other than those expressly authorized by statute. For purposes of this section, a statute that does not refer to firearms, ammunition, or components or combination thereof, shall not be construed to provide express authorization."
[http://gunla.ws/va1]

C.   Reciprocal Carry

By statute, Virginia will recognize all other state's license to carry, provided that:

"1. The holder of such permit or license is at least 21 years of age; and
2. The permit or license holder carries a photo identification issued by a government agency of any state or by the U.S. Department of Defense or U.S. Department of State; and
3. The holder displays the permit or license and such identification upon demand by a law-enforcement officer; and
4. The permit or license holder has not previously had a Virginia concealed handgun permit revoked."

Anyone contemplating reciprocal carry should check with the official list maintained by the Virginia State Police at the point in time the reciprocal carry is to occur. A list of states, which Virginia has a reciprocal carry agreement with can be accessed at: [http://gunla.ws/va2]

D.   Duty to Inform Officers

Virginia does not require individuals to inform a LEO of a permit or license to carry but if an Officer asks about a weapon, by law, an answer must be supplied. You are required to have Your license/permit with you at all times that you carry. [http://gunla.ws/t4mb]

E.   Assault Weapons Law

Virginia defines an assault weapon as "any semi-automatic center-fire rifle or pistol which is equipped at the time of the offense with a magazine which will hold more than 20 rounds of ammunition or designed by the manufacturer to accommodate a silencer or equipped with a folding stock, or a shotgun with a magazine which will hold more than seven rounds of the longest ammunition for which it is chambered". Virginia restricts the sale and possession of assault weapons to US citizens who are at least 18 years old for a rifle/shotgun or 21 years old for a pistol. Restrictions on carrying assault weapons may apply. [http://gunla.ws/va3]

F.   NFA Items

Virginia permits ownership of all NFA items, provided they are legally obtained pursuant to federal law. MGs must be registered with the state police within 24 hours of acquisition. It is legal to use suppressors for hunting. Some DDs are prohibited outside of law enforcement. [http://gunla.ws/1c6h

G.   Carrying Firearms in Vehicles

Virginia permits anyone who is legally allowed to possess firearms to carry a handgun without a permit, provided it is secured

404

in a locked container or compartment. [http://gunla.ws/va4]

H. Self-defense Laws

Virginia has a Castle Doctrine but no SYG law. There is no duty to retreat when in Your dwelling. You may use force, including deadly force, in defense of yourself or others if You reasonably believe it is necessary to prevent imminent death, SBI, the commission of a forcible felony, or to stop the unlawful & forcible entry into Your dwelling if You reasonably believe the intruder intends to harm an occupant of the dwelling. [http://gunla.ws/va5]

I. Criminal Provisions

Under Virginia law, a license to carry a handgun is not valid in any of the following places or circumstances, whether Virginia issued it, or a person is carrying pursuant to a reciprocity agreement between his or her state of license and Virginia:

- Hunting while under the influence of alcohol or illegal drugs
- While on the private property where the owner has prohibited possession
- In places of worship
- Court houses
- School property and at school functions
- Jail or Juvenile Detention Facilities
- On the grounds of any state government building occupied by the executive branch
- Domestic abusers must surrender their firearms within 24 hours of being served with a final family abuse protective order
- State police will have a booth at every gun show and

will offer to conduct background checks for $2 for people conducting private transfers. These background checks will be completely optional

For a list of places where carrying firearms is prohibited, see: [http://gunla.ws/va6]

J.   Do "No Gun Signs" Have the Force of Law?

No. "No Firearms" signs in Virginia do not have the force of law unless they are posted on property that is specifically mentioned in state law as being off limits to those with a permit/license to carry. However, as a possessor with a real property interest, a retailer, has the right to limit, and qualify the right to enter the property, subject to not carrying a handgun. It would be improper to enter, and the licensee would be subject to ejection for possession of a handgun thereat. Failure to leave once requested would subject the licensee to criminal charges.

K.   Carry in Restaurants That Serve Alcohol

Yes. You are allowed to carry into any establishment that serves alcohol, including bars. You are prohibited from carrying while you consume alcohol or are under the influence of alcohol. [http://gunla.ws/96tz]

L.   Open Carry

Open carry is generally allowed without a permit for people 18 years of age and older. The following cities and counties have exceptions that disallow the open carry of "assault weapons" (any firearm that is equipped with a magazine that will hold more than 20 rounds of ammunition or is designed by the manufacturer to accommodate a silencer or equipped with a folding stock) or

406

shotguns equipped with a magazine that holds more than 7 rounds: the Cities of Alexandria, Chesapeake, Fairfax, Falls Church, Newport News, Norfolk, Richmond, and Virginia Beach and in the Counties of Arlington, Fairfax, Henrico, Loudoun, and Prince William. These restrictions do not apply to valid concealed carry permit holders. [http://gunla.ws/wi8b]

WASHINGTON
GUN LAWS

Introduction

Washington is located in the far Northwest. It is bordered to the north by Canada, to the south by Oregon, to the west by the Pacific Ocean, and to the east by Idaho. Over half of the residents of Washington State live in the Seattle Metropolitan Area. Open carry of a loaded handgun is legal in Washington with a valid license to carry, and open carry of an unloaded handgun is legal even without a license.

A.   State Constitution

Regarding the right to bear arms, the Washington Constitution states:

> "The right of the individual citizen to bear arms in defense of himself, or the state, shall not be impaired, but nothing in this section shall be construed as authorizing individuals or corporations to organize, maintain or employ an armed body of men." [http://gunla.ws/wa1]

B.   Scope of Preemption

The controlling language of Washington's preemption statute is set forth as follows:

"The state of Washington hereby fully occupies and preempts the entire field of firearms regulation within the boundaries of the state, including the registration, licensing, possession, purchase, sale, acquisition, transfer, discharge, and transportation of firearms, or any other element relating to firearms or parts thereof, including ammunition and reloader components." [http://gunla.ws/wa2]

C.   Reciprocal Carry

By statute, Washington will recognize another state's license to carry if that state recognizes Washington's license:

"A person licensed to carry a pistol in a state the laws of which recognize and give effect in that state to a concealed pistol license issued under the laws of the state of Washington is authorized to carry a concealed pistol in this state if: (i) The licensing state does not issue concealed pistol licenses to persons under twenty-one years of age; and (ii) The licensing state requires mandatory fingerprint-based background checks of criminal and mental health history for all persons who apply for a concealed pistol license." [http://gunla.ws/wa3]

Since there is no national carry license, as with the other states, some states are reciprocal with Washington and some are not. Anyone contemplating reciprocal carry should check with the official list maintained by the Washington AG at the point in time the reciprocal carry is to occur, which may be viewed here: [http://gunla.ws/wa4]

D.   NFA Items

MGs and SBSs — unless purchased before July 1, 1994 —

are illegal for non-law-enforcement possession. Suppressors, DDs and any other weapons are lawful to possess and use if registered with the ATF(E). SBRs are lawful to possess and use if registered with the ATF(E). [http://gunla.ws/ppk8]

E.   Seattle Gun Tax

As of 1/1/16, the city of Seattle imposes a $25 tax on the sale of firearms, and a 5 cent per round tax on the sale of ammunition. This tax is currently being challenged in court as violating the state's preemption law, but has been allowed to take effect in the interim. [http://gunla.ws/2hus]

F.   Carrying Firearms in Vehicles

Washington generally prohibits carrying firearms in vehicles without a permit. It is illegal to carry a loaded long gun in a vehicle. A permit is required to carry a handgun, and even then a handgun may only be carried if: the pistol is on the licensee's person, (ii) the licensee is within the vehicle at all times that the pistol is there, or (iii) the licensee is away from the vehicle and the pistol is locked within the vehicle and concealed from view from outside the vehicle. [http://gunla.ws/wa5]

G.   Self-defense Laws

Washington has a Castle Doctrine but no SYG law. There is no duty to retreat when in Your dwelling. You may use force, including deadly force, in defense of yourself or others if You reasonably believe it is necessary to prevent imminent death, SBI, or the commission of a forcible felony. [http://gunla.ws/wa6]

F. Universal Background Checks

Background checks are mandatory for all firearm sales, and transfers between private parties must go through a licensed dealer, except for transfers between family members. [http://gunla.ws/jcs0]

I. Criminal Provisions

Carrying a Firearm in Washington State:

(1)(a) Except in the person's place of abode or fixed place of business, a person shall not carry a pistol concealed on his or her person without a license to carry a concealed pistol.

(b) Every licensee shall have his or her concealed pistol license in his or her immediate possession at all times that he or she is required by this section to have a concealed pistol license and shall display the same upon demand to any police officer or to any other person when and if required by law to do so. Any violation of this subsection (1)(b) shall be a class 1 civil infraction under chapter 7.80.

(2)(a) A person shall not carry or place a loaded pistol in any vehicle unless the person has a license to carry a concealed pistol and: (i) The pistol is on the licensee's person, (ii) the licensee is within the vehicle at all times that the pistol is there, or (iii) the licensee is away from the vehicle and the pistol is locked within the vehicle and concealed from view from outside the vehicle. [http://gunla.ws/941050]

Under Washington law, a license to carry a handgun is not

valid in any of the following places or circumstances:

- In any public or private elementary or secondary school, or school-provided transportation
- Note: Airsoft gun owners in Seattle: It is unlawful to knowingly carry or shoot any spring gun, air gun, sling or slingshot in, upon or onto any public place. For purposes of this section, "public place" means an area generally open to the public, regardless of whether it is privately owned, and includes, but is not limited to, streets, sidewalks, bridges, alleys, plazas, parks, parking lots, transit stations, transit vehicles and buildings [http://gunla.ws/12a14]
- A jail, a law enforcement facility, or any other place used for the confinement of a person arrested, charged with, or convicted of an offense
- Horse racetracks
- Outdoor music festivals
- At/on most college campuses
- Presentation of weapon, with intent to intimidate
- Purchasers of handguns are added to a state database
- Areas of buildings used in connection with court proceedings, including:
  - Courtrooms
  - Jury rooms
  - A judge's chambers
  - Offices and areas used to conduct court business
  - Court waiting
  - Corridors adjacent to areas used in connection with court proceedings

For a list of places where carrying firearms is prohibited, see: [http://gunla.ws/wa7]

J. Duty to Inform LEO Immediately on Contact?

No. You must have your permit/license with You at all times that You are carrying a concealed pistol. You must present Your license/permit upon request from a LEO. [http://gunla.ws/e0it]

K. Do "No Gun Signs" Have the Force of Law?

No. "No Firearms" signs in Washington do not have the force of law unless they are posted on property that is specifically mentioned in state law as being off limits to those with a permit/license to carry. However, as a possessor with a real property interest, a retailer, has the right to limit, and qualify the right to enter the property, subject to not carrying a handgun. It would be improper to enter, and the licensee would be subject to ejection for possession of a handgun thereat. Failure to leave once requested would subject the licensee to criminal charges.

L. Carry in Restaurants That Serve Alcohol

Yes, if you possess a license/permit to carry. You are only allowed to carry in parts of the restaurant where those under 21 years of age are allowed. You are prohibited from carrying in a bar or the bar section of a restaurant. It is illegal to carry while consuming alcohol or while intoxicated. [http://gunla.ws/s4zt]

M. Open Carry

Open carry is legal, but you must have a valid permit/license to carry a loaded handgun in any vehicle in Washington. Open carry of a loaded long gun in a vehicle is illegal, regardless of CPL possession. Places as listed in the "Criminal Provisions" above apply to those who open carry. The minimum age for open carry is 21. [http://gunla.ws/fmyt]

WEST VIRGINIA GUN LAWS

West Virginia is surrounded by Maryland, Pennsylvania, Ohio, Kentucky, and Virginia. Due to the positioning of the state, it is often included in multiple regions of the U.S., including the South and the Mid-Atlantic. Open carry is legal in West Virginia at age 18 even without a license to carry.

A.   State Constitution

Regarding the right to bear arms, the West Virginia Constitution states:

> "A person has the right to keep and bear arms for the defense of self, family, home and state, and for lawful hunting and recreational use." [http://gunla.ws/wv1]

B.   Scope of Preemption

The controlling language of West Virginia's preemption statute is set forth as follows:

> "(a) ...Neither a municipality nor the governing body of any municipality may limit the right of any person to purchase, possess, transfer, own, carry, transport, sell or store any revolver, pistol, rifle or shotgun or any ammunition or ammunition components to be used therewith nor to so regulate the keeping of gunpowder so as to directly or indirectly prohibit the ownership of the ammunition." [http://gunla.ws/wv2]

C.   Reciprocal Carry

West Virginia allows anyone 21 or older to carry a handgun without a permit, concealed or openly. West Virginia now allows adults between the ages of 18-20 to apply for a provisional concealed carry permit, which requires applicants to undergo firearms training, unless applicants are 21 and up.

By statute, West Virginia will recognize another state's license to carry if that state recognizes West Virginia's license:

"A holder of a valid out-of-state permit or license to carry a concealed handgun, as issued by another state with which the State of West Virginia has executed a reciprocity agreement, shall be recognized as valid in this state, if the following conditions are met: (1) The permit or license holder is 21 years or older; (2) The permit or license is in his or her immediate possession; (3) The permit or license holder is not a resident of the State of West Virginia; and, (4) The State of West Virginia has executed a valid and effective reciprocity agreement with the issuing state pertaining to the carrying and verification of concealed handgun licenses and permits issued in the respective states. (b) A holder of a valid permit or license from another state who is authorized to carry a concealed handgun in this state pursuant to provisions of this section is subject to the same laws and restrictions with respect to carrying a concealed handgun as a resident of West Virginia who is so permitted, and must carry the concealed handgun in compliance with the laws of this state." [http://gunla.ws/wv3]

Anyone contemplating reciprocal carry should check with the official list maintained by the West Virginia AG at the point in time the reciprocal carry is to occur. West Virginia's reciprocity agreement can be viewed online. [http://gunla.ws/wv4]

416

D.   NFA Items

West Virginia permits ownership of all NFA items, provided they are legally obtained pursuant to federal law. It is legal to use suppressors for hunting. CLEOs are required to sign an application for the transfer of any item regulated under the NFA within 30 days if the applicant is not prohibited by law from receiving it. [http://gunla.ws/pvpc]

E.   Carrying Firearms in Vehicles

West Virginia permits anyone who may legally possess a firearm to carry it unloaded in a motor vehicle, provided it is clearly visible from the outside. From July 1 to September 30 each year, unloaded guns must also be secured in a case when carried during certain times of the day. [http://gunla.ws/wv5]

F.   Self-defense Laws

West Virginia has both Castle Doctrine and SYG laws. There is no duty to retreat from anywhere You have a legal right to be. You may use force, including deadly force, in defense of yourself or others if You reasonably believe it is necessary to prevent imminent death, SBI, or to stop the unlawful & forcible entry into Your dwelling if You reasonably believe the intruder intends to harm an occupant or commit a felony inside the dwelling. [http://gunla.ws/wv6]

G.   Constitutional Carry

As of 5/24/16, West Virginia now permits anyone who is at least 21 years old and not prohibited from owning a firearm to carry a handgun without a permit, openly or concealed. Possession and open carry of handguns is legal at age 18, but adults between the ages of 18 and 21 must obtain a permit in order to carry a concealed firearm. Persons under the age of 18 may carry on family premises or on other property with permission of the owner or lessee.

H. Criminal Provisions

Under West Virginia law, a license to carry a handgun is not valid in any of the following places or circumstances:

- Brandish or use a firearm in a way or manner to cause, or threaten, a breach of the peace
- On any school bus
- State capital complex
- Courthouse
- Jails, detention facilities or State Division of Corrections facilities
- A public or private elementary or secondary education building, grounds, structure, or facility, or at any school-sponsored function, unless carry is necessary for a valid educational purpose with permission from the board of education or principal or if You are dropping off or picking up students (firearm must not leave the vehicle) [http://gunla.ws/5qnc]
- Where the owner, or lessee of private property has prohibited the carrying of any firearm

For a list of places where carrying firearms is prohibited, see: [http://gunla.ws/wv7]

I. Duty to Inform Officers

No. While carrying a firearm, You must have your license/permit in Your immediate possession and must display it upon request from a LEO. [http://gunla.ws/bv5s]

J. Do "No Gun Signs" Have the Force of Law?

No. "No Firearms" signs in West Virginia do not have the force of law unless they are posted on property that is specifically mentioned in state law as being off limits to those with a permit/license to carry. However, as a possessor with a real property interest, a retailer, has the right to limit, and qualify the right to enter the property, subject to not carrying a handgun. It would be improper to enter, and the licensee would be subject to ejection for possession of a handgun thereat. Failure to leave once requested would subject the licensee to criminal charges.

K. Carry in Restaurants That Serve Alcohol

Yes. West Virginia has no law prohibiting the carrying of a firearm into establishments that serve alcohol. However, if the owner or manager of the establishment requests that You disarm or leave, You must do so. Failure to obey such signs or verbal warnings constitutes trespass.
[http://gunla.ws/d56t

L. Open Carry

Open carry is legal. A permit to carry is available, but is not required to carry a handgun either openly or concealed. Places as listed in the "Criminal Provisions" above apply to those who open carry. The minimum age for open carry is 18.
[http://gunla.ws/z1o3]

WISCONSIN GUN LAWS

Introduction

Wisconsin is bordered by Michigan and Lake Superior to the north, Minnesota and Iowa to the west, Illinois to the south, and Lake Michigan to the east. Wisconsin's industries include health care, manufacturing, and agriculture. Open carry is legal in Wisconsin at 18 even without a license to carry, although handguns stored in vehicles may not be hidden from view unless the owner has a valid license to carry.

A.   State Constitution

Regarding the right to bear arms, the Wisconsin Constitution states:

> "The people have the right to keep and bear arms for security, defense, hunting, recreation or any other lawful purpose." [http://gunla.ws/wi1]

B.   Scope of Preemption

The controlling language of Wisconsin's preemption statute is set forth as follows:

> "No political subdivision may enact an ordinance or adopt a resolution that regulates the sale, purchase, purchase delay, transfer, ownership, use, keeping, possession,

bearing, transportation, licensing, permitting, registration or taxation of any firearm or part of a firearm, including ammunition and reloader components, unless the ordinance or resolution is the same as or similar to, and no more stringent than, a state statute." [http://gunla.ws/wi2]

C.   Reciprocal Carry

Wisconsin provision for the carrying of a concealed firearm:

(a) "A licensee or an out-of-state licensee may carry a concealed weapon anywhere in this state except as provided under subs. (15m) and (16) and ss. 943.13(1m)(c) and 948.605(2)(b)1r." [http://gunla.ws/wi3]

Anyone contemplating reciprocal carry should check with the official list maintained by the Wisconsin Department of Justice at the point in time the reciprocal carry is to occur. States add *and* delete states with reciprocity agreements over time. Wisconsin's reciprocity agreements can be viewed online. [http://gunla.ws/wx2c]

D.   Duty to Inform Officers

No. Wisconsin does not require individuals to inform a LEO of a permit or license to carry but if an Officer asks about a weapon, an answer must be supplied. You must possess a license/permit any time You are carrying a handgun. Upon request from a LEO, You must display Your license/permit. [http://gunla.ws/58jc]

E.   NFA Items

At this time the law addressing possession, transfer and transport of NFA items is in a state of flux and clarification and reform are being sought. MGs are prohibited unless for "scientific purpose, possession as a curiosity, ornament, or keepsake (if the gun is not usable as a weapon), or possession (other than a MG adapted to use pistol cartridges) for a purpose manifestly not aggressive or offensive." A person may be authorized by the chief of police of any city or the sheriff of any county to sell, possess, use, or transport a MG. No person may sell or offer to sell, transport, purchase, possess or go armed with a SBS or SBR. Exceptions include armed forces or National Guard personnel in line of duty and LEOs.

F.   Carrying Firearms in Vehicles

Wisconsin generally prohibits carrying firearms without a license. Carrying handguns openly without a permit is now legal, but a permit is required to carry them concealed. Long guns must be unloaded and "discernable to ordinary observation" from outside the car. [http://gunla.ws/wi4]

G.   Self-defense Laws

Wisconsin has a Castle Doctrine but no SYG law. There is no duty to retreat when in Your dwelling, place of business, or motor vehicle. You may use force, including deadly force, in defense of yourself or others if You reasonably believe it is necessary to prevent imminent death, SBI, or to stop the unlawful & forcible entry into a dwelling, place of business, or occupied motor vehicle. [http://gunla.ws/wi5]

H.   Criminal Provisions

Under Wisconsin law, a license to carry a handgun is not valid in any of the following places or circumstances:

- Any portion of a building that is a police station, sheriff's office, state patrol station, or the office of a division of criminal investigation special agent of the department
- A prison, jail, house of correction, or secured correctional facility
- A public or private elementary or secondary education building, grounds, structure, or facility, or at any school-sponsored function, unless You are a retired or off duty police officer
- A secure mental health facility for the detention, evaluation and institutional care of persons as defined by § 46.055
- The Wisconsin Resource Center on the grounds of the Winnebago Mental Health Institute as defined by §46.056
- The law on MGs is unclear; they are prohibited in most circumstances but there are exceptions
- Tasers and tear gas, and certain types of mace are prohibited
- Any secured portion of a mental health institution pursuant to §51.05
- Any portion of a building that is a county, state, or federal courthouse
- Any portion of a building that is a municipal courtroom if court is in session
- Any portion of an airport beyond a security checkpoint

- At the private residence of a person who has notified any carrier of a concealed firearm that firearms are prohibited

For a list of places where carrying firearms is prohibited, see: [http://gunla.ws/wi6]

I.   Do "No Gun Signs" Have the Force of Law?

Yes. If a property or establishment has a "No Guns" sign or the person in lawful possession communicates to you that guns are not allowed, You are prohibited from carrying on to the property or into the establishment. Failure to obey such signs or verbal warnings constitutes trespass. [http://gunla.ws/bwlz]

J.   Carry in Restaurants That Serve Alcohol

Yes, if you possess a license/permit to carry. You are allowed to carry into any establishment that serves alcohol, including bars. You are prohibited from carrying while you consume alcohol or are under the influence of alcohol. [http://gunla.ws/qllp]

K.   Open Carry

Open carry of loaded handguns and long guns is permitted without a license. The minimum age for open carry is 18. [http://gunla.ws/j36j]

Note: On March 8, 2017, the Wisconsin Supreme Court ruled that Madison's Metro Transit rule forbidding firearms on public buses violated the state's preemption law. Therefore, You are permitted to carry a firearm on public buses. [http://gunla.ws/nqls]

424

WYOMING GUN LAWS

Introduction

Wyoming is located in the West of the United States and includes the foothills of the Eastern Rocky Mountains and the High Plains. Wyoming is the least populous state and is bordered on the north by Montana, on the east by South Dakota and Nebraska, on the south by Colorado, on the southwest by Utah, and on the west by Idaho.

A.   State Constitution

Regarding the right to bear arms, the Wyoming Constitution states:

"The right of citizens to bear arms in defense of themselves and of the state shall not be denied." [http://gunla.ws/wy1]

B.   Scope of Preemption

The controlling language of Wyoming's preemption statute is set forth as follows:

"The sale, transfer, purchase, delivery, taxation, manufacture, ownership, transportation, storage, use and possession of firearms, weapons and ammunition shall be authorized, regulated and prohibited by the state, and regulation thereof is preempted by the state."

[http://gunla.ws/wy2]

C. Reciprocal Carry

The requirements for obtaining a license to carry is that the applicant:

(i) Is a resident of the United States and has been a resident of Wyoming for not less than six (6) months prior to filing the application. The Wyoming residency requirements of this paragraph do not apply to any person who holds a valid permit authorizing him to carry a concealed firearm authorized and issued by a governmental agency or entity in another state that recognizes Wyoming permits and is a valid statewide permit;

(ii) Is at least twenty-one (21) years of age;

(iii) Does not suffer from a physical infirmity, which prevents the safe handling of a firearm;

(iv) Is not ineligible to possess a firearm pursuant to 18U.S.C. section 922(g) or W.S. 6-8-102;

(v) Has not been: (A) Committed to a state or federal facility for the abuse of a controlled substance, within the one (1) year period prior to the date on which application for a permit under this section is submitted; (B) Convicted of a felony violation of the Wyoming Controlled Substances Act of 1971, W.S. 35-7-1001 through 35-7-1057 or similar laws of any other state or the United States relating to controlled substances and has not been pardoned; or (C) Convicted of a misdemeanor violation of the Wyoming Controlled Substances Act of 1971, W.S. 35-7-1001 through 35-7-

1057 or similar laws of any other state or the United States relating to controlled substances within the one (1) year period prior to the date on which application for a permit under this section is submitted.

By statute, Wyoming will recognize another state's license to carry if that state recognizes Wyoming's license:

"A person who wears or carries a concealed deadly weapon is guilty of a misdemeanor ... unless: ... (iii)The person holds a valid permit authorizing him to carry a concealed firearm authorized and issued by a governmental agency or entity in another state that recognizes Wyoming permits and is a valid statewide permit." [http://gunla.ws/wy3]

Since there is no national carry license, as with the other states, some states are reciprocal with Wyoming and some are not. Anyone contemplating reciprocal carry should check with the official list maintained by the Wyoming State Police at the point in time the reciprocal carry is to occur. Wyoming's reciprocity agreements can be viewed here: [http://gunla.ws/rrjy]

D.   Constitutional Carry

As of 7/1/11 Wyoming has enacted a constitutional carry law, although it only applies to Wyoming residents. Wyoming permits Wyoming residents who are at least 21 years old and legally allowed to possess a firearm to carry a handgun without a permit, openly or concealed. [http://gunla.ws/wy4]

E.   NFA Items

Wyoming permits ownership of all NFA items, provided they are legally obtained pursuant to federal law. It is illegal to hunt with a fully-automatic weapon or a suppressor.

F.   Carrying Firearms in Vehicles

Wyoming permits anyone who may legally possess a firearm to carry a loaded handgun in a motor vehicle without a permit. Wyoming residents can carry handguns openly or concealed, but nonresidents without a permit may only carry handguns if they are visible from outside the car and not concealed on their body. It is illegal to hunt, shoot, or attempt to kill any wildlife from any public highway.

G.   Self-defense Laws

Wyoming has a Castle Doctrine but no SYG law. There is no duty to retreat when in Your dwelling. You may use force, including deadly force, in defense of yourself or others if You reasonably believe it is necessary to prevent imminent death, SBI, or to stop the unlawful & forcible entry into Your dwelling. [http://gunla.ws/wy5]

H.   Criminal Provisions

Under Wyoming law, a license to carry a handgun is not valid in any of the following places or circumstances, whether it is issued by Wyoming, or a person is carrying pursuant to a reciprocity between his or her state of license and Wyoming:

- Any facility used primarily for law enforcement operations
- Any detention facility, prison, or jail
- Any courtroom, although this does not apply to the judge of said courtroom
- Any meeting of a governmental entity

428

- Any meeting of the legislature or a committee thereof
- Any elementary or secondary school, college or professional athletic event/facility not related to firearms
- Any elementary or secondary school facility
- Any college or university facility, except with written consent of the security service of that college or university
- Any place for public worship, without written consent of the administrator
- Any place prohibited by federal law
- In all state parks, campgrounds, recreational grounds, historic landmarks, or historic sites unless otherwise designated by the Fish and Game Commission

For a list of places where carrying firearms is prohibited, see: [http://gunla.ws/wy6]

I.   Duty to Inform Officers

No. Permitees must carry their permit, together with valid identification at all times when they are carrying a concealed firearm. You must display both the permit and proper identification upon request from any LEO. [http://gunla.ws/wfnm]

J.   Do "No Gun Signs" Have the Force of Law?

Yes. If a property or establishment has a "No Guns" sign or the person in lawful possession communicates to you that guns are not allowed, you are prohibited from carrying on to the property or into the establishment. Failure to obey such signs or verbal warnings constitutes criminal trespass. [http://gunla.ws/35ob]

K.   Carry in Restaurants That Serve Alcohol

Yes. You can carry a concealed firearm in a restaurant that serves alcohol. Places like Fridays or Chili's unless they have a "No

Gun Sign," then You are prohibited from carrying into the establishment. This does not include a bar or the bar area of a restaurant – You are prohibited from carrying a concealed weapon in these areas. You are not allowed to carry while You consume alcohol or are under the influence of alcohol. You are permitted to *open carry* at any establishment that serves alcohol. [http://gunla.ws/srul]

L.   Open Carry

Open carry is legal in Wyoming. No permit is required for residents. Non-residents must possess a permit or license issued by a state that Wyoming honors and that is a "valid statewide permit" to carry in Wyoming. Places as listed in the "Criminal Provisions" above apply to those who open carry. Any person 21 years of age or older, who is not a prohibited possessor, may carry a weapon openly or concealed without the need for a license.

PART VIII: CARRY IN OTHER STATES BY CURRENT AND RETIRED LAW ENFORCEMENT OFFICERS

I.   Introduction

After the September 11 terrorist attacks on the United States, all aspects of national and international safety and security were reexamined. One result of this top-to-bottom review questioned not having state and local police officers able to carry a concealed firearm while off duty in other states. The policy behind allowing qualified and retired LEOs to do so, was reinforced through training (shooting requirements) and a basic understanding of the use of deadly force. The Law Enforcement Officer's Safety Act was passed and signed into law in 2004 (LEOSA of 2004).

II.   Federal Right for Qualified Active and Retired LEOs to Carry

This LEOSA of 2004 was placed in the United States Code 18 U.S.C. § 926(D) [active qualified] and §926(C) [retired qualified], which is Chapter 44 covering firearms and federal penal violation of firearms law. The LEOSA of 2004, as codified, mandates that despite any state law provision to the contrary prohibiting a qualified active or retired LEO from carrying into the state, it is unenforceable because federal law trumps state law provisions under the Supremacy Clause.

In other words, none of the fifty (50) states can prevent a qualified current or retired officer from carrying into the state by state or local law. It is void, although that does not mean a police officer in another state could not disagree and still arrest You. This does not seem likely. All of the reported legal cases to date focus on a handful of states that have refused to issue identification to retired police officers and qualify them with their firearm.

III. Officers this Applies To

A. Active LEOs

An active LEO of one state may carry a firearm into another state on unofficial business and while not working. He or she may do so, so long as they meet the following criteria:

- The firearm is concealed.
- Authorized by a governmental authority to "engage in or supervise the prevention, detection, investigation, prosecution, or the incarceration of any person for, any violation of law."
- "Has statutory powers of arrest."
- "Is authorized by the agency to carry a firearm."
- "Is not under any disciplinary action by the agency which could result in suspension or loss of police powers."
- "Meets standards, if any, established by the agency which require the employee to regularly qualify in the use of the firearm."
- "Is not under the influence of alcohol or another intoxicating or hallucinatory drug or substance." This would apply to addiction while carrying in another state.
- "Is not prohibited by Federal Law from receiving a firearm." In other words, even in the absence of a disciplinary case, a police officer who had a protective order issued against him or her, after notice, would be Brady-disqualified and not be able to carry a concealed firearm in another state, as this is one of several federal

provisions prohibiting possession or receipt of a firearm.

■ Carries "the photographic identification issued by the governmental agency for which the individual is employed as a LEO."

B.   Retired LEOs

A retired LEO of one state may carry a firearm into another state on unofficial business and while not working so long as he or she meets the following criteria:

■ The firearm is concealed
■ "Separated from service in good standing service with a public agency as a law enforcement officer."
■ Before retirement or separation "was authorized by law to engage in or supervise the prevention, detection, investigation, or prosecution, detection, investigation, or prosecution of, or the incarceration of any person for, any violation of the law."
■ "Had statutory powers of arrest."
■ Before retirement or separation "served as a law enforcement officer for an aggregate of 10 years or more." Or "separated from service with such agency, after completing any applicable probationary period of such service, due to a service-connected disability, as determined by such agency."
■ "During the most recent 12-month period, has met, at the expense of the individual, the standards for qualification if firearms training for active law enforcement officers, as determined by the former agency of the individual, the State in which the individual resides or, if the State has not established such standards, either a law enforcement agency with the State in which the individual resides or the standards used by a certified firearms instructor that

is qualified to conduct firearms qualification for active duty officers within that State."

■ "Has not been officially found by a qualified medical professional employed by the agency to be unqualified for reasons relating to mental health and as a result of this finding will not be issued photographic identification."

■ "Has not entered into an agreement with the agency from which the individual is separating from service in which that individual acknowledges he or she is not qualified under this section for reasons relating to mental health and for those reasons will not receive photograph identification."

■ "Is not under the influence of alcohol or another intoxicating or hallucinatory drug or substance." This would apply to addiction while carrying in another state.

■ "Is not prohibited by Federal Law from receiving a firearm." In other words, even in the absence of a disciplinary case, a police officer who had a protective order issued against him or her, after notice, would be Brady-disqualified and not be able to carry a concealed firearm in another state, as this is one of several federal provisions prohibiting possession or receipt of a firearm.

■ The photographic identification along with qualification is a bit more complex for qualified retired/separated/ disabled officers no longer working for an agency.

Agency of Employment and Qualification:

(1) For this to apply, there must be photographic identification issued by the agency from which the individual separated from employment as a Law Enforcement Officer; and

(2) The agency "indicates that the individual has, not less recently than one year before the date the individual has, not less recently than one year before the date the individual is carrying the concealed firearm, been tested or otherwise found by the agency to meet the active duty standards for qualification in firearms training as established by the agency to carry a firearm of the same type as the concealed firearm."

Agency of Employment and Qualification Elsewhere:

(1) For this to apply, there must be photographic identification issued by the agency from which the individual separated from employment as a Law Enforcement Officer; and

(2) "A certification issued by the State in which the individual resides or be a certified firearms instructor that is qualified to conduct a firearms qualification test for active duty officers within that State that indicates that the individual has, not less than 1 year before the date the individual is carrying the concealed firearm, been tested or otherwise found by the State or a certified firearms instructor that is qualified to conduct a firearms qualification test for active duty officers with that State to have met:

(a) "The active duty standards for qualification in firearms training, as established by the State, to carry a firearm of the same type as the concealed firearm."
Or

(b) "If the State has not yet established such standards, standards set by any law enforcement agency within that

State to carry a firearm of the same type as the concealed firearm."

IV.   Excluded Firearms

Other than the requirement to carry concealed, there are several types of firearms and ammunition that may not be carried under the Act, as codified. As a general rule, NFA weapons are excluded, which are short-barrel rifles, shotguns, machine guns, suppressors, and AOW, such as pen guns. Any firearm that is regulated by the NFA and subject to a tax stamp is excluded from carry under the Act as placed in the U.S. Code. Stated differently, a firearm that may be carried under the Act is as defined for general long guns and handguns under the non-NFA provisions of the U.S. Code.

V.   Exceptions to the Concealed Carry by a Qualified Active or Retired LEO

A.   Federal Statutory Exceptions

This federal statutory provision is available to active and retired police officers who meet the criteria and is not without limitation. Because of the constitutional dimensions associated by the right to maintain private property and state sovereignty, there are two major exceptions where a qualified or retired LEO cannot carry a firearm if not allowed:

- Private Property: The person or entity controlling this Private Property has restrictions on the carry of firearms.
- State or local government buildings: This unit of government has prohibited or restricted the carry of firearms.

436

1. Private Property

Where such restrictions exist, unless the off-duty LEO is *excepted* from coverage, it is not permissible to carry a firearm under this federal right. In some states, if a landowner has posted "No Firearms", it is a criminal act to carry thereon. In other states, it would just be a basis to have an off-duty LEO asked to leave the property. Failure to do so thereafter, would likely be criminal trespass and perhaps constitute a civil tort.

See Chapter 22 for treatment of private property and the chapters of the respective states You will be carrying in, as set forth in Part VII.

2. State or Local Governmental Land or Installations

On state or local governmental land, the firearm may be subject to confiscation, and the off-duty officer arrested, ticketed, or removed from the property. **In these places, the qualified off duty officer must be aware of and follow the law of the state as it relates to the rights of private property owners and local and state governmental to regulate firearms on their property and in their installations. This federal right is not recognized in these places and it is as if the law enforcement officer stood as a civilian.**

See Part V for treatment of state, local, and other regulation and the chapters of the respective state You will be carrying in set forth in Part VII.

B. Other Federal Penal Laws

A qualified or retired LEO must adhere to all federal penal law. In general, the LEO is treated as a civilian and cannot carry under this federal provision in the following places:

- **Federal buildings or on federal property**, without a state exception allowed under federal law or an exception provided under the federal penal code, such as on federal lands incident to lawful and permitted.
- **Aircraft or Amtrak** unless following the check provisions afforded under federal law which required disclosure to the carrier, and compliance with specific packaging and the firearms being unloaded.
- **School Zones** unless allowed under the federal and state penal provisions.

VI. Miscellaneous

There are a number of related concepts a qualified active or retired LEO should understand to comply with the general legal parameters of the LEOSA of 2004 and not wind up violating such or properly evaluating risk in carrying under the LEOSA of 2004:

A. Immunity

It is key for qualified active or retired LEOs to understand that except for expansion of the right to carry by virtue of being a police officer, it does not grant other authority. This would mean the ability to act under color of law and have immunity for any act or omission with a firearm carried in another state. There is also no statutory power of arrest.

This is not to say that using a firearm in a way that would be afforded to a civilian carrying such lawfully would not give the

438

police officer a justification in the way of this affirmative defense available to civilians. However, this would attach in the context of a criminal proceeding. Therefore, the qualified active or off duty LEO may have to endure criminal trial if charged and make this case to the jury.

The advice of one state that has particularly strict firearms laws, New Jersey, is a police officer acting under the LEOSA of 2004 not become involved except as strictly allowed by a given state's penal laws. Instead, a qualified active or retired police officer should call the local police to handle the matter.

B.   License to Carry (a/k/a CCP or CCW)

For LEO's who do not qualify to carry under the LEOSA of 2004, and are not otherwise disqualified under state or federal law, he or she may be able to obtain a resident or non-resident license to carry a handgun and lawfully carry in another state. As a general rule a license to carry, no matter if resident or non-resident, has far more places where it is not honored within a given state.

See Part V for treatment of state, local, and other regulation and the chapters of the respective state You will be carrying in set forth in Part VII.

C.   Interstate "Official Police Business" Compacts

Finally, state or local LEOs on official duty or who have to be duty ready within a certain amount of time after landing, may carry firearms into other states. A common example would be to pick up a prisoner being held in other states. This is accomplished by complying with the TSA requirements to fly armed and allowed state-to-state by compacts to allow this for official business purposes.

This has no connection to the LEOSA of 2004 or a state-issued CCP or CCW.

VII. Conclusion

Under the LEOSA of 2004 a qualified active or retired law enforcement officer may carry a concealed firearm under a provision of federal law, no matter if there is state or local law to the contrary. The qualified active or retired law enforcement officer must follow any private property rules of a landholder in the state, local and state requirements for their lands and facilities, along with federal penal law, unless excepted (i.e., he or she cannot fly armed, but could check a firearm in luggage as a civilian could do).

PART IX: RECIPROCITY TABLES

The threshold part of any reciprocal carry is determining reciprocal states. This is more or less commonly available information because most states post some type of list or reciprocity table on an official state website. And it is easy to assume once reciprocity is determined this is the end of the analysis.

In other words, as the thinking goes, Your state, State X's license (resident or non-resident license) is recognized by State Y, which is a border state. Therefore, when You drive there it is the same as being in State X. Nothing could be further from the truth. That is what the GLBS Guide is all about.

The book provides guidance about how to determine what You need to do in State Y before getting there. Further, it sets forth the ways a firearm, including a handgun for carry in a reciprocal state, may be transported to and through states where there is no reciprocity agreement.

Thus, determining reciprocity is the threshold and rather easy consideration. For this reason, because it should be a first and last consideration–to make sure State Y is reciprocal–a table is provided but only at the end. This is to emphasize that determining reciprocity alone is a minute faction of what it takes to lawfully carry a handgun in a reciprocal state.

Utilized and considered in this light, varying reciprocity tables are useful and are provided in real time at [http://gunla.ws/reciprocity]. Use these tables as a part of Your research.

This GLBS manual in print or e-format is designed to be used in conjunction with its companion interactive website along with first-hand research before any carry, purchase or possession of any firearm, as this material is for educational purposes only. The website contains links to official sources, which themselves are not always up to date. No reciprocity map or like list is ever complete because of statutes, case law, rules, ordinance, custom, and daily changes that occur throughout any given place. Thus, no reliance should be placed on this table without independent research to the requisite level to ensure You have identified and have a working understanding of the controlling laws.

To utilize our online, up-to-date U.S. reciprocity map, please visit this link: [http://gunla.ws/reciprocity].

Alabama

Alabama Honors Permits From:
Alabama honors all other state licenses or permits, except from Vermont. Alabama also honors permits from The District of Columbia, Guam, Puerto Rico, and the Virgin Islands.

Alaska

Alaska Honors Permits From:
Alaska honors all other state licenses or permits. Residents of Vermont may carry with a Vermont driver's license or state issued photo ID. Alaska also honors permits from The District of Columbia, Guam, Puerto Rico, and the Virgin Islands.

Arizona

Arizona Honors Permits From:
Arizona honors all other state licenses or permits. Residents of Vermont may carry with a Vermont driver's license or state issued photo ID. Arizona also honors permits from The District of Columbia, Guam, Puerto Rico, and the Virgin Islands.

Arkansas

Arkansas Honors Permits From:
Arkansas honors all other state licenses or permits, except from Vermont. Arkansas also honors permits from The District of Columbia, Guam, Puerto Rico, and the Virgin Islands.

California

California Honors Permits From:
California does not honor any other state licenses or permits.

Colorado

Colorado Honors Residential Permits From:
Alabama, Alaska, Arizona, Arkansas, Delaware, Florida, Georgia, Idaho, Indiana, Iowa, Kansas, Kentucky, Louisiana, Michigan, Mississippi, Missouri, Montana, Nebraska, New Hampshire, New Mexico, North Carolina, North Dakota, Ohio, Oklahoma, Pennsylvania, South Dakota, Tennessee, Texas, Utah, Virginia, West Virginia, Wisconsin, Wyoming.
Further, Colorado does not honor non-resident permits; You must be a resident of the state Your permit is issued from for it to be valid.

Connecticut

Connecticut Honors Permits From:
Connecticut does not honor any other state permits.

Delaware

Delaware Honors Permits From:
Alaska, Arizona, Arkansas, Colorado, Florida, Idaho (enhanced permit only), Kentucky, Maine, Michigan, Missouri, New Mexico, North Carolina, North Dakota, Ohio, Oklahoma, South Dakota, Tennessee, Texas, Utah, West Virginia.

District of Columbia

District of Columbia Honors Permits From:
District of Columbia does not honor any other state permits.

Florida

Florida Honors Permits From:
Alabama, Alaska, Arizona, Arkansas, Colorado, Delaware, Georgia, Idaho, Indiana, Iowa, Kansas, Kentucky, Louisiana, Maine, Michigan, Mississippi, Missouri, Montana, Nebraska, New Hampshire, Nevada, New Mexico, North Carolina, North Dakota, Ohio, Oklahoma, Pennsylvania, South Carolina, South Dakota, Tennessee, Texas, Utah, Virginia, West Virginia, Wyoming. Further, Florida does not honor non-resident permits; You must be a resident of the state Your permit is issued from for it to be valid.

Georgia

Georgia Honors Permits From:
Alabama, Alaska, Arizona, Arkansas, Colorado, Florida, Idaho, Indiana, Iowa, Kansas, Kentucky, Louisiana, Maine, Michigan, Mississippi, Missouri, Montana, New Hampshire, North Carolina, North Dakota, Ohio, Oklahoma, Pennsylvania, South Carolina, South Dakota, Tennessee, Texas, Utah, West Virginia, Wisconsin, Wyoming.

Hawaii

Hawaii Honors Permits From:
Hawaii does not honor any other state licenses or permits.

Idaho

Idaho Honors Permits From:
Idaho honors all other state licenses or permits, except from Vermont. Idaho also honors permits from The District of Columbia, Guam, Puerto Rico, and the Virgin Islands.

Illinois

Illinois Honors Permits From:
Illinois does not honor any other state licenses or permits.

Indiana

Indiana Honors Permits From:
Indiana honors all other state licenses or permits, except from Vermont. Indiana also honors permits from The District of Columbia, Guam, Puerto Rico, and the Virgin Islands.

Iowa

Iowa Honors Permits From:
Iowa honors all other state licenses or permits, except from Vermont. Iowa also honors permits from The District of Columbia, Guam, Puerto Rico, and the Virgin Islands.
Further, Iowa honors non-resident permits if the holder is at least 21.

Kansas

Kansas Honors Permits From:
Kansas honors all other state licenses or permits including non-resident licenses provided the person is at least 21 years old. Kansas also honors permits from The District of Columbia, Guam, Puerto Rico, and the Virgin Islands. Residents of Vermont may carry with a Vermont driver's license or state issued photo ID.

Kentucky

Kentucky Honors Permits From:
Kentucky recognizes all other state licenses and permits including non-resident permits, except Vermont. Kentucky also honors permits from The District of Columbia, Guam, Puerto Rico, and the Virgin Islands.

Louisiana

Louisiana Honors Permits From:
Alabama, Alaska, Arizona, Arkansas, Colorado, Florida, Georgia, Idaho, Indiana, Iowa, Kansas, Kentucky, Maine, Michigan, Minnesota, Mississippi, Missouri, Montana, Nebraska, Nevada, New Hampshire, New Mexico, North Carolina, North Dakota, Ohio, Oklahoma, Pennsylvania, South Carolina, South Dakota, Tennessee, Texas, Utah, Virginia, Washington, West Virginia, Wisconsin, Wyoming.

Maine

Maine Honors Permits From:
Alaska, Arizona, Florida, Georgia, Idaho, Iowa, Indiana, Kansas, Kentucky, Louisiana, Michigan, Missouri, Mississippi, Nebraska, New Hampshire, North Carolina, North Dakota, South Dakota, Ohio, Oklahoma, Tennessee, Utah, Virginia (Must also possess

government issued photo ID).

Further, residents of Vermont may carry with a Vermont driver's license or state issued photo ID. Maine does not honor non-resident permits; You must be a resident of the state Your permit is issued from for it to be valid.

Maryland

Maryland Honors Permits From:
Maryland does not honor any other state licenses or permits.

Massachusetts

Massachusetts Honors Permits From:
Massachusetts does not honor any other state licenses or permits.

Michigan

Michigan Honors Permits From:
Michigan honors all other states resident (bot not non-resident) licenses or permits, except from Vermont. Michigan also honors permits (resident or non-resident) from Guam and the Virgin Islands

Minnesota

Minnesota Honors Permits From:
Alaska, Delaware, Idaho (enhanced permit only), Illinois, Kansas, Kentucky, Louisiana, Michigan, Nevada, New Jersey, New Mexico, North Dakota (class 1 only), Rhode Island, South Carolina, South Dakota (enhanced permit only).
Further, Minnesota honors non-resident permits from all the above states.

Mississippi

Mississippi Honors Permits From:
Mississippi honors all other states permits and licenses, including non-resident licenses, except from Vermont. Mississippi also honors permits from The District of Columbia, Guam, Puerto Rico, and the Virgin Islands.

Missouri

Missouri Honors Permits From:
Missouri honors all other states permits and licenses, including non-resident permits, except and Vermont. Missouri also honors permits from The District of Columbia, Guam, Puerto Rico, and the Virgin Islands.

Montana

Montana Honors Permits From:
Alabama, Alaska, Arizona, Arkansas, California, Colorado, Connecticut, Florida, Georgia, Idaho, Indiana, Illinois, Iowa, Kansas, Kentucky, Louisiana, Maryland, Massachusetts, Michigan, Minnesota, Mississippi, Missouri, Nebraska, Nevada, New Jersey, New Mexico, New York, North Carolina, North Dakota, Ohio, Oklahoma, Oregon, Pennsylvania, South Carolina, South Dakota, Tennessee, Texas, Utah, Virginia, Washington, West Virginia, Wisconsin, Wyoming.
Further, Montana honors non-resident permits from all the above states.

Nebraska

Nebraska Honors Permits From:
Alaska, Arizona, Arkansas, California, Colorado, Connecticut, District of Columbia, Florida, Hawaii, Idaho, Illinois, Iowa (non-

professional), Kansas, Kentucky, Louisiana, Maine, Michigan, Minnesota, Missouri, Montana, Nevada, New Jersey, New Mexico, North Carolina, North Dakota (enhanced permit only), Ohio, Oklahoma, Oregon, Rhode Island, South Carolina, South Dakota (enhanced permit only), Tennessee, Texas, Utah, Virginia, West Virginia, Wisconsin, Wyoming.

Further, Nebraska honors non-resident permits from all the above states if the holder is at least 21.

Nevada

Nevada Honors Permits From:
Alaska, Arkansas, Arizona, Idaho (enhanced only), Florida, Illinois, Kansas, Kentucky, Louisiana, Massachusetts, Michigan, Minnesota, Mississippi, Montana, Nebraska, New Mexico, North Carolina, North Dakota, Ohio, Oklahoma, Oregon, South Carolina, South Dakota (enhanced only), Tennessee, Texas, Utah, Virginia, West Virginia, Wisconsin, Wyoming.

Further, Nevada recognizes non-resident permits from all the above states.

New Hampshire

New Hampshire Honors Permits From:
Alabama, Alaska, Arizona, Arkansas, Colorado, Florida, Georgia, Idaho (resident or nonresident), Indiana, Iowa, Kentucky, Louisiana, Maine, Michigan, Mississippi, Missouri, North Carolina, North Dakota, Ohio, Oklahoma, Pennsylvania, Tennessee, Utah, Virginia, West Virginia, Wyoming.

Further, New Hampshire does not recognize non-resident permits, except from Idaho.

New Jersey

New Jersey Honors Permits From:
New Jersey does not honor any other state licenses or permits.

New Mexico

New Mexico Honors Permits From:
Alaska, Arizona, Arkansas, Colorado, Delaware, Florida, Idaho (enhanced only), Kansas, Louisiana, Michigan, Mississippi, Missouri, Nebraska, Nevada, North Carolina, North Dakota, Ohio, Oklahoma, South Carolina, Tennessee, Texas, Virginia, West Virginia, Wyoming.
Further, New Mexico recognizes non-resident permits from all the above states if the holder is at least 21.

New York

New York Honors Permits From:
New York does not honor any other state licenses or permits.

North Carolina

North Carolina Honors Permits From:
North Carolina recognizes all permits from all other states, except from Vermont. North Carolina also recognizes permits from the District of Columbia, Guam, Puerto Rico, and the Virgin Islands.

North Dakota

North Dakota Honors Permits From:
Alabama, Alaska, Arizona, Arkansas, Colorado, Delaware, Florida, Georgia, Idaho, Indiana, Iowa, Kansas, Kentucky, Louisiana, Maine, Michigan, Minnesota, Mississippi, Missouri,

Montana, Nebraska, Nevada, New Hampshire, New Mexico, North Carolina, Ohio, Oklahoma, Pennsylvania, South Carolina, South Dakota, Tennessee, Texas, Utah, Virginia, Washington, West Virginia, Wisconsin, Wyoming.

Ohio

Ohio Honors Permits From:
Ohio honors all other state licenses or permits, including non-resident permits, except from Vermont. Ohio also recognizes permits from The District of Columbia, Guam, Puerto Rico, and the Virgin Islands.

Oklahoma

Oklahoma Honors Permits From:
Oklahoma honors all other state licenses or permits, including non-resident permits. Oklahoma also recognizes permits from The District of Columbia, Guam, Puerto Rico, and the Virgin Islands. Residents of Kansas and Vermont can carry in Oklahoma without a permit.

Oregon

Oregon Honors Permits From:
Oregon does not honor any other state licenses or permits.

Pennsylvania

Pennsylvania Honors Permits From:
Alaska, Arizona*, Arkansas, Colorado, Florida*, Georgia, Indiana, Iowa, Kansas, Kentucky, Louisiana, Michigan, Mississippi*, Missouri, Montana, New Hampshire, North Carolina, North Dakota (Enhanced permit only), Ohio, Oklahoma, South Dakota, Tennessee, Texas, Utah*, Virginia*, West Virginia, Wisconsin,

451

Wyoming.
* = Permits from these states are only valid for people who are NOT residents of Pennsylvania.

Rhode Island

Rhode Island Honors Permits From:
Rhode Island does not honor any other state licenses or permits.

South Carolina

South Carolina Honors Permits From:
Alaska, Arizona, Arkansas, Florida, Georgia, Idaho (enhanced permit only), Kansas, Kentucky, Louisiana, Michigan, Missouri, New Mexico, North Carolina, North Dakota, Ohio, Oklahoma, South Dakota (enhanced permit only), Tennessee, Texas, Virginia, West Virginia, Wyoming. Further, South Carolina does not recognize non-resident permits.

South Dakota

South Dakota Honors Permits From:
South Dakota honors all other state licenses or permits, including non-resident permits, except from Vermont. South Dakota also recognizes permits from The District of Columbia, Guam, Puerto Rico, and the Virgin Islands.

Tennessee

Tennessee Honors Permits From:
Tennessee honors all other state licenses or permits, including non-resident permits, except from Vermont. Tennessee also recognizes permits from The District of Columbia, Guam, Puerto Rico, and the Virgin Islands.

Texas

Texas Honors Permits From:
Alabama, Alaska, Arizona, Arkansas, California, Colorado, Connecticut, Delaware, Florida, Georgia, Hawaii, Idaho, Illinois, Indiana, Iowa, Kansas, Kentucky, Louisiana, Maryland, Massachusetts, Michigan, Mississippi, Missouri, Montana, Nebraska, Nevada, New Jersey, New Mexico, New York, North Carolina, North Dakota, Ohio (only if issued/renewed after 3/23/15) Oklahoma, Pennsylvania, Rhode Island (only if issued by the AG), South Carolina, South Dakota, Tennessee, Utah, Virginia, Washington, West Virginia, Wyoming.

Utah

Utah Honors Permits From:
Utah honors all other state licenses or permits, including non-resident permits, except from Vermont. Utah also recognizes permits from The District of Columbia, Guam, Puerto Rico, and the Virgin Islands.

Vermont

Vermont Honors Permits From:
Vermont allows anyone who is at least 21 and can legally possess a firearm to carry concealed without a permit.

Virginia

Virginia Honors Permits From:
Virginia honors all other state licenses or permits, including non-resident permits provided the holder is at least 21. Virginia recognizes permits from The District of Columbia, Guam, Puerto Rico, and the Virgin Islands.

Washington

Washington Honors Permits From:
Idaho (enhanced only), Kansas, Louisiana, Michigan, North Carolina, North Dakota (Class 1 permits only), Ohio, Oklahoma, Utah.

West Virginia

West Virginia Honors Permits From:
Alabama, Alaska, Arizona, Arkansas, Colorado, Delaware, Florida, Georgia, Idaho, Indiana, Iowa, Kansas, Kentucky, Louisiana, Michigan, Mississippi, Missouri, Nebraska, Nevada, New Hampshire, New Mexico, North Carolina, North Dakota, Ohio, Oklahoma, Pennsylvania, South Carolina, South Dakota, Tennessee, Texas, Utah, Virginia, Wisconsin, Wyoming. Further, West Virginia honors non-resident permits from all the above states.

Wisconsin

Wisconsin Honors Permits From:
Alabama, Alaska (only if permit issued after 1/14/13), Arizona, Arkansas, California, Colorado, Connecticut, Georgia, Hawaii, Idaho, Illinois, Indiana, Iowa, Kansas, Kentucky, Louisiana, Maryland, Massachusetts (only if Class A Massachusetts Permit), Michigan, Minnesota, Mississippi, Missouri (only if permit issued after 8/28/13), Montana, Nebraska, Nevada (only if permit issued after 7/1/11), New Mexico, New York, North Carolina, North Dakota, Ohio (only if permit issued after 3/23/15), Pennsylvania, South Carolina, South Dakota (only if Enhanced or Gold License), Tennessee, Texas, Utah, Virginia (non-resident permits only), Washington, West Virginia (only if permit issued after 6/8/12),

454

Wyoming, Puerto Rico, U.S. Virgin Islands.
Further, Wisconsin honors non-resident permits from all the above
states if the holder is at least 21.

Wyoming

Wyoming Honors Permits From:
Alabama, Alaska, Arizona, Arkansas, Colorado, Florida, Georgia,
Idaho, Indiana, Iowa, Kansas, Kentucky, Louisiana, Maine,
Michigan, Mississippi, Missouri, Montana, Nebraska, Nevada,
New Hampshire, New Mexico, North Carolina, North Dakota,
Ohio, Oklahoma, Pennsylvania, South Carolina, South Dakota,
Tennessee, Texas, Utah, Virginia, West Virginia, Wisconsin.
Further, Wyoming honors non-resident permits from all the above
states if the holder is at least 21.

PART X: RECIPROCAL CARRY WORKSHEETS

In this final part of the GLBS Guide is a Preparation Worksheet in PDF format that You can print and use as You research and prepare for carry of a handgun in a reciprocal state. The more You "work it," the more You will assimilate the laws that You will be bound to follow.

In addition, the Preparation Worksheet is structured so that it elicits connections You might not otherwise make if You are new to the topic of reciprocal carry. The more of these You make, the easier each future reciprocal carry research will become – the law is a seamless web with no good place to start or end. But this will help You develop the knack for how it all fits together, recognizing sometimes that there is no answer or that the law is in conflict.

Following that worksheet is a before-You-go checklist to help You not make any last-minute mistakes that might impede Your reciprocal carry, or worse yet, cause criminal or civil exposure. This checklist runs the gamut, and it (along with the Preparation Worksheet) will be used to the extent You are comfortable with the state of the law in a reciprocal state and risk preference.

While this may seem like a great deal of work, and indeed it is, so is the responsibility of gun ownership and carrying a handgun in another state in a cavalier way, given a mistake could result in serious criminal and/or civil liability.

Finally, to make the most of the experience, an After Action Form is provided so that You can memorialize questions, concerns, problems, benefits, and the like from the reciprocal-carry experience to use in the future to evaluate what worked, what did not, and, on balance, the ultimate weighing: is self-defense versus violating a law worth the experience?

RECIPROCAL CARRY PREPARATION WORKSHEET

Instructions: Use this form as You review the book in preparation for interstate travel to and carry in a reciprocal state. Fill in and adopt the form as You conduct Your independent research into the matter.

Q   How will You transport Your handgun and comply with the law (See Chapter 3)?

Q   Is the state a reciprocal state? (Check with Your licensing state and the reciprocal state by using the hyperlinks in the book.)

Notes:_____.

Q   If not, is this state one where You may obtain a non-resident license in order to engage in reciprocal carry in that state (Utah and Florida have well-known non-resident programs)? If so, which state and what is the training schedule and is physical presence in the state required?

Notes:_____.

Q   If Your reciprocity is based on a non-resident license, is there any question about its acceptance in the reciprocal state versus acceptance of that issuing state's resident license? (Alabama has an open question about differences between resident and non-resident license programs of other states.)

Notes:_____.

Q   If there is limited (or no) preemption, have You investigated any local ordinances, rules and regulation at this level? (Check the repositories that contain some ordinances by accessing the hyperlinks found throughout the GLBS Guide.)

Notes:_____.

Q   Did You obtain such local laws, and review and understand any provisions related to firearms or reciprocal carry?

Notes:_____.

Q   Has the primary criminal law been looked up to determine what illegal acts are exempted by those who have a license? (Check and follow the hyperlinks provided for each state to reference to criminal law, which sometimes excludes certain acts from being criminal with a license.)

Notes:_____.

Q   Is it necessary to explore any ambiguities in the statutory law by looking to see how appellate courts have interpreted such, if at all? (Free case-law databases exist, such as FindLaw.com.)

Notes:_____.

Q   Is the reciprocal state "known" as a pro-gun or anti-gun state and does this affect Your considerations on a risk/benefit analysis? (The NRA grades politicians on their gun voting record.)

Notes:_____.

Q   Are there unique considerations in this state that are unfamiliar or that cause You concern, such as ammunition restrictions or magazine-capacity bans?

Notes:_____.

Q   Is there any unique place that You will encounter that needs additional research, such as Native American tribal lands or federal lands? (A hyperlink is provided to ATFE, which references the US Code and Code of Federal Regulations governing firearms.)

Notes:_____.

Q   Have You prepared a list of places where carry is prohibited or qualified with a CCW so You can identify that in advance before entering into such a place or event? (For instance, in Arizona You could not carry and consume alcohol in a place selling it without committing a crime.)

Notes:_____.

Q   Are You engaging in any particular activity where additional state or federal rules may apply (i.e., hunting in any state requiring a non-resident hunting license or a machine-gun shoot, requiring approval from ATFE for interstate transportation of an NFA weapon)?

Notes:_____.

Q   Have You obtained any state book written on the laws, practice and customs of carry in that state? (Bloomfield Press has most such books in stock.)

Notes:_____.

Q   Have You cross-checked questions or concerns with online resources, such as the NRA?

Notes:_____.

Q   Is there some specific reason to consult with counsel in advance?

Notes:_____.

Q   Do You know and have You researched an attorney in the reciprocal state to engage in the event that a problem occurs?

Notes:_____.

BEFORE-YOU-GO FINAL CHECKLIST

Instructions: Go through this checklist 24 hours before You depart for Your reciprocal-carry event. In the event this is a weekend or holiday, use a 48 to 72-hour timeline. This allows for additional provisions to be obtained, such as a hard-sided case. Review the checklist a final time as You leave Your home. Refine and change as necessary to fit Your needs.

Q   Do You have the proper container for interstate transport and check-in or notice provisions, if any? (In the book, there are hyperlinks to TSA and Amtrak, among others for this purpose.)

Notes:_____.

Q   What is Your attorney contact name?

Notes:_____.

Q   Do You have Your license or permit along with government-issued identification?

Notes:_____.

Q   Have You checked and rechecked the handgun to ensure it is unloaded, following the safety rules?

Notes:_____.

Q   Did You map out from start to finish the way to lawfully interstate transport the firearm, engage in reciprocal carry, and return to the place from which You left, staying always compliant with the law?

Notes:_____.

Q   If You are hunting, have You applied for a non-resident license? Do You have it with You?

Notes:_____.

Q   If You are taking firearms other than a handgun, but also including the handgun, are any of them illegal in the reciprocal state?

Notes:_____.

Q   Do You know Your blood type if You are injured in a hunting accident?

Notes:_____.

Q   Do You have a plan if You are involved in a deadly-force encounter?

Notes:_____.

Q   Do You have the key to the locked container in a secure place?

Notes:_____.

Q   Have You checked Your carry-ons and clothing, if flying or traveling by train, to ensure that You do not have any ammunition, magazines, knives, or related but prohibited items?

Notes:_____.

AFTER-ACTION NOTES/REPORT

Instructions: If any question arose before, during or after the reciprocal carry, check the topic for further consideration. Write Your answer. Reflect on it for a few days and go back and see if You have additional insights. Index these for future preparation for reciprocal carry.

Q   What was the biggest mistake You made for the reciprocal carry?

Notes:_____ .

Q   What is the most important part of the task You made in preparing, or what did You discover (i.e., license expired, ammunition restriction)?

Notes:_____ .

Q   What thing(s) went wrong as it relates to transportation of the handgun to the reciprocal state?

Notes:_____ .

Q   What thing(s) went more smoothly as it relates to transportation of the handgun to the reciprocal state?

Notes:_____ .

Q   What item concerned You about the reciprocal carry as it unfolded?

Notes:_____ .

Q   What, if anything, did You do while returning to Your state of residence differently than You did leaving?

Notes:_____.

Q   What would You change about the experience if You could go through with it now?

Notes:_____.

Q   Other:

Notes:_____.

_____

_____

_____

_____

_____.

PART XI: QUESTIONS & ANSWERS

What is reciprocal carry?

There is no federal law that allows civilians to carry a handgun in another state. The legal means by which this right exists is a compact (agreement) between two states. Such an agreement is one that recognizes the other state's license or permit to carry a handgun. This changes from time to time as states who enter into such agreement and may withdraw at any time. Without such an agreement, there is no reciprocity or right to carry a handgun in another state by recognizing the other state's license.

What is state-based preemption, and why is it important to me?

State preemption is one of the first matters You should consider in a reciprocal state carry. If there is state preemption, then only the state may pass criminal (and sometimes civil) laws regulating the carry of handguns. If there is not state-based preemption then the laws may vary from one political subdivision (county, town, et cetera) to another. So on one side of a street in a divided town the criminal and civil laws regarding carrying a handgun may differ. In these states, carrying a handgun across the state is very difficult to do legally.

What is the most common myth about reciprocal carry?

The most common myth is that when carrying in another state, the licensee follows the laws of the state that issues the license. In a reciprocal state, all that occurs is this state recognizes the other state's license for carry. However, the out-of-state licensee must follow the laws of the state he or she is in at the time of reciprocal carry.

Are there different types of licenses?

There are many different types of licenses as it relates to firearms and handguns in particular. A license or permit to carry a handgun generally applies to any handgun the licensee carries on his or her person. However, there may be a license or registration of handguns by a state or local government for the carry of handguns. There is a license to hunt. And there is a federal license of sorts as it relates to Title II firearms, such as short barrel rifles and shotguns, machine guns (pre-May 19th, 1986), suppressors, and AOWs. In addition, federal law requires an approval by ATFE to carry a title II weapon into another state.

What is the biggest misunderstanding about deadly force?

The biggest misunderstanding about the exercise of deadly force is related to retreat, standing Your ground and the Castle Doctrine. Practically speaking, if there is a reasonable way to retreat without being injured or risking injury, the exercise of deadly force is improvident. This is because even if no criminal charges are considered or filed, there is still a significant risk of civil suit for which the costs of defense alone can ruin the life of the person exercising deadly force in paying to defend a wrongful death or personal injury case that in most cases, is not covered by insurance. The reason insurance does not cover such incidents is self-defense (the decision to shoot) is intentional not negligent.

Is there one key mistake gun owners make with carrying a handgun for self-defense?

There is a singular mistake most gun owners make in obtaining a license or permit and carrying a handgun for self-defense. This is neglecting legal education about deadly force and carry itself (such as where within a state it is illegal even with a license, such as a federal building) and training with a carry gun. Without both of these, carrying a handgun for self-defense is a risky proposition at best.

466

Should I tell a police officer I am carrying a firearm in a traffic stop?

There is not a singular answer to whether a person should disclose a carry handgun in a routine traffic stop. There are some generally accepted or required positions. In some states, disclosure is required. In other states, it is not. Where it is not, it is a discretionary call for the person stopped. If he or she will be obtaining a license or registration in proximity to a carry handgun, then it should be disclosed to avoid an officer thinking a person is trying to pull a firearm on the police officer. In other cases, it may not come up and is no more dangerous than the running vehicle itself as such is inherently dangerous depending on how it is used. If You do choose to inform the officer, make sure You do it in a tactful and non-threatening manner. Saying "I would like to inform You that I am lawfully carrying a firearm" sounds a lot better than "I have a gun". You should keep Your hand on the wheel at all times, tell the officer where Your gun is located, then ask how they would like You to proceed. It is important to appear as cooperative and non-threatening as possible. Carrying a handgun for self-defense is a thinking person's matter, and if You are not willing to do so, You should seriously consider the propriety of carrying a handgun, else You may wind up in prison.

Can I possess a firearm in a state the does not recognize my license?

A person may transport a firearm from any lawful place it is possessed to any other lawful place so long as it is not in the passenger area, such as in a trunk, unloaded, in a locked container, and separate from the ammunition. However, the route through the state where the firearm is illegal must be direct to the state where the firearm will be used or transported to. The more indirect the route and time in the state where that firearm is illegal, the more likely a criminal or civil issue is to arise.

What is the best handgun to carry?

The answer is there is no direct answer. There are a number of considerations that answer this question for any given person. The first is reliability and ability to use the firearm as it is intended. A cheap firearm that a person does not know how to operate is a poor choice for a handgun. Second, a handgun that is too big or heavy to carry is generally a poor choice. The firearm that is the most reliable and one a person will carry regularly and consistently due to size and weight is the best choice. One common rule of thumb is to carry the most powerful handgun that You can reliably conceal and control. Choice of firearm may also depend on Your attire, as it is easier to conceal a larger gun when wearing many layers of clothing than when dressed only in shorts and a T-shirt. The most important consideration is to carry a gun that is reliable and with which You are comfortable and confident. As it is sometimes stated, "a man should not show up at a gun fight (read convenience store that is being robbed), without a gun (read reliable self-defense firearm that a person can manipulate and use with precision)."

Does the ammunition I carry in my self-defense handgun matter?

The ammunition that is used in a carry gun can make or break a civil or criminal defense. For instance, a poor choice for a self-defense round is ball ammunition, commonly known as full metal jacket. This is typically covered with a material such as copper with a lead center and is rounded. This type of ammunition can penetrate many layers of barriers after the bad guy and travel a great distance and still be terminal. The notion that a hollow point round is not appropriate for self-defense is an outdated concept. These rounds are designed so that when the projectile hits the target (i.e., the bad guy who is committing a forcible felony, attacking in the home, or puts the victim and certain third parties at risk of serious bodily injury or death by his criminal act), it expands to make its surface area greater, which both causes more damage and helps to dump velocity and energy into the target, to reduce the chance of the bullet over-penetrating the target and harming the person in the next room or across the street. For this reason, hollow points are also

468

more effective at stopping bad guys quickly. It should be noted that although hollow points will not over penetrate as often as FMJ ammo, any round that has enough energy to stop an attacker will be able to penetrate several layers of drywall or other siding. In the ideal situation, a person's self-defense ammo is the same as the local or state police use, which is certain to be a hollow point. It is inadvisable to use reloads for defense ammo, both for reliability issues, and because a zealous prosecutor may use them to portray You in a negative light to a jury in a criminal prosecution scenario, as a vigilante who makes his own "extra lethal" ammunition to wreak havoc, as opposed to someone engaged in lawful self-defense.

Can a state have more restrictive gun laws than federal gun laws?

A state may have more restrictive gun laws than federal law. Congress has stated it is not preempting the field of firearms regulation (making it the only body who can pass firearms laws) but co-occupies this area of law-making with the state. Under the Second Amendment right to keep and bear arms, the United States Supreme Court has only limited states from banning an entire class of firearms citizens prefer for self-defense, namely handguns. That is the extent of federal protection of the right. For this reason, "assault weapons" bans and magazine capacity restrictions appear to pass constitutional muster under the Second Amendment.

If allowed in my state, should I open carry a handgun?

There are two key reasons a person should open carry versus concealed carry if allowed by a state or the law is silent on this matter. The first and most common and prudent is for deterrence purposes. A bank security guard in uniform is taken as a much more credible security tactic than is an unarmed security officer. This is deterrence because criminals often avoid places where they know a person may impede their felonious act by shooting him or her. The second reason is a public policy statement the person wants to make about the importance of the right to keep and bear arms. However, a person known to be armed by open carry identified by the criminal in a split second is much more likely to be the first person shot and killed or injured by the felon. On the whole, complete concealed carry (no printing through clothing) is the appropriate way for one to defend himself/herself in the event of being in the wrong place at the wrong time.

Why do we have gun laws at all?

This a complex question with varying "correct" answers that could fill many books. However, the answer is a variant of the following: Throughout all recorded history, all societies have had some form of laws. In the modern era, many inherently dangerous items have laws to regulate their possession and/or safe operation. For instance, cars have driver's licensing requirements to ensure a driver without a minimum level of skill does not mistakenly use this heavy moving item as a giant moving bullet of sorts and mow over pedestrians. This is why there is a driving test, and safety mechanisms on cars like turn signals and horns.

However, because guns are primarily made for offensive and defensive use--to kill animals and people--they have been identified for additional regulation and scrutiny. Also, because in theory, firearms are not strictly necessary to the survival of humans, they have emotional components that drive laws that says why have them made and lawful to own at all.

This is very similar to nuclear power (uranium). It too is not necessary as a power source for the survival of the species, so there are emotional dynamics to its law-making and strict licensing. Like a firearm, misuse can maim or kill hundreds or thousands. But when used properly, nuclear power is one of the safest forms of energy, and on average emits less radiation than coal power. The more there is a side for or against particular items, which are inherently dangerous but not strictly necessary to survival of human-kind, typically the more laws, rules, and regulations that are passed.

Chain saws, pools, and heart disease injure or kill humans each year on a far greater scale. However, there is no real group to organize against processing lumber in sustainable forests, pools for recreational and sport use, or elimination of junk food. So many people are for such in one way or another You just do not hear about bans, licensing, or restrictions in any meaningful way.

470

Does the Second Amendment preempt all state and local rules and regulations?

No. It was not until the year 2010, that the U.S. Supreme Court formally spelled out in the *McDonald* case that the Second Amendment of the United States Constitution applied to the states. Therefore, a state could not ban an entire class of firearms preferred by its citizens for self-defense, namely handguns. The U.S. Supreme Court has declined taking cases that expand the parameters of the right to keep and bear arms. In addition, through the Gun Control Act, Congress has indicated it would not preempt (take over) gun law making but share it with the states. Therefore, unless a state banned the purchase and possession of a handgun entirely, gun rights come from other federal and state laws under the modern view.

What are the laws about guns in the workplace?

They vary widely from no laws to specific statutes and cases. Many states have statutes that allow firearms in the workplace or work property, such as an employee's car. The competing rights are the employer's rights to make rules governing safety and security on their property versus the right to keep a firearm at least in one's car or there would be really no right to carry a handgun by employees during the work week going to and from work. There is no OSHA rule governing firearms in the workplace. However, various political groups, such as Chambers of Commerce have vigorously fought against firearms in the workplace for employers. Most states that do have such a provision to allow firearms in the workplace have many exceptions that employers often "determine" they fall within in order to have a policy against this, meaning the employee faces discharge and then suing the employer over the meaning of the law and exceptions.

Are there differences between men and women gun owners?

This is a "loaded" question about which there would be little consensus. However, anecdotal evidence suggest women are far more desirous of having firearms for self-defense purposes than hunting or collecting. In addition, they are seeking education about laws and training on a statistically higher basis than men. In addition, the trade group for the firearms industry has tracked women as the fastest growing segment of the firearms market.

PART XII: ABOUT THE AUTHOR

Bryan L. Ciyou is a trial and appellate attorney at the Indianapolis law firm of Ciyou & Dixon, P.C. He earned his BA with distinction and graduated through the honors program, along with his JD, *cum laude*, at Indiana University in Bloomington, Indiana. One of his key practice areas is Firearms Law wherein he represents a wide array of clients, including licensed manufacturers and dealers with criminal or regulatory/compliance matters, gun show promoters and businesses with firearms legal issues, and individuals involved in deadly force encounters. Bryan also consults across the United States with lawyers and those in the industry.

Bryan has authored several books on Firearms Law--the *Indiana Firearms Law Reference Manual* and the annual reference manual, *Gun Laws By State.* The latter compiles the thousands of gun laws and driving concepts and simplifies this complex interaction of local, state, and federal gun laws that bind citizens and LEOs who carry firearms off duty in other states. He also authored a portion of *Inside the Minds: Strategies for Defending Firearms Offense Charges*, published by Thomson Reuters, structured to assist America's practicing criminal defense and other attorneys working in this area of law.

The local, state, and national media have featured Bryan's a-political works and opinions numerous times. In addition, everyone from attorneys, judges, police officers, news reporters, legislators, and everyday people wanting to know more and accurate information regularly reference his books. He is a frequent lecturer on gun laws and has been active on the legislative front in different ways, such as advising lawmakers in drafting proposed legislation, considering current laws, and testifying about the impact of firearms legislation and regulation at the local, state and national level. In addition, he frequently teaches groups, ranging from ordinary citizens, LEOs, and lawyers, covering a wide variety of topics, such as current trends and the components of defending or analyzing a deadly force encounter. Bryan was also a presenter at the NRA's 17th Annual National Firearms Law Seminar, covering material titled the "Federal Firearms Disqualifications and the Restoration of Rights" in April of 2014.

Bryan is actively involved in shooting sports and has trained at some of the country's best facilities, such as Gunsite, under the tutelage of renowned instructors. He is a lifetime member of the National Rifle Association, the Second Amendment Foundation, and Safari Club International.